We Saved Each Other

"Dogs in Our World" Series

Canine Crania: Your Dog's Head and Why It Looks That Way (Bryan D. Cummins with Kaelyn Racine, 2024)

The Peace Puppy: A Memoir of Caregiving and Canine Solace (Susan Hartzler, 2024)

My Broken Dog: Living with a Handicapped Pet (Sandy Kubillus, 2024)

Canine Agility and the Meaning of Excellence (Beth A. Dixon, 2024)

We Saved Each Other (Christopher Dale, 2024)

Police Dogs of Trinidad and Tobago: A 70-Year History (Debbie Jacob, 2024)

The Force-Free Dilemma: Truth and Myths in Modern Dog Training (Nicola Ferguson, 2024)

Dogs of the Railways: Canine Guardians, Companions and Mascots Since the 19th Century (Jill Lenk Schilp, 2023)

Horror Dogs: Man's Best Friend as Movie Monster (Brian Patrick Duggan, 2023)

I Know Your Dog Is a Good Dog: A Trainer's Insights on Reactive, Aggressive or Anxious Behavior (Linda Scroggins, 2023)

The Most Painful Choice: A Dog Owner's Story of Behavioral Euthanasia (Beth Miller, 2023)

Your Service Dog and You: A Practical Guide (Nicola Ferguson, 2023)

Dog of the Decade: Breed Trends and What They Mean in America (Deborah Thompson, 2022)

Laboratory Dogs Rescued: From Test Subjects to Beloved Companions (Ellie Hansen, 2022)

Beware of Dog: How Media Portrays the Aggressive Canine (Melissa Crawley, 2021)

I'm Not Single, I Have a Dog: Dating Tales from the Bark Side (Susan Hartzler, 2021)

Dogs in Health Care: Pioneering Animal-Human Partnerships (Jill Lenk Schilp, 2019)

General Custer, Libbie Custer and Their Dogs: A Passion for Hounds, from the Civil War to Little Bighorn (Brian Patrick Duggan, 2019)

Dog's Best Friend: Will Judy, Founder of National Dog Week and Dog World *Publisher* (Lisa Begin-Kruysman, 2014)

Man Writes Dog: Canine Themes in Literature, Law and Folklore (William Farina, 2014)

Saluki: The Desert Hound and the English Travelers Who Brought It to the West (Brian Patrick Duggan, 2009)

We Saved Each Other

How Rescue Dogs Help Us Through Hardship

Christopher Dale

Dogs in Our World
Series Editor Brian Patrick Duggan

McFarland & Company, Inc., Publishers
Jefferson, North Carolina

Unless otherwise noted, all photographs
are from the author's collection.

ISBN (print) 978-1-4766-9433-7
ISBN (ebook) 978-1-4766-5225-2

LIBRARY OF CONGRESS AND BRITISH LIBRARY
CATALOGUING DATA ARE AVAILABLE

Library of Congress Control Number 2024009157

© 2024 Christopher Dale. All rights reserved

*No part of this book may be reproduced or transmitted in any form
or by any means, electronic or mechanical, including photocopying
or recording, or by any information storage and retrieval system,
without permission in writing from the publisher.*

Front cover image: © Evgenii Bakhchev/Shutterstock

Printed in the United States of America

*McFarland & Company, Inc., Publishers
Box 611, Jefferson, North Carolina 28640
www.mcfarlandpub.com*

For Vector, and for Nicholas.
Love you both, all the way and every day.

Table of Contents

Preface   1

1. Partners in Grime: A Desperate Dog's Journey to His Humbled Human—and Vice Versa   5
2. Trauma: Seeing, I, Dog   25
3. Trauma: Two Birds with One Bone   39
4. Addiction: A Hopeless Drug Addict and a Doomed Dog Walk into a Bar…   56
5. Addiction: Johnny, Be Good   70
6. Mental Health: Guide, Dog   84
7. Mental Health: Rx Rescue   97
8. Marriage and Relationships: V for Victory   111
9. Marriage and Relationships: Yes We Canine   122
10. Parenthood: Doggie Bro-Bro   137
11. Parenthood: Foster/Mom   152
12. Grief: Good Grief   167
13. Grief: Ophelia (You're Breaking My Heart)   180

Epilogue: Vectorious   194
Chapter Notes   201
Bibliography   207
Index   213

Preface

It takes one to know one. As a clinically depressed recovering drug addict with a rare visual disability, I am all too familiar with this phrase, which expresses the lonely line between sympathy and empathy.

My loved ones support me, validate me, root for me. But they seldom do so from the tight bond of personal experience—and never, as yet, from firsthand struggles with the trifecta of variable-laden maladies I've lived with my entire adult life.

During my decade as a freelance writer turned author, I've tried to construct, through precisely chosen words, bridges to narrow these empathy gaps. I've attempted to make "normies," my wife chief among them, better understand the compulsion to drink and drug to oblivion; or the relapse-remit grapple with dark, even suicidal hopelessness; or, perhaps most difficult, navigating a blurry world others get to enjoy in high-definition—an insult-to-injury compounding of frighteningly poor eyesight and frustratingly incomplete knowledge of what I'm missing. And while these efforts to linguistically alleviate my alienation have been more selfish than selfless—more therapy via Word doc than attempts to help fellow isolated individuals—I'd like to think I struck a resonant note here and there.

Just as importantly, though, I've learned that my blanket assumption about empathy was, if not incorrect, at least incomplete. I've found evidence of experience-driven identification forming fast and firm despite reluctance or resistance—exceptions where empathy sprouts and flourishes from infertile grounds of indifference or antipathy.

That proof is currently snoozing on my bed as I type. His name is Vector.

My wife, Patty, was never a dog person. She didn't grow up with dogs, was never particularly enamored by dogs and, elongating her arm's-length outlook, is mildly allergic to dogs. By contrast, dog ownership was always high on my list of adult wants. Specifically, it was fourth—right behind getting clean and sober, not killing myself in a depressive fog and, for lack of a physical cure, mentally coping with my visual deficit.

When it came to man's best friend, I "got it." Patty just ... didn't.

Fast forward a face-licking, couch-cuddling decade, and Patty is a bona fide (bone-a-fide?) dog person. Maybe not as fido fanatical as me, but her conversion is total. She's a doting dog mom. She's all in. She gets it—and by "it," I mean far more than allergy meds.

It didn't just take one to know one. It took Vector to *make* one.

Patty's transformation, though, involved an intangible greater than the sum of its parts. Greater than her husband's pleading or her new dog's utter cuteness. The secret ingredient was Vector's backstory—a homeless, hopeless and ultimately tailless tale whose happy ending with us became the genesis for this book. We'll explore Vector's against-all-odds survival in Chapter 1, the first of 13 attempting to place into words the ineffable value, virtue and victories tied to our formerly desperate dogs. There's magic there, and through a mix of memoir and interviews, this book comprises a well-intending (but woefully incomplete) effort at putting that pixie dust on paper.

In doing so, I decided to focus on big problems. Problems like addiction, mental illness, trauma, grief. Problems like mine. And I did

Patty and Vector in February 2014: from dog-averse to doting dog mom in mere weeks.

this with the understanding that Vector is the only living being, bar none, that has loved me—completely and without the complications of forgive-but-don't-forget grudges or judgments—every day he has known me.

Such unconditional loyalty pays dividends far beyond assurances of affection, deserved or otherwise. Vector's unalterable faith and fealty became a foundation providing tangible relief from my three main afflictions, plus numerous lesser ones. It has provided perspective and comfort in especially challenging times (such as losing a loved one) and helped strengthen my closest human relationships.

Always, part and parcel to Vector's potency was his own desperate struggle to survive—and the knowledge that this existential fight was rewarded with a lengthy love-filled life thanks, incredibly, to me. Rescue dogs do more than make us feel good for them; they make us feel good about ourselves. If all dogs go to heaven, rescue dogs earn the fluffiest clouds.

Did Vector solve the incurable affliction of addiction? Eradicate my depression once and for all? Vanquish the fear and frustration associated with my visual impairment? Of course not. But his harrowing history and sublime salvation have helped me make tremendous strides toward combatting each and, in the process, informed and enriched my two most important roles: husband and father.

I was curious to find similar stories of resilience, redemption and relief. I was hopeful that others were, like me, rescued by their rescues. And this time, I found flashes of empathy everywhere.

An abused dog who almost single-handedly dragged her human from the depths of drug addiction. A Beagle spared the horrors of lab experimentation to become the only constant in a neglected, transient high schooler's life, inspiring her to accomplishments few achieve by early adulthood.

A mutt who spent six months in a trash dumpster to become not only a rallying point for a family beset by mental illness, but also a doggie diagnostic tool. A 17-year love story spanning one woman's troubled past through settled, satisfying present, earning her four-legged companion four months' worth of simultaneously heartwarming and heartbreaking goodbye letters.

Throughout, we find rescue dogs compelling their humans to be better people. To push forward despite headwinds, to persist despite setbacks, to build self-esteem through the estimable acts of feeding, sheltering and loving an innocent, mistreated being.

We find rescue dogs helping couples more deeply appreciate their partners, and serving as teaching-moment touchstones for parents looking to instill life lessons in their children. And we see these endearing dogs convince their humans to extend their love to other down-and-out dogs via adoption, fostering, or even starting their own rescue organizations.

I am a slow learner. As such, too many of these epiphanies congealed in my brain only late in Vector's life. Since I wanted him to be around while I finished what he started, I wrote this book fervently and at a feverish pace considering my 50-hour-a-week non-writing-related career.

Still, time does not stop to allow for 75,000 words of prose to be written and rewritten, agonized over and edited. Life happens in that 12- to 18-month stretch of time—which, for dogs, is more like six to 10 years. Vector was already getting up there as I began this project; by its conclusion he is flat-out old. That transition inevitably became part of this narrative—and, I believe, a powerful part. I am privileged to witness the golden years of a life the universe tried to snuff out in its cradle.

Before we begin, a special thanks to all the benefactors that brought us our beloved, barking family members. We owe an unpayable debt to the rescue teams, no-kill shelter personnel, volunteer veterinarians and foster parents who draw life-saving lines from death's door to our front doors. You saved their lives so they could enrich ours, and I can speak for each of this book's subjects when I express my heartfelt gratitude.

To the folks who don't "get it" when it comes to dogs, I'll ask you to add a "yet" to that label and keep reading. I implore you to give paws a chance.

There are folks profiled in this collection whose doggie skepticism shot well past my wife's into the realm of loathing and paranoia. Today they are among the most impassioned dog people imaginable. The reasons for this are more than adorable floppy ears and wagging tails, more than mere good company or compatible companionship. These dogs did more than make them love dogs; they helped them love themselves.

Join us in far more than a celebration of all things canine. Join us in joy. It doesn't take a dog person to know a dog person. It just takes a rescue dog to become one.

1

Partners in Grime

A Desperate Dog's Journey to His Humbled Human—and Vice Versa

My dog should be dead.

And it shows, from head to tail. Or rather, nose to nub.

Let's start with the former. His snout has a deep scar of unknown origin, though our vet's best guess is a bite wound that, per his words, "must have bled, a lot." Continuing along his adorable, too-small-for-his-body head, his expressively pointy ears have chunks missing at the tips.

This time, the culprit is not a fellow canine but a parasite, which infected him with the worst case of ehrlichia—an autoimmune disorder similar to Lyme Disease—that this same septuagenarian vet had seen in his decades-long career. In addition to crippling arthritis, ehrlichia can restrict blood flow to the extremities, leaving places like the edges of ears susceptible to atrophy so severe that they wilt away and, eventually, crumble off.

Moving past his head, something seems off. Three paws look fine, but the back left one looks … smaller. A closer examination reveals that it's missing a toe. Whether this came about by car, canine or carelessness, God only knows.

Finally his tail—or, rather, what little remains of it. In a dog-owning landscape that increasingly frowns upon tail clipping, I've been left explaining myself more times than I can count. "It's not clipped," I'll reassure the concerned party. Then the less-than-reassuring follow-up: "It was bitten off."

I've tried to envision the scenario where my 22-pound dog lost his tail but not his life. Was the tail a consolation prize for an equally desperate dog? If his tail hadn't been severed—seemingly leaving his counterpart with a full mouth—would the next bite have been a deathblow to his neck? Is he alive *despite* his tail being bitten off, or *because* of it? And even so, how did he not bleed out, or die from an infection, or…?

He is undersized for his "breed," a type of mutt that has emerged from several breeds living in close, unsupervised quarters for decades. Most of his ilk have 10 pounds on him, making the mean streets even meaner.

He was about three years old when we brought him home, from a brief stay with a foster family, on September 25, 2013. That date will become significant—indeed, this book's very origin—later. For now, the takeaway is the seeming impossibility of him surviving three years of hopelessness before arriving where he was always supposed to be: home, with us, forever.

How on Earth is he here—on my couch, in my backyard, in my family? How did an anonymous cur walk through hell to find recognition, let alone salvation?

How did an invisible, nameless non-entity become among the best things that has ever happened to me?

My dog should be dead. Instead, he's a miracle.

In early 2013, a gaunt mutt was scavenging for food, water and shelter in what for stray dogs is an especially unforgiving environment. Puerto Rico's climate, poverty and geography add up to an ungodly 500,000 estimated satos—local Spanish slang for "stray dog" or "mongrel"—roaming the island's streets and beaches.[1]

To put that in perspective, the country with the world's highest number of homeless dogs is India. The Asian subcontinent nation has as many as 62 million homeless dogs, largely concentrated in its congested, often squalid inner cities—slum dogs, minus the millionaire part.[2]

Still, India's human population of 1.4 billion places its human-to-stray ratio at 22.5 to 1. By contrast, Puerto Rico is home to just 3.2 million people. That's *less than seven humans per sato*. Per capita, then, Puerto Rico's sato crisis is upwards of *three times worse* than the country with the world's most egregious stray dog problem. Even stray-heavy countries with far lower human populations—say, Thailand, with about a million stray dogs and 71 million people—don't have per capita figures even approaching those of Puerto Rico.

Similar scenarios play out across much of the Caribbean—islands where economies are fueled by tourism but whose residents are, mostly, simply too poor to look after so obscene a number of desperate dogs. Inviting all-inclusive resorts sit a stone's throw from abject poverty; tourists enjoy themselves while locals can barely feed themselves. The protracted human emergency supersedes the longstanding canine one, which goes unaddressed and, litter by litter, grows exponentially worse.

Puerto Rico has one such locale that sums this scenario up with piercing precision. Near the island's southeastern corner is an unassuming

1. Partners in Grime

beachside town named Yabucoa. Dotted with quaint seaside inns like the Parador Palmas de Lucia, the area seems like a quiet counterbalance to San Juan's bustling, built-up urbanity. Somewhere to relax, sunbathe and swim at the main beach, Playa Lucia.

To locals, though, Playa Lucia isn't a slice of heaven, but rather a heaping helping of hell. To them, the comforting, romantic Spanish gives way to a grating, galling English nickname.

Welcome to Dead Dog Beach.

The top Google result in a search for "Dead Dog Beach" is the online library of a photographer named Sophie Gamand. Gamand is also a fierce advocate for strays and shelter dogs—the type of everyday hero we'll meet more of later in this chapter.

The first photo of Gamand's Dead Dog Beach collection recalls a long-dead steer in a desert—a long-snouted, fleshless, sun-parched skull on the sand. Only this sand is beach not desert, and that skull isn't a cow. It's man's best friend. Or at least, it was.

Frightened. Emaciated. Heat-stroked. Maimed. Dead Dog Beach is an affront to civilization, one whose very name snaps listeners to abrupt attention. It is made all the more grotesque upon the realization that these desperate scenes play out in thousands of other pockets throughout this doggie deathtrap of an island. Dead Dog Beach isn't just a macabre

Dead Dog Beach: a canine killing field and an affront to civilization (photograph by Ralph Quinonez, courtesy the Sato Project).

moniker; it's a microcosm—a head-turning entrée to a heartbreaking, territory-wide tragedy.

There is, simply, nowhere for them to go. Despite being roughly the size of Connecticut—not a large state but certainly not the smallest—Puerto Rico has just five municipal animal shelters. Packed by twos, threes and fours in dirty, decrepit conditions multitudes past maximum occupancy, the chances for survival in the island's shelters are, perhaps, even lower than those outside of them. Euthanasia rates reach as high as a staggering 97 percent; in fact, many dogs never even see the inside of a crammed cage, instead taken "straight out back"—code for put down.

This is just one symptom of an island in protracted crisis. Puerto Rico's poverty rate is *44 percent*[3]—inexcusable considering residents are citizens of the world's wealthiest nation. After all, Puerto Rican problems are American problems.

A brief summation: In 2017, $70 billion in debt, Puerto Rico filed for bankruptcy, a financial collapse whose consequences remain unsettled and untenable. That September, Hurricane Maria slammed into Puerto Rico as a monstrous Category 4 storm, inflicting $90 billion in damage and killing over 3,000—a death toll exceeding both Pearl Harbor and 9/11. Homes were destroyed. Roads were impassable. The power grid was decimated. The American president threw rolls of paper towels, and the world moved on.

But nature wasn't done. On January 7, 2020, a magnitude 6.4 earthquake crippled critical infrastructure. As aftershocks trembled for weeks, many Americans canceled getaways to a destination that urgently needed revenue. My family was among them.

It wouldn't have mattered anyway. We all know what happened next: the global showstopper of Covid-19. More death and hopelessness and lost tourism revenue.

Last but not least is a distinction separating the island from most Caribbean locales. As noted, Puerto Ricans are U.S. citizens, meaning they can move to the mainland whenever they want. Or rather, if they have the means.

In 2014, 84,000 Puerto Ricans migrated to the U.S. mainland. Only 20,000 did the opposite. So even before its snowballing tragedies, about 230 people were departing daily; Puerto Rico's population shrank 1.8 percent that year. After Hurricane Maria the 12-month migration figure doubled, reaching 130,000. By 2020, Puerto Rico had shed 440,000 people—12 percent of its population.[4]

Here, demographics matter. With nearly half the population in poverty, the poorest typically can't just board a plane and resettle on the mainland. The people leaving, then, are the ones with skills, with means.

1. Partners in Grime

Doctors and lawyers. Plumbers and mechanics. There's a term for this: the Puerto Rico brain drain.[5] Given the obvious choice between an economic wasteland or an economic powerhouse, educated middle-class residents are leaving in droves—a collectively devastating exodus for Puerto Rico.

Puerto Rico's chronic destitution, recent destruction and spiraling desperation have nothing to do with my dog, or the half-million like him currently roaming its streets and beachfronts. But they also have everything to do with him, and with them. Because when humans can't afford to care for themselves, they certainly can't afford to care for stray dogs.

And that brings us back to my yet-nameless dog. Given Puerto Rico's cascading crises, I am unsure whether his odds back in 2013 were incalculable, or whether I merely can't bear to attempt the arithmetic. They were, let's agree, less than slim but ever-so-slightly greater than none.

I also can't bear to imagine what his first three years of life in that hot, humid hellhole were like. But I must confront it, even if that means descending into quasi-fiction—into the likely yet non-verifiable life of an anonymous, seemingly doomed Puerto Rico street dog. The respect he has earned mandates my understanding, however incomplete or speculative.

Sometime around 2010, a tiny puppy—almost certainly the runt of his litter—entered the world, likely along with a half dozen or so siblings.

The odds are that nobody noticed. If they did, they didn't care enough to keep him around for long. If they do have a dog, few in Puerto Rico can afford to keep five or six more. So they kept the mom—the dog they already knew and assumedly loved—and not the others.

What to do? The shelters are full, and any family and neighbors who could afford a dog already had one, since they are literally everywhere for the taking. So teeming with strays is Puerto Rico that, for satos, real rescue almost always means a forever home on the U.S. mainland. There are no vacancies here—no room at the inns nor the island at large.

Sometimes, a lucky family of satos gets rescued all at once. This was not the case with mine. The most we know about his mother is that she probably survived long enough to nurse him, at least for a little while. The most we know about his siblings is that, statistically, he's likely the only one who made it out alive.

And from there ... the big ifs. Where did he go? Did anyone even casually care for him—perhaps setting out some food and water once in a while—or was he sifting through trash and slurping putrid puddles? Did he ever have a home, *ever*, even for a few months prior to his rescue? Or did he spend upwards of 1,000 days outside on an island whose coolest month, January, still averages an oppressive 84 degrees?

When it poured—as it does with frequency in such tropic locations—where did he shelter himself? Under an urban awning? A dumpster? A car? Is *that* how he lost his tail? Was it smashed by tires and ultimately removed—God, what an awful thought—by his own teeth?

A sato's life is a limitless combination of dangerous, soul-crushing obstacles that, eventually, converge at a single point: death. There is no long-term survival without rescue. Given his injuries, my dog certainly spent at least some time on the streets, undersized among canines and overmatched by conditions. He hung on for dear life on the very margins of existence.

But time was running out.

At some point, ticks and heartworms planted infectious seeds that, sooner rather than later, would have finished him had the elements not done so first. He contracted heartworm and ehrlichia, both fatal if left untreated. His days were numbered as the parasitic clock counted down to zero, a figure mirroring any sato's odds over an extended period.

Then, my boy got lucky.

Somehow, a group of folks with a steady job took a liking to him. Maybe they saw his mangled tail, scarred snout and missing toe and, finding his condition pitiful even among his struggling streetmates, decided they couldn't turn a blind eye to this particular pooch. I'd like to think he lost a tail only to gain attention—and that this attention saved his life.

His good fortune turned out to be even more fortuitous, because he hadn't stumbled upon a group of supermarket cashiers or hotel workers. These kind souls were air traffic controllers at San Juan's Luis Muñoz Marín International Airport. My dog had happened upon people willing to help at a place that, in theory, could catapult him out of his misery.

Suddenly, he was no longer anonymous. He was acknowledged, recognized. While they didn't take him into their homes or even their workplace, that recognition came with regular food and water. And soon enough, it came with something else.

They called him Vector.

vector [VEK-ter] verb. (1) To guide in flight by issuing appropriate headings. (2) to change direction of (the thrust of a jet or rocket engine) in order to steer the craft.

It was among the most appropriate names in the history of dogdom. The air traffic controllers had a way with words as well as a heart.

But heart wasn't enough, because Vector's would soon be infected with worms. He was a goner without the sheer luck of his current location. At their place of work, these nice people had witnessed others do what they could to get dogs off this island.

1. Partners in Grime

Puerto Rico's stray dog problem is so severe—and so ubiquitous—that a sato often needs more than a kind stranger to lay out some kibble. My dog—my Vector—needed kind strangers with *connections*. He needed someone to pick him out from the hordes of hopeless hounds ... *and* he needed that someone to *know someone else*. To know someone with the resources to get him the hell out of there. And given his parasitic time bombs, he needed that someone *now*.

The odds are astronomical. Vector should have met his maker.

Instead, he met Chrissy.

Chrissy Beckles is a Golden Gloves amateur boxing champion, an unsurprising revelation upon making her company. She looks and sounds the part.

She is energetic and endearing, but also intense—intimidating even. Like a boxer sizing up a stronger opponent, Chrissy is focused to the point of tunnel vision, and relentless to the point of obstinacy. If you told her moving forward might kill her, she'd take it as a dare rather than a threat.

Chrissy Beckles is too pugnacious to be pragmatic, which is exactly what her vocation requires. One round at a time. Stick and move, but never retreat. Get knocked down, but never knocked out. That's how she came to dirty her hands in the insurmountable, Sisyphean task of saving satos.

In 2007, she traveled to Puerto Rico for the first time. She was there with her husband, Bobby, a stuntman visiting the island during a film production. There, Bobby witnessed an example of the frightening frivolity with which the island's satos are discarded: he saw a vehicle run over a dog ... *on purpose*. A jarringly casual act undoubtedly played out daily throughout the island.

Chrissy's experience was equally heartbreaking and horrifying. She describes seeing puppies no more than a few weeks old so hungry they were chewing rocks in a futile attempt at nourishment.

But unlike so many before her, Chrissy left the island with something she couldn't shake: herself. Her makeup did not permit her to do nothing. Fighters fight, period. In short order, Chrissy began donating to and volunteering for several animal rescue organizations across Puerto Rico, including *Amigos de los Animales* (Friends of the Animals) and *Manos por Patas* (Hands for Paws).

A year later, she took matters from her own hands to her own home. She and Bobby adopted a sato from a shelter in Arecibo, west of San Juan. A nod to Chrissy's distinctive blend of altruism and combativeness, they named the tough little mutt Boom Boom.

But the larger issue can feel, simply, impossible in its enormity. A handful of rescue organizations with minuscule resources versus

Chrissy Beckles, founder of the Sato Project, with her beloved Boom Boom (photograph by Sophie Gamand, courtesy the Sato Project).

hundreds of thousands of dogs multiplying litter by litter. Progress was akin to drops in an ocean—a thin bandage over a severed jugular.

This was not a winnable fight. But Chrissy Beckles doesn't know how to quit. She follows the creed of a quote from one of her idols, Muhammad Ali, "Impossible is nothing." That, plus a well of compassion as deep as her stubbornness, is how the Sato Project was founded.

Frustrated with the pace of progress, Chrissy formed her own rescue organization in November 2011. By early 2012, her efforts despite a shoestring budget were so remarkable that the United States' paper of record profiled her. From the March 24 issue of *The New York Times*:

> [Chrissy] has become the unlikely but unrelenting savior of Dead Dog Beach. Operating out of her apartment in Brooklyn, and with minimal financial support, she has taken 81 dogs from the beach, paid for their medical care and placed 60 of the dogs healthy enough to make the trip to the continental United States in adoptive homes.

Then, the narrative's kicker:

> Without Ms. Beckles's intervention, all of the dogs would likely be dead from starvation, sickness or worse.[6]

A decade later, the Sato Project's 2021 end-of-year report spoke volumes about what Chrissy and her growing team had accomplished. In its

1. Partners in Grime 13

first ten years, the organization rescued more than 6,000 satos. That number is all the more impressive considering that, again, for satos the only real rescue comes with getting off that island forever.

To make that possible, the Sato Project—a non-profit started by one woman determined to do something about the horrors she saw—flies dogs on commercial airlines and chartered planes. Hoisting hundreds of once-doomed dogs to forever families on the U.S. mainland, these events have become known as Freedom Flights. Followers of the Sato Project on social media can watch all that goes into these flights in real time, from crate preparation in Puerto Rico to handing over dogs to their adopters at airports in the New York Metropolitan area.

The Sato Project also has tried to stem the flood of futility on the island itself. At last count, the organization has spayed, neutered and vaccinated over 8,300 dogs, and distributed nearly 150,000 tons of humanitarian and animal welfare supplies following Puerto Rico's series of natural disasters.

The Sato Project's profile has grown along with its footprint. Its merchandise fundraisers have become so popular among adopters and supporters that it took three separate drives to get my hands on my now-cherished logoed hat.

To adopt their dogs, don their merch and raise awareness to Puerto Rico's plight, Chrissy and her team also have solicited celebrities, including popular fashion designer Marc Jacobs. Thanks to Puerto Rico-born singer Roselyn Sanchez, on December 31, 2022, the organization was profiled on *Dick Clark's New Year's Rockin' Eve*, which draws tens of millions of U.S. viewers. And for several years running, each February sees a handful of satos compete in the annual Puppy Bowl, broadcast by *Animal Planet* prior to the Super Bowl.

In summer 2022, the organization launched Sanctuary by the Sato Project, a care center where newly rescued strays can heal together—a first step on their journey to forever homes on the U.S. mainland. Among other benefits, the environment takes some pressure off the scores of volunteer foster families the Sato Project has dotted across the island. It also allows them to better focus their post-rescue care. Another terrific idea, born in love and executed with purpose.

In just over a decade, then, it is safe to say that the Sato Project has done just about everything humanly possible to alleviate Puerto Rico's stray dog crisis. The effort has been nothing short of Herculean.

But it isn't nearly enough.

That isn't a knock—quite the opposite in fact. The everyday miracle of Chrissy Beckles and the Sato Project is one of persistence despite the intractable permanence of the problem facing them. Each day, they muster total dedication to what is, essentially, attempting to bail out a sinking boat with a teaspoon.

The circumstances are too dire, and the deluge of dogs too inundating, to solve Puerto Rico's stray dog problem over the short term. Nevertheless, the tiny successes are counted saved sato by saved sato—one spared soul at a time.

And in 2013, one of those sato souls was my sato soulmate.

Preparing a Freedom Flight, which carries Puerto Rico's satos to forever homes on the U.S. mainland (courtesy the Sato Project).

1. Partners in Grime

In the spring of 2013, the Sato Project's general inbox received an email.

"A group of workers at San Juan Airport had been looking after a small stray at the complex's outskirts," recalls Chrissy. "One of them was leaving for another job, and was concerned about what would happen to the dog."

The air traffic controllers undoubtedly saw tens or even hundreds of street dogs each day, but had taken a particular liking to this one. Perhaps they were projecting onto one sato their unachievable desire to care for them all. Perhaps this little runt was just especially assertive when it came to begging. Whatever the reason, the group had given him a name. And now, they were giving him a chance.

"After we exchanged messages, they ended up bringing him to our veterinary office," Chrissy recalls. After three years facing near-impossible odds, Vector had gotten almost impossibly lucky.

Then and there and against all odds, Vector's struggle to survive abruptly ended. He was sheltered in a clean, humane cage, received ample nutritious food and fresh drinking water. He was cared for by an experienced, altruistic veterinarian, who treated his wounds and, upon testing his blood, administered antibiotics to treat his ehrlichiosis. He was treated for a particularly stubborn case of heartworm—one that would eventually recur post-adoption.

He was one of the first 500 or so dogs saved by the organization—a Sato Project OG. Having stumbled upon the airport by chance, then taken in by a rescue organization still in its infancy, he was among the luckiest of the lucky.

And then, in September, Vector's big day came. Or at least, his first big one. While some satos leave Puerto Rico bound directly for a forever home, Vector was temporarily taken in by a foster parent in Manhattan.

"He fit perfectly into our family pack," said Cheryl Claude, Vector's foster mom. "Our cat Nokie, and pups Cody and Boomer, all accepted him right away, which isn't always the case with a fresh foster." The environment—Cheryl's loving, modest home—clearly wasn't the problem.

She shows me a photo of Vector curled up on her daughter's bed. He looks both younger and older—browner certainly, and without the paunch of old age. But his eyes reveal a shell-shocked spirit that has endured the nearly unendurable. He is exactly as I remember him in September 2013. He is broken.

It showed. When we first met Cheryl, she described the difficulties she'd had simply leashing Vector for a trip downstairs from her apartment to relieve himself. Everything—his past, the flight, this loud, honking new environment—was too much for him.

Outside he tremored. Inside he curled up like a little brown bagel, nervous and mistrusting. That Cheryl also had two bigger, permanent dogs likely didn't help, however generous the gregarious Cody and Boomer were toward him.

Still, he was off that island. People like Cheryl are an essential part of that process—pit stops en route to permanent solutions. As days and weeks passed without a forever family in sight, she could have given up on a mutt as damaged as Vector. She did not.

Meanwhile, my wife, Patty, and I had found what we thought was a promising match. A woman in our area was fostering an adorable little doggie. His cute ears and endearing eyes spoke to us from Petfinder.com. We called the number and arranged a meeting that, we hoped, would lead to adoption shortly thereafter.

His name was … Muffin. And fortunately, Muffin's mama muffed the meeting. She was a no-show, and wasn't answering her phone. Maybe Muffin got under her skin and into her heart. While it would have been nice to know the reason—a simple "Sorry, other arrangements have been made" text message would have sufficed—Patty and I are eternally grateful for the Muffin misfire. Because just a few weeks later, getting snubbed would never feel so wonderful.

Our first reaction was pretty much everyone's first reaction. "What a weird name," Patty mused, reading a moniker that, at the time, recalled a famous line from *Airplane!* ("What's your vector, Victor?") and, later, would seem like gallows humor amid the deadliest pandemic in a century.

We called the number on the listing—like most aspiring adopters, we'd never heard of the Sato Project back in 2013—and arranged to meet him. The thorough process seemed somewhat prying, but we now realize they were merely trying to find a home where a long-abandoned dog wouldn't be alone 12 hours a day while his parents were at work. Chrissy, Cheryl and the rest of the Sato Project had come too far to find an imperfect home for Vector—or, for that matter, any saved sato.

We passed the pre-screen. While we both worked, my wife did so from home a few days a week and, when she didn't, my retired, widowed father was more than happy to walk, feed and cuddle with a dog.

On Saturday, September 21, we drove into New York City to meet Vector. The interview was mutual; we were hoping the dog would be a fit, and Cheryl was carefully assessing whether we were a duo deserving of Vector.

We parked, approached Cheryl's building, got in the elevator. At Cheryl's floor, the doors slid open. The first noise we heard was the now-familiar "chit-chit-chit" of our boy's nails tapping against a hardwood floor. A dog described over the phone as "fragile, nervous, and still very much recovering" had taken it upon himself to trot toward Cheryl's open apartment door, round the corner, and greet the two strangers that now stood, mouth agape at his complete and utter cuteness, before him.

Patty claims it was me who broke the stunned silence. Apparently I mustered an elongated "Awwwwww!" in a cadence similar to that evoked by an infant doing something adorable. I do not remember this. What I do remember is that I was in love, instantly.

I barely remember the interview. What I do recall is that this scared sato let his new would-be mom pick him up and pose for what would become the first of thousands of family photos. Shortly thereafter, he did something that even Cheryl, who'd fostered her share of tepid rescues, found surprising. After studying me for a few moments, Vector hopped onto the couch where I was sitting, gingerly approached me ... and placed his little sato head right on my not-so-little thigh.

"He likes you," Cheryl said.

"I like him too," was all I managed to reply.

We left the apartment. Unable to contain our excitement, we called the Sato Project half an hour later, hoping that Cheryl had already been in touch with them.

She had. It was good news.

Vector was ours.

Vector's tragic pre-rescue trajectory draws parallels with my own life—one that, like his, almost abruptly ended at a young age.

When I was 27, I climbed to the roof of a five-story building, took a lengthy gaze over the edge...

... and didn't jump.

That evening in 2007 was the low point of a steep, monthslong depressive spiral. Fear had descended to paranoia, anxiety to near-incessant panic attacks, restlessness to full-blown insomnia. I was in the throes of an eight-day stretch of sleeplessness, well on my way to hospitalization for exhaustion and malnourishment.

In its emergency stages, depression slows sufferers' synapses and deceives them into thinking their circumstances are hopeless. By that night, the illness had fogged my mind, clouded my judgment and, finally, obliterated my will to go on. I was done, and I wanted to be over.

I still don't know why I didn't do it. Memories from this period are, perhaps fortunately, fragmented and fuzzy. But certainly, there was no cinematic toeing of the ledge, no welling of tears at the impact this violent act might have on others. I was too numb for any such drama.

My survival that night was more random than romantic. Perhaps I figured I might somehow survive the fall. Perhaps I was just too cowardly to end it—spared by my own crippling, disease-driven mortification. Perhaps it doesn't matter. And while it was the first time I gravitated toward an early grave, it would not be the last.

So like Vector, I could very well be dead. At least I would have had the dignity of being a statistic. Of being remembered. Mourned. Missed.

My 34-year road to Vector was both shocking and unsurprising. It was chaotic in real time but linear in retrospect. It was a lot of hell and, finally, a little bit of hope.

It didn't start well. Shortly before my third birthday, my mother became pregnant. It was a girl, due in the fall of 1982. Neither would get there. My mother died in August of preeclampsia. She was 24; the fetus was seven months.

Childhood was rough. Everyone else seemed to have two parents, a house and siblings, while I had none of these markers of conventional normalcy. My existence felt inferior, lonely in a roomful of people. I sat silent and acted as "fine" as possible.

Still, I might have turned out OK. High school brought a bigger pond to swim in and collect compadres. There were semblances of normalcy emerging. Next was New York University, whose urban setting offered anonymity for square pegs like me. I needed somewhere to hide in plain sight, blend into a crowd, and ultimately find my own niche. It's easier being a small fish in the Big Apple. I was pretty good with words, and opted for a journalism major in a school renowned for that field.

Things got even better. Sophomore year, I was at a party at Rutgers, New Jersey's state university, when a cute little Asian-American girl approached me.

"Chris?" she said.

"Yeah … do we know each other?"

Her name was Patty, and we'd taken piano lessons from the same teacher as children. A quarter-century later, our seven-year-old son now takes piano lessons.

My writing was improving, my girlfriend was brighter and better looking than I thought possible, and the dynastic late–90s Yankees were rattling off three consecutive World Series championships. I got my diploma, and a job at a public relations firm. I started moving up the ranks. Patty was looking more and more like a permanent partner. Life was good.

And then, one day, it stopped.

Two years after graduating college, I started going blind. I would continue along that path for 18 mortifying months.

It started with a routine checkup, when neither eye could read the 20/20 line. Cue the "One or two?" tests associated with eyeglass prescriptions. Throughout, my response was disconcerting: "None of the above." Soon, I was similarly underperforming on a visual field examination, which detects blind spots in our sightlines.

Airplanes and doctor's offices have something in common: there's usually nothing to worry about until the staff seem worried. When the doctor read the field test printout, his eyes widened.

We'll dive deeper into my ocular ordeal next chapter, the first of two addressing trauma. For now, suffice to say that the ensuing year and a half involved specialists with increasingly sophisticated titles. My optic nerve was deteriorating before their eyes—and taking my eyes with it. The 20/30 line disappeared, then the 20/40. A year into my mysterious medical misadventure, the 20/50 line became unrecognizable.

Then, at about 20/60, it stopped getting worse. It has stayed at least largely stable for the past two decades.

Humans take in about 90 percent of the information around them through their eyes. So while fear of blindness isn't an excuse to completely unravel, it's hard to argue that it isn't a viable reason. Still, I held it together for a while. I recommitted to work and reconnected with long-ignored friends. I moved into a nicer place in Brooklyn. In 2006, Patty and I got engaged.

But things weren't OK. I was too anxious, too ill-equipped. I was faking it to make it, glomming cues and hints from cohorts, attempting to grow up via osmosis. That only took me so far before it took me down. Or rather, up—to the top of the aforementioned five-story building.

Incredibly, four months later I was walking down the aisle, a gaunt, sickly-looking man-child marrying an attractive, mature-beyond-her-years woman. I pressed forward, borrowing normalcy from the most grounded person I'd ever met: my bride.

It just wasn't to be. I was too damaged.

I started drinking more heavily. Alcohol became a short-term salve for everything from anxiety to insomnia. I drank to fit in, to feel comfortable, to sleep soundly. Meet Chris, the slurring, self-medicating cliché.

By 28, I was on a fast track to full-fledged alcoholism. Booze was beginning to steer me toward situations where I could drink openly with friends or clandestinely without them.

Alcohol was taking the wheel. Then cocaine hijacked the car and drove it off a goddamn cliff.

To an insecure chronic depressive, introducing something as euphoric as cocaine had a predictable result: the powder keg of pleasure left me near-instantly addicted. The spiral was steep and sharp; I hit the bottom hard, and scuttled along the canyon floor. Gratefully, though, by making addiction's gauntlet more brutal, cocaine expedited my momentum toward addiction's four common destinations: jails, institutions, death or recovery. I would experience the first two before finding the last one.

A one-paragraph summary of my cocaine career: Three years. Roughly $100,000. Unemployed, then unemployable. Volatile in character but predictable in action. Nearly divorced several times, and *really* nearly divorced once.

And then, mercifully, it—or rather, I—was done, courtesy of the New York City Police Department. That was October 10, 2011, and I haven't had a drink or drug since.

I began attending Alcoholics Anonymous meetings. I stayed sober for a week, then a month. Ever so slightly, a door cracked open and a glimpse of hope shone through. For the first time in my adult life, I was getting better rather than worse.

For whatever reason, after failed rehabs and previous toe-dips into AA, this time recovery stuck. I showed up, shut up and studied up, and was rewarded with the rapid ascent of a well-practiced early recovery. As 2012 turned into 2013, likely Vector's most desperate days, I was celebrating a year—a *year!*—clean and sober. I was going to make it.

But staying sober and staying married are two entirely separate stories, and one that led me—that led *us*, Patty and I—directly to Vector.

One partner's early recovery from addiction can, for the non-addict partner, be such a confounding, frustrating and seemingly directionless period that an instruction manual is warranted. In fact, that was the purpose of my previous book, *Better Halves: Rebuilding a Post-Addiction Marriage*.

The difficult-to-swallow truth is that my addiction had made Patty a worse person. The experience had placed scars on her soul that did not exist prior to my rampant substance abuse. Spouses see, hear and feel too much during their partners' protracted debauchery to emerge from so harrowing a crisis unscathed. She was angrier, less trusting, more cynical.

What transpired is something I call the "partner's paradox": Through no fault of her own, Patty was a worse person, but (a) didn't recognize it, and (b) wouldn't have known what to do about it even if she had.

We had to reinvent our marriage—to become Chris & Patty 2.0—but had no idea how to get there. We'll explore this theme in Chapter 8. For now, it's enough to state that society does not provide nearly enough resources for partners of those with substance abuse—active or recovering. Patty needed guidance to help her heal along a separate yet parallel path. Such guidance eluded her, as it does far too many in her confounding situation.

So we fought. A lot. There were a few times when neither of us thought this was going to work, and one or two times when we nearly separated. Most of it derived from simply not knowing any better.

It was clear Patty and I had work to do. More conflict was inevitable, and we needed something to distract us and deflect tension, tears and trauma at this crucial crossroads in our lives together. Something simple in a complicated time. Something to agree on. Something to rally around, root for and dote upon.

We needed Vector.

On September 25, 2013, Patty and I made one of the smartest decisions of our lives. Then we made one of the dumbest.

That afternoon we brought Vector home, a move that ranks high on our marriage's milestones list. But that night, we nearly set the record for "World's Briefest Dog Owners."

The evening started wonderfully. Leaving her Manhattan office, my wife retrieved her car, drove over to Cheryl's apartment, and officially became Vector's mom. She looped his harness through the passenger side seat belt and headed home. Unsurprisingly and understandably, he shook the whole way.

Since I don't work in New York City, I was waiting at the northern New Jersey home we'd purchased earlier that year. I met them in the driveway and led our trembling sato inside. He was clearly frazzled, his nerves frayed anew from a car ride with a stranger to a strange place.

He came inside, poked around, did a once-around the living and dining rooms, the den and the kitchen. He had the first of thousands of treatsies, and even drank a little water. Both seemed like a sign of budding, albeit tenuous, trust.

Soon, we figured he had to pee. The fence in the backyard wasn't finished yet, so the harness and leash were a must. We hooked him up and headed out the door. Half a block later, Vector lifted his leg against a tree. Good, we thought. That's normal.

Then, he yanked against the leash toward the direction of the house. "No, buddy, let's walk a little more," I said.

But Vector tugged harder. The leash became taut. And then ... Vector wriggled out of his harness and bolted away into the autumn night. His tiny haunches disappeared over a small hill, darting around the bend toward our house. Christ, was he fast.

We sprinted home, hoping he'd be waiting on the porch. He was not. He was nowhere.

He was gone.

In what today would seem like a poor-taste Paw Patrol impression, we threw on the spelunker-esque, light-affixed headgear we'd purchased during the previous year's devastating Superstorm Sandy, which had left swaths of the northeast U.S. without power for over a week. We searched the backyard, then the rest of the block, then the next. Nothing.

By the time we returned home an hour later, I was actively crying—a grown man in a stupid hat bawling his eyes out.

Then, Patty had an idea. We'd already placed the blanket Cheryl had packed with him out on the porch, hoping he'd pick up the scent and gravitate toward it. Now, Patty employed a more alluring aromatic weapon: meatloaf. She placed it outside. Then, in case the sight of humans would dissuade the clearly panicked pooch, we retreated indoors.

Fifteen minutes later, the most relieving rap of our lives sprang us from our seats. It was Vector. He'd devoured the meatloaf, and had batted the screen door. To this day, the dispute rages whether my wife's culinary mastery was solely responsible for Vector's second—and final—salvation, or whether he actively decided to give this whole forever family thing a shot.

It was probably the former. I hope it was the latter. But it doesn't matter, because Vector was home—and this time for good.

Did Vector single-pawedly save our marriage? Of course not. But he was the perfect pooch at the perfect time. In giving him a forever home, we were actively stating our intention to keep that home intact. To stick it out. To stay together. We weren't quite ready to create a life—that would take another couple of years—but we were ready to save one. Vector cemented our dedication to each other, and to goodness in general, at a make-or-breakup time. He turned a recovering couple into an aspiring family.

Through the years, Vector has become far more than a shock absorber, a symbol, a salve. To me, who in our minds he calls Daddams (pronounced *duh-DAHMS*), he's a "bestie and son, rolled into one." To Patty, who (again, in our heads) he calls Mummumsie, he is a dedicated cuddler and foot warmer. And in 2016, he was proudly thrust into another crucial role: big brother to our son, Nicholas.

Bringing Vector into our lives has yielded immeasurable rewards since the first time his claws chit-chit-chitted across our hardwood floors. It has led to much more love, and to so much more than love. We cannot envision our family without him, despite knowing that his absence—and the sorrowful silence it will create—is lurking ever closer.

But alas, if there is a co-star in this particular narrative—or, at least, a supporting actor of note—that inglorious distinction falls upon me. In a book exploring the profoundly positive impacts rescue dogs can have on people with mental illnesses and relationship struggles, I alone among Vector's family members am qualified, however unenviably, to play the

1. Partners in Grime   23

Vector in October 2013, one month after joining our family: an anxious, exhausted being, hopeful but haunted.

part of human guinea pig. As a depressive, traumatized, half-blind addict, I can honestly say that it's a role I step into with humility.

I am, for our purposes here, a mere case study volunteer. A constant in an evolving equation. A baseline against which to gauge the extent that one undersized, underprivileged mutt has helped one underwhelming human.

And somehow, I always knew he'd help.

Weeks before falling in love with Vector at first sight (which I most certainly did), I was already in love with the *idea* of him. A rescue dog for a rescued person. A rescue dog for a rescued marriage. A living, sniffing symbol of the ability—canine and human alike—to survive, salvage and persevere.

Through his life, Vector's impact on me has been both momentous and multi-faceted. It has flowed from what Vector is, what he is not, and what he represents. It is the unlikelihood of his long, happy life—and my joyously benevolent role in that life—that has made my rescue dog a monkey wrench, one whose pacifying powers seem to shapeshift to suit whatever ailment currently plagues me most.

Sometimes I need to be reminded of my scrappy sato's seemingly limitless reserve of resilience, a never-say-die fortitude in the face of perils that, typically, make my problem du jour seem comparably trivial. Often, Vector unmistakably (if unknowingly) delivers his message of downtrodden one-upmanship with a simple sideways glance, his pupils shifting to reveal the whites of his large eyes in what suspiciously resembles an eyeroll. "I've been through far worse," the look suggests, "and I'm still here, not only surviving but thriving."

Sometimes I need to borrow his Buddhist detachment—his inherent doggie ability to take life one distinct moment at a time, rather than letting a few setbacks steamroll the promise of the present. Here, Vector's status as a calm, content being once at death's door makes his overarching message—something to the tune of "just take it easy, daddams"—all the more impactful.

And sometimes I just need a sounding board who can't understand what he's hearing, nor fashion a response. Sometimes I just need to vulgarly vent, or self-servingly whine, or even shed a few pent-up tears. At these moments—and there are many—Vector offers acknowledgment and love without making me feel judged and self-conscious. He makes me feel *heard*, which is sometimes more important than being understood. He is the only soul on Earth capable of performing this trick, however illusory it may be.

Over the next dozen chapters, we'll address a half-dozen issues that hinder us humans, from mental illnesses and addiction to grief and … well, our fellow humans. Each theme comprises a memoir chapter involving Vector and I, followed by one featuring interview subjects whose rescue dogs have played significant roles alleviating their specific struggles.

In their own ways, all of the people we'll meet have been rescued by their rescues, as I was—and as I continue to be.

2

Trauma

Seeing, I, Dog

"Hi Wilma!" my then-six-year-old son, Nicholas, enthusiastically exclaimed upon opening the front door. Ever since he could reach the doorknob, he'd become our family's official greeter.

In bursts Wilma, off leash and off to the races. The two-year-old rescue dog is the pride and joy of Eric and Andrea, two close friends who, bless their hearts, consistently forget our preference that she be restrained when they come over, at least for the first half-hour or so.

Regardless, this was a nothingburger—a venial sin absolved by decades of dear friendship. Besides, Eric's penchant for living brashly and boisterously—a sort of details-be-damned gregariousness sometimes mistaken for thoughtlessness—is among the reasons we love him.

"Wilma T! I pity the fool!" I chimed in, parlaying her middle initial into a corny 1980s C-list celebrity reference. Officially, her name is Wilma T. Dog; the "T" stands for "The," an homage to Wile E. Coyote of Looney Tunes fame.

Wilma has substantial percentages of both Pit Bull and Poodle, but really she's just like Vector: a twenty-something-pound mutt. In fact, a DNA test declares Wilma 26 percent "Supermutt," denoting a jumble of breed percentages so minuscule they cannot be confidently pinpointed.[1]

Wilma bounds into our home, does an exciting-new-place dash through the living room, den and kitchen, returns to greet me with a generously salivated lick across my face. She attempts a similar pooch smooch for Nicholas—paws on his shoulders as her head darts in—but he falls backward onto his behind. Undeterred, Wilma falls with him, planting a sloppy kiss on her helpless target.

Stunned, Nicholas' brow starts to furrow, his eyes well just a bit…

… but he doesn't cry. His face straightens, then beams, giggling along with his already-laughing dad. A big boy moment for a kid accustomed to getting jostled by his often rambunctious but always well-intending four-legged brother. No harm intended, none given.

While this transpired, Nicholas' sato sibling sidled in the background, unsettled yet unable to do anything about this faster, younger canine cruising his home turf. Just a few years ago, Vector never would have let another dog get within licking distance of his little brother. Now, at an arthritic age 11, it's impossible to discern how much of Vector's uneasy inaction is due to his semi-familiarity with Wilma, and how much is simply an older, hobbled dog avoiding conflict unless he deems it absolutely necessary.

Because knowing Vector, conflict was certainly on his mind. Some dogs see another dog and want to play; mine sees another dog and wants to play executioner. And while Vector's outward aggression toward his fellow canines has diminished as his gait slows and coat grays, his disdain is permanent.

Soon enough, the inevitable occurs. Wilma saunters up to Vector, who gives some ground before tensing up and digging in. Wilma's innocent (if somewhat naïve) approach continues, and a traditional doggie introduction ensues: a thorough butt-sniffing.

One Mississippi…. Grrrrr….

Two Mississippi…. Snap!

Vector lunges and lashes with the speed and strength of a dog half his age. Stunned by the unexpected aggression, Wilma backs away. Not wanting to find out what happens next, I promptly separate the two. Harm definitely intended; none given, fortunately.

"And that, my friend," I remind Eric, "is why we leash."

Fifteen minutes later, a now leashed Wilma and Vector once again come into close quarters, this time under the dining room table. It is détente via distraction; the peace between surly sato and aloof guest holds only because the former is too busy begging for scraps for another chomp at the latter's cheek.

It's simple: Vector loves food slightly more than he hates dogs. For a decade running, a full belly has been my boy's permanently paramount priority.

Before he loses some of the luster applied during last chapter's unabashed tribute, let me clearly state that Vector is a great dog.

He's just not always a good one. This is because his protracted period of desperation in one the world's worst places for stray dogs, Puerto Rico, has left Vector with proclivities that have lasted a lifetime.

But the point isn't Vector's trauma-ingrained tendencies. It's Vector's contentedness *despite* them. The point is pointlessness—his ability to make his trauma, with a little help from his family, as insignificant as possible. Forever home is far more important than forever flaws.

2. Trauma: Seeing, I, Dog

It's a lesson I continue to learn, often the hard way and always incompletely.

"That's … 20 over 100," said the optical assistant.
"That's … really bad news," I replied, with gallows humor.
Twenty over 100. That means I need to be five times closer than a normally-sighted person to see clearly. That's halfway to legally blind—and with eyeglasses *on*, no less.

That exam, in 2021, was my worst to date. I'd been in the 20/60–70 range for nearly two decades.

"Here we go again," I thought, give or take a few expletives.

My eyesight is the one thing I would change about myself—and that's coming from a clinically depressed recovering cocaine addict. It started in 2003, with two terrifying words scrawled atop an examination report.

"Mass lesion."

A visual field test checks for scotomas (blind spots) in a patient's eyesight. Mine showed worrisome black spaces spanning a quadrant in each eye. Frequently, bilateral scotomas are caused by a tumor pressing against the optic chiasma, where the optic nerves cross; an MRI was ordered to scan for such a malignant interloper. A few nerve-wracking days later, the doctor called. Not a tumor.

But not in the clear, either. Soon, my vision diminished to 20/30—about 50 percent of normal corrected acuity.

Thus began a mortifying 18-month medical misadventure to determine why a 24-year-old was seemingly going blind. The issue was my optic nerve; comparing the eye to a camera, my problem concerned the cable, not the lens.

Neurologists. Ophthalmologists. Neuro-ophthalmologists. When you're stumping doctors with seven-syllable titles, there's reason to worry.

Chart tests. Field tests. Colorblindness tests. Failed, failed, and failed miserably. Electrophysiology exams. More MRIs. A spinal tap when one doctor suspected multiple sclerosis. He was wrong—another bullet dodged. Meanwhile, my eyesight slipped to 20/40. Then 20/50. Then 20/60. Then…

… it just stopped. Satisfying diagnosis aside, the remainder of my eyesight was spared, at least for the time being.

What hadn't been spared was my psyche.

I don't know whether I'd have developed crippling anxiety, chronic depression and drug addiction without so severe a blow to my mental well-being. What I do know is that the connection between my eyesight and those conditions is strikingly linear.

My vision loss curtailed, I reengaged with life. I recommitted to my career, moved out of my childhood home, married my longtime girlfriend. I tried to fast-track an adulthood delayed by a protracted medical scare and its growth-stunting fallout.

It just didn't work. Gripping anxiety, insufferable insomnia, deep-fog depression. Finally, the suicidal gesture discussed in the previous chapter. All of it has a genesis in the inescapable detriment I wake up with every morning.

Partial sensory disabilities are largely invisible to others. While I'm nowhere near needing a white cane or guide dog, each day I face the world with an incomplete picture of my surroundings, lacking full functionality without most people even noticing. Alienated and anonymous, I get by with 8-bit vision in an HD world.

Despite my most eloquent efforts, my visual disability remains elusively indescribable. I can't see what I can't see and, therefore, cannot fully grasp what I'm missing. Conversely, showcasing what I *am* seeing is impossible, because everyone can only see the world through their own eyes, damaged or otherwise.

The result is a medically unique condition fomenting a correspondingly customized loneliness. Comprehensive empathy with another human is unobtainable. And unlike my arrested addiction and medicated, psychiatrist-treated depression, my visual disability never gets better. My eyesight is stuck on the "shitty" setting.

It is unalterably perpetual. So is its mental toll.

For starters, the prolonged period of unexplained vision loss bred anger, resentment and cynicism. I'll admit it: that this fate befell me, at such a young age, pisses me off something fierce. It is intolerable and unfair. And as much as depression treatment and addiction recovery push against this ultimately useless narrative, part of me hasn't forgiven the universe. I want my eyesight back, goddammit.

Further, my misfortune wouldn't have been so traumatic had doctors just *listened* to me. Time and again, the same smart people with the same smart-people pedigrees took the easy way out when stumped. It was, I was told, mostly in my head. I had a visual deficit, yes, but one exaggerated by panic. The not-so-implied message: You aren't going blind, you're going crazy. Only once it *stopped* getting worse did these same folks realize that, indeed, 20/60 was my visual ceiling.

In fact, my eyesight hadn't actually stopped declining. It just stopped declining *quickly*. It went from taking months to lose a line to years to lose a fraction of one. For proof, I need look no further than a book I used to rapidly read but now struggle to peruse. Again, only I can see what I see … and what I see isn't what I used to see.

Worst of all is the dread. Not fear of living with my current detriment, but the specter of further deterioration. Regardless of how "clinically stable" my eyesight might seem, I've certainly lost more vision over the years. This "examination elusiveness" is itself frightening. Even the most modern detection methods struggle to pinpoint mild vision loss. There's a lot of fear, and a lot of loneliness, in that.

A Sword of Damocles dangles over my already-frayed optic nerve. I don't have much more to lose without forfeiting any semblance of normalcy. My roughest days—an even-worse-than-usual stretch due to eyestrain, too much sun or other stressors—evoke a pit-in-the-stomach panic. Is this difficult day an even-less-acceptable preview of the near future?

Even "good vision" days are … well, not particularly good. I've flagged down a bus from afar, only to realize it was a truck. I've made crude inside jokes to friends only to realize that, on closer inspection, they were complete strangers. I've violated the small-font instructions of countless documents and street signs.

It's just … relentless. And immovable. And irreversible. It requires navigating countless impossible scenarios, from following PowerPoint presentations in meetings to baseball games from the stands. My blown-up computer screen text, my too-close-to-the-TV chair. My feigned happiness when someone gifts me a paperback when enlarged-text e-readers are a must. My eyesight is an indignity bombarding me with simple tasks I simply cannot perform.

Even now, after 20 years, I go through obsessive stretches. I'll catch an even-blurrier-than-usual glimpse, test my eyesight against self-established baselines, and it's off to the cycle-repeating races. Eyestrain and headaches. Anxiety and anger. Dejection and depression. My physical disability reverts to its yearslong role as mental malady catalyst. Vision loss, anxiety and depression become intertwined, their boundaries—like my vision itself—blurred, even indistinguishable.

Unsurprisingly, there are real-world consequences. Anguish over my eyesight often "pre-fills" the amount of frustration, annoyance or pain I can handle. Some days, my disability is about all I can deal with and, when additional stressors inevitably arrive, I overreact. I wake up fed up, an ill omen for the busy day ahead. "This is unacceptable and unfair," screams my internal monologue. "So screw all this, and screw all of them, too. This is useless."

Useless. My eyesight caters to depression's primary emotional ingredients: hopelessness, futility, worthlessness. There's a fine line between "it is not good" and "*I* am not good." And if my eyes will never get better, this diseased mindset says, *I* will never get better.

Suffice to say I don't have much wiggle room here—physically or mentally. And that brings us back to 2021. To 20 over 100. To a 42-year-old with a decade of sobriety and a promising career. To a husband and father with a hell of a lot to lose.

The next day I visited an optometrist. For someone long dependent on optic nerve specialists, it felt like amateur hour. Eyesight, meet eyeroll.

But not this time. The optometrist fiddled with my lenses, conducted his "1 or 2?" and "2 or 3?" progression tests…

… and got my eyesight back to where it was, 20/70-ish. It was my first big scare in a while. It will not be my last.

My eyesight will continue to cause fear, stress, frustration, isolation. It will smack me with daily examples of my "less than" existence. It will drive me toward depression and, sometimes, I will take the ride.

Living with so marked a detriment is a perpetual exercise not in eliminating its mental impact but mitigating it. My eyesight and psyche are too compatible, and too compromised, for a knockout win. My victories are narrower, and come via majority decision—or rather, *my* decision to move forward, in-focus or otherwise.

There are no long-term answers, only short-term solutions. I will live as well as I can for as long as I can. With an issue so complex, so entangled with my very being, I must keep it that simple.

For Vector, no such extended qualification is necessary. His status as a trauma sufferer is inherent, obvious, implied in what he is. Rescue dogs are, well, *rescued*. Delivered by humans from untenable, often unsurvivable situations—and such situations cause trauma.

No being, however blessed with the amnesia of a less sophisticated brain, emerges from what Vector went through on the streets of Puerto Rico without trauma. And by trauma, I don't mean physical scars like his bitten-off tail, deep snout wound or conspicuously missing toe. I don't mean his caught-just-in-time heartworm or the chronic ehrlichia that plagues him to this day. I don't even mean the curled up, quivering anxiety he displayed for his first few weeks with Patty and me.

No, those harms are, respectively, physical consequences and acclimation-related nerves. Trauma is what gets instilled in a being for longer than it takes to get accustomed to new surroundings, however more promising than the previous setting.

For Vector, trauma is what rears its head nearly every time any other dog, including his houseguest Wilma, gets too close for his warped sense of comfort. A slow-rolling growl, a raised upper lip. A lunge stopped only by my double-handed tug on a taut leash. *Christ*, he's strong for such a little mutt.

We discovered Vector's vehemently anti-canine stance early in our time with him—and nearly at a very dear cost. I was a very new dog owner, and I did a very stupid thing: I took a rescue dog from the streets and, after months of cuddling and isolation from other pooches, plopped him right down in the dog run at our local park.

The trouble started ... oh, about 10 seconds later. A tail-wagging French Bulldog innocently trotted up to Vector for a butt-sniffing, let's-be-friends introduction. It was rebuffed with a nip, a leap ... and a last-second save as I lifted the frightened Frenchie to safety—a no-no turned necessity since it was between me and Vector, who was milliseconds from clamping down on its neck.

A heartfelt apology to the French Bulldog's owner, and a heart attack-inducing lesson learned. No more dog runs for this sato.

I'd like to report that Vector's "no (other) dogs allowed" policy grew more lenient over the years. It simply did not. There are very few dogs Vector has ever been truly OK with. One is his "aunt," Xena, who we'll meet in Chapter 12. A few other dogs who frequent our home—pets of friends and family—have earned Vector's begrudging tolerance, a "stay over there and we're cool" doggie détente.

The rest? Look the fuck out, fido. Twenty-two pounds of terror, flying fangs-first at your jugular. The size of the other dog means nothing to Vector, meaning his aggression runs the gamut from attempted murder (Chihuahuas and Cairn Terriers) to attempted suicide (German Shepherds, Rottweilers, etc.). He lunged at a Great Dane once, which apparently was hysterically funny to everyone who witnessed it ... save for yours truly.

Lord knows I've tried to get Vector to be more accepting of other dogs ("more accepting," in Vector's case, would basically mean him recognizing another dog's right to co-exist in the same park, or even the same planet). I've tried easing him into a meet and greet, leash slacked to show I have confidence in him. I've tried easing him into a meet and greet, leash taut so he knows I'm right there for backup. I've tried showing love to both him and another dog at the same time.

Failed, failed, and get-the-hell-away-from-my-daddams failed.

His penchant for all things food-related is another survivalist holdover. Or at least, the *extent* to which Vector is steered by his stomach is likely due to an extended period when going to great lengths for a meal was the difference between life and death.

All dogs are motivated by food, at least to some degree. Vector takes it to the nth degree. While most dogs equate extra food as a highly attractive commodity, Vector sees *all* food through the lens of a being accustomed to not knowing where his next meal is coming from. He's wired to go for food full throttle.

Could we have trained him better? Absolutely. I'll be the first to admit that I'm a softy when it comes to my Veckie, as if authoring this book didn't make that entirely obvious. But while obedience school may have improved Vector's incessant begging at the dinner table, those everyday settings are inconsequential compared with some of his other food-centric fiascos.

It is in these culinarily convenient circumstances that the street dog in Vector truly resurfaces. Like when he mugged a three-year-old at a backyard barbecue for a hotdog. (OK, maybe "mugged" is an exaggeration. More like "theft by intimidation.") Or stolen any number of edible items out of his younger human brother's unsuspecting hands.

Indeed, it's the times when Vector *isn't being watched*—if only for a few seconds—that his sato sneakiness comes to the forefront.

Once, I was doing a few dishes, a chore that takes all of five minutes. I finished up, dried my hands, walked five paces into the living room … and

Vector on Father Day 2017: impossible around dogs, insatiable around food, and adorable in general.

2. Trauma: Seeing, I, Dog

there was a white bag with a hole in it. It took me several minutes to realize that Vector had gone into my messenger bag, stolen a piece of crumb cake I'd bought from our favorite bakery, ripped open the bag ... and devoured *every last crumb* of it. By that, I mean there was no sign of a crumb cake—a white, powdery bakery item prone to lots of ... well, crumbs—on our dark living room rug. Only a white bag with a hole in it. This perfect confectionary crime (we called him "Crumb Bum" for weeks afterward) took Vector less time than it took me to do a few dishes.

But Vector's most outrageous (and funniest) capers have transpired when we weren't home. There are places he's reached for a morsel—a too-high cabinet atop a too-high narrow counter, for example—that seem nearly impossible for a dog his size to access. Often, these escapades have two layers of implausibility; for example: "How did he get up there ... and how did he open that without thumbs?" Once, he opened a heavy drawer (which should require thumbs) with a child safety lock on it (which again, should require thumbs), pushed aside a heavy glass lid and then ate ... dry rice. Like, a *lot* of dry rice. Midday walks were interesting for the next week or so.

Once, he opened the pantry door, dragged the garbage into the kitchen, knocked it over, devoured whatever was reasonably edible ... and nervously pooped on the floor next to the mess.

These proclivities aren't going anywhere. Vector's distaste for other dogs and his mega-taste for food are trauma-based issues that are too ingrained, too intractable. Vector with other dogs just isn't going to happen, nor is Vector behaving himself even mildly around anything edible.

We know these things are permanent because Vector's impermanence is upon us. At his advanced age, he will not suddenly become interested in making new friends or passing up some clandestine chow. He's a food-driven people pooch, period.

And in living with his trauma, what Vector has taught me is one simple lesson: these permanent imperfections are perfectly OK.

As much as I want to see life as a linear exercise in improvement—a notion buttressed by my longstanding, group-centric recovery from addiction, which pedestalizes progress—some things simply never get better.

What doesn't kill you doesn't always make you stronger. Some things simply nick away at life without amassing the proverbially fatal 1,000 cuts. Some things are imperfect and permanent, and we just have to live with them. Not overcome them, but move forward despite them.

So it is with my eyesight and the angst it causes. And so it is with Vector's excessive food motivation and intolerance for other dogs.

Regarding Vector, reaching such a conclusion is merely a

consideration of time. Because he simply doesn't have enough of it left to reverse those longstanding trends.

Assessing my situation is far less cut and dry, but at its heart is that my eyesight and its associated trauma are too mortifying, too multifaceted and altogether too monumental to conquer. Both physically and emotionally, my visual disability is too big *not* to fail. I am never going to be completely comfortable or accepting of my defective (and still slowly deteriorating) vision. There will always be significant amounts of fear and anxiety, and some degree of resentment, stemming from this.

The physical detriment will never get better, and almost certainly get worse. The emotional anguish has a demarcation line past which I'll likely never mature. Twenty years of living with this have taught me that, mentally, there's a limit to how OK with my eyesight I'll ever be.

The recovering addict in me sees this realistic realization as self-defeating, even pusillanimous. This "Recovery Chris" logic contends that the tools used to achieve physical sobriety can further my emotional sobriety indefinitely. And I'm happy to report that this mindset is mostly accurate.

Mostly—but not completely. There are things no amount of 12 Step-work, therapy or other self-help tools will budge, at least past a certain point of mental health. My eyesight has proven Exhibit A for such exceptions.

Being OK with not being OK isn't something that comes naturally to me. My recovery from addiction and depression, as well as my repaired marriage (see Chapter 8), have ingrained in me the notion that hard work and altruistic intentions will yield prodigious progress with personal problems. And nothing is more personal to me than my eyesight.

But that mindset is simply wrong, at least in this select circumstance. Regarding my eyesight and its trauma, working toward progress-oriented growth isn't the solution, but merely a recipe for more problems—for continued frustration, unrealistic expectations, and recurring dismay. Meeting these emotions with a pugilistic attitude have only led to repeated gut punches. I'm better off dodging and ducking, not digging in and slugging.

There's a difference between giving up and accepting your limitations; I must realize that my visual disability and the emotional traps it sets occupy the latter category. Dwelling on it doesn't make it better; it only gives it more space in my head to further mess with my mind.

Perseverance doesn't always involve conquering, or even freedom. Sometimes it just involves surviving and thriving despite an intractable, permanent obstacle.

It's a complicated lesson. And I learned it from a dog.

2. Trauma: Seeing, I, Dog

In fact, there are two lessons here—one per each of Vector's trauma-related proclivities. Let's look at his food fetish first.

As a writer, I'm constantly challenging myself to pass the "who cares?" hurdle. It's basically a test that asks whether what I'm writing is really worth writing—that it's actually going to resonate with readers. Vector's all-out attitude toward food procurement has presented me with a different type of "who cares?" test. As in "who cares if he never really gets over it?"

There are exceedingly few scenarios where Vector's inability to control himself around food really matters. Unless he manages to break into a chocolate store or a grape orchard, it's not going to usher in his doggie demise. And besides, considering his history I'm sure he's eaten worse.

So it is with my eyesight—or, rather, the emotional trauma it causes. Earlier, I declared that I must meet so complex an issue with simplicity. My vision and its fallout bring so many knotted problems and fears that unraveling them is self-defeating.

Sometimes, the best you can do with swirling worries and persistent frustrations is to shrug them off one day at a time—to place a perpetual pin in a problem with no permanent solution. Sometimes, I just need to acknowledge that I've come this far—strong marriage, wonderful child, promising career—despite my disability, and that tomorrow I'll go a step farther. It's always going to be a (if not *the*) source of anxiety and discouragement and resentment … but so far it hasn't landed a knockout blow.

Vector can live a full life even if his stomach (at least in his opinion) is eternally empty. I can lead a full life even with a haranguing dialogue of "what ifs" swimming in my mind, and objects often swimming in my line of sight. It's a big, fat thing to say "who cares" to, but I try—and the grit and guts I know Vector embodies help me flip my demons a daily middle finger. Fuck off, fear, I got shit to do today.

Unlike his aggression toward food, of course, Vector's aggression toward other dogs could certainly be dangerous. He could get himself killed or kill another dog, neither of which is acceptable.

But while this trauma-centric behavior remains unresolved, it has not gone unaddressed. There are guardrails in place. There is me, my wife, his grandpaw (my dad). We all know to warn off fellow dog owners in the park. And when our "No, please, he doesn't like other dogs" requests go unheeded, Vector goes apeshit. So we brace, embarrassingly yank him away and…

… nothing. It passes. He goes back to sniffing, marking and meandering. He goes back to a dog with a terrible past living his best possible present.

Every time Vector shows teeth at a passing dog, I am reminded of both the dichotomy of life and our ability to live with uncleanable stains on our souls. At home, and with the vast majority of other humans, Vector is the sweetest dog on Earth. Gentle, non-threatening, passive. But his trauma has changed his attitude toward one specific set of fellow beings; it just happens to be other canines. It's an unfortunate, lifestyle-limiting holdover from his violent pre-salvation past.

Holdover, yes. But hangover? No. The curious dog passes, and Vector calms down. A defect that will never disappear recedes to the background, and life goes on. Vector does not detach from these dustups with malice, or fondness, or even indifference. He detaches from them *entirely*—without giving them a second thought.

Of course, he's totally cheating. Anyone who's left the house for five minutes and had their dogs greet them like they were gone five days knows our pooches live moment to moment. Vector's ingrained trauma—the genesis of his unbecoming behavior—is a result of living through an extended, life-threatening emergency. At this point it is essentially nurture-instilled nature, a sort of learned instinct. By contrast, Vector's trauma-triggered confrontation with another dog doesn't fester in Vector's brain because it pretty much can't. It is an excitable exception to his now-wonderful life rather than a violent facet of his formerly frightening one. Vector moves on because he has a lot of great things to move on to.

Asking me to detach from my eyesight—physically or emotionally—is, of course, impossible. But I must take Vector's example by making an active effort to forget the most recent embarrassment, limitation or new sign of potential deterioration. This thing is going to affect me no matter what; I just can't let it run my goddamn life. We've seen what happens when it does—crippling anxiety, despondent depression, low-bottom addiction.

I strive toward this ideal without ever realizing it. But realizing it isn't the point. Living as well as I can as long as I can is. And in Vector, I have a companion who has already accomplished this goal.

As I write this, Vector is four months past his ninth "gotcha day." He was about three when we got him, so that makes him 12. Considering his horrible history and chronic ehrlichia, every single day we have with Vector from this point forward is gravy.

Recently, Vector's septuagenarian vet retired. As we left his office for the final time, his parting remarks were to express that helping to keep Vector alive this long was truly a joy for him. That expression of graciousness from a consistently stand-up guy has an underlying message: "I wasn't sure he'd make it to my retirement."

In my house, Vector is playing with house money. In my heart, he is already victorious. The universe tried to prevent him from senior citizenship. Vector 1, Universe 0.

My final score is still unsettled. I've mentioned that I'm not so much worried about my eyesight tomorrow as my eyesight 20 and 30 years from now. If I'm barely capable of mentally and emotionally handling my current level of impairment, how will I cope with becoming *more* blind as the decades pass?

I don't know. But what I do know is I have the perfect role model. In Vector, I have a soulmate who is already a senior, and whose longstanding, chronic health issues continue to take their toll. His arthritis is getting worse, as is his hearing and vision. His gait is slower, his leaps lower, his skin sagging.

But you know what? He still gets by just fine. And most importantly, he still has joy in his life. He doesn't always hear me when I walk in the door, but when he does he's the same excited dog thrilled that daddy's home. Here, the fact that dogs stay mostly mentally consistent throughout their lives—that Vector is basically the same dog he was a decade ago, something that most certainly can't be said for my son—only punctuates the reassurance of this new, older Vector still being, for the most part, the same old Vector. His body is slowly falling apart, but his ability to still do *most* of the things he loves—albeit more slowly—makes getting out of his doggie bed in the morning more than worth it. He's well past his physical peak, but far from done—and far from dejected.

Unencumbered by a sense of time, dogs don't seem to possess the ability to mourn for themselves. As forlorn as Vector would be if I didn't come home one night, he isn't in tune with his own history enough to, for example, consciously notice that he used to run faster, leap higher, or have more energy generally. This partial amnesia serves dogs well in old age. Instead of pining for the past and fearing the future, as we humans largely do in old age, dogs simply enjoy the time they have left as much as caninely possible.

The takeaway is clear: "You'll be all right, dad. Or as all right as you allow yourself to be."

And in the meantime, he's here to help deal with the traumatic trials and tribulations of life as a visually impaired person. Earlier, I mentioned that one emotional symptom of my poor eyesight is that it prefills the level of stress I feel capable of handling on any given day. And given my 50-hour-a-week day job, uber-hobby (this), indefatigable young son and house that seems to always have something falling apart, there are a hell of a lot of stressors in my world besides not being able to see it clearly.

Being simultaneously fed up and inundated is a recipe for disaster, or at least displeasure. Despite feeling done with everything, I often finding myself having to do ... well, everything. In those situations seemingly anyone can be the tipping point toppling my waning, already-had-it-up-to-here composure. Clients, colleagues, cashiers. Wife, child, friends.

But not Vector. Even in my most frazzled state, I've never been capable of manufacturing anger against him. He is an innocent, blameless being. In an ideal world, one could make the same statement about children; but any parent (including me) knows that simply isn't the case. So here, Vector is unique in my household: he is a family member I see every day and never get tired of, not even for a second. Clients demand, colleagues annoy. Kids touch nerves and couples quarrel. But dogs never bring out the worst in us. This is especially valuable on days when the worst in me is boiling hot and bubbling barely under the surface.

On such despicable days, I don't take Vector for a walk. I do not wish to control him in those scenarios. More specifically, I do not feel capable of guiding him in those scenarios.

Rather, I take him out, unleashed, to our pleasant, fenced-in backyard. It is Vector's domain, a place where he can sniff and scratch and stretch and sunbathe without any fear or concern. Nowhere is Vector more his authentic, imperfect doggie self than in our backyard.

There, I take measure of this mutt. This old, arthritic, scarred, tailless street dog. He is still here, and still happy, despite everything. He has not let the terrifying things that have befallen him rob him of a joyful present.

I hope for some peace via osmosis, and head back into the house. Another day with my PTSD pal.

3

Trauma

Two Birds with One Bone

Among the happiest headlines ever born of disaster came on an infamous date: January 6, 2021.

Later that day, protestors who incorrectly believed President Donald Trump had been cheated out of reelection would storm the U.S. Capitol Building. Overshadowed by that day's attempt to violently undo a free and fair election was a headline posted earlier that morning to *The Washington Post's* website.

"So Many Pets Have Been Adopted During the Pandemic That Shelters Are Running Out."[1]

History can only be viewed from the present, and this news seems logical in retrospect. As we emerge from the deadliest pandemic in a century, the dramatic uptick in pet adoptions during the Covid-19 crisis has become part of a fixed national narrative. People were alienated, frightened and lonely, and they wanted companionship, cuddles and cuteness during the protracted lockdowns. Of course they did.

But that wasn't the initial reaction. At first, the fact that shelters were running out of animals actually seemed counterintuitive, especially given Covid's cratering of the economy.

"We thought people would stop adopting because they would need to conserve their money," said Cindy Sharpley, founder and director of Last Chance Animal Rescue, a nonprofit animal shelter in Waldorf, Maryland. "But that hasn't happened. It's been just the opposite. They're going like hot cakes." Per *The Washington Post's* reporting, Last Chance's adoptions jumped about 40 percent in 2020 compared with 2019, with most adoptees being dogs. Nearby Lucky Dog Animal Rescue in Arlington, Virginia, helped nearly 3,400 animals find homes in 2020, up from about 1,800 the previous year.

The article goes on to discuss the types of shelter shortage stories that would soon become common knowledge, including an anecdote where an adopter filled out nine applications before finding a rescue. It also shares data from Shelter Animals Count, which tracks activity at more than 1,000 shelters nationwide, citing a 15 percent year-over-year increase in adoptions from 2019 to 2020.

Shelter Animals Count's 15 percent figure roughly aligns with a survey conducted by the American Society for the Prevention of Cruelty to Animals. In late May 2021, the ASPCA reported that, per a poll of 5,000 representative U.S. households, nearly one in five had adopted a pet during the pandemic.[2] That result points to an astonishing 23 million American households adopting pets during the Covid-19 crisis. The most noteworthy of these households was the First Family, with President Joe Biden and First Lady Jill Biden adopting a dog, Commander, in December 2021.

Encouragingly given understandable fears (and scattered reports) of "adopter's remorse" among animal advocates, the ASPCA poll noted that the vast majority of new pet adopters—90 percent for dogs, 85 percent for cats—were not considering returning their new family members. While still too high, this 10–15 percent attrition rate tracks with pre-pandemic levels. In August 2021, the Animal Humane Society seconded the sentiment of stable return rates, despite widespread anecdotal reporting of recent adopters returning or even abandoning dogs and cats.[3]

With the pandemic somewhat waning and Americans fully reemerging from their homes, *The Washington Post* did a follow-up story exactly a year and a day later. The January 7, 2022, headline reads like the best possible of problems: "Americans Adopted Millions of Dogs During the Pandemic. Now What Do We Do with Them?"[4]

It's an important question, but not as critical as the salvation of so many dogs and cats found during an otherwise mortifying, macabre and altogether miserable time for us humans. For them, whatever comes next is undoubtedly preferable to the alternative. It's better that a dog is alone in a loving home for a few hours, a byproduct of reopened offices, than packed into a shelter cage. Pet owners were making accommodations for their four-legged family members far before the advent of Covid-19. Those who become adopters during the prison-life pandemic will figure it out as they reengage with the world.

And they better, because animal shelter populations discouragingly surged again throughout 2021, and continued climbing into 2022.[5] By January 2022, Best Friends Animal Society estimated there were 60,000 more dogs and 40,000 more cats in need of homes than in January 2021.[6] Unfortunately, at least some of this glut was due to returned Covid adoptees—typically due to financial constraints, as the pandemic stretched bank accounts for a second consecutive year.[7] In mid–2022, high inflation caused a further uptick in returned pets.[8]

3. Trauma: Two Birds with One Bone

Still, one overarching takeaway remains: humans in crisis turned to animals in crisis. That we did so may seem obvious in hindsight—but at the time, it wasn't. With the economy in tatters, saving money was extremely important. But saving our sanity—saving our*selves*—was paramount, even existential.

The scale to which we saw rescue animals as a key aspect to keeping calm and carrying on is telling, and the individual stories are compelling. Here is but one, which exemplifies how intimately trauma and rescue dogs can go hand in paw.

To say Deanna Cheng was not a dog person is like saying Superman wasn't much for kryptonite.

For the vast majority of her life, Deanna suffered from a deep fear of canines. But unlike, say, an alcoholic/addict like me steering clear of bars, Deanna didn't see the distance she kept from dogs as healthy. She was an otherwise rational person with an irrational phobia, and it weighed on her.

Deanna's childhood helped set the stage. Her mother wasn't into animals, and her sister was an asthmatic, making most potential pets a nonstarter. Her dad would quash any lightly entertained notion of getting a dog by exaggerating the negatives: big hassle, can't go on vacation, need to clean up after it. Combined, the whole clan was basically a great big doggie don't.

Then, as a young girl, Deanna visited a relative who had a large dog. The dog bit her, and it was the first of several unfortunate incidents between her and canines.

"I had always only had charged experiences with dogs," she remembers. The resulting fear was self-reinforcing—a snowball effect that gathered momentum as she got older. "When you're afraid of dogs, everyone will say something like 'they feel your fear.' Which is frustrating because … well, I *am* afraid of them." Not only was this repeated pointing out of the obvious unhelpful, but the embarrassment made Deanna even more reluctant to be near dogs at all.

"It became a loop," she said. She wanted to neither be near dogs nor be lectured about her fear of them. So she just avoided them entirely.

But of course, that's not really possible. In the United States, more than 65 million households are home to between 83.7 and 88.9 million dogs, and many people won't just lock Fido in the basement while their friend Deanna comes over for dinner.[9] So she adapted as best she could.

"I had friends' dogs who I was OK around after knowing them for a while," she relates. "But I still didn't 'get it.'"

For dog people—assumedly including most people reading this book—that's a big "it." The best Deanna could muster was a from-afar respect for dogs. She didn't identify with the deep emotional bond humans can form with their barking, tail-wagging family members.

"I really didn't know why people had them. I thought it was just a…" she pauses, as if choosing her words carefully so as not to insult her dog-loving interviewer (me) "…time suck. I just didn't get it on any level."

In 2018, Deanna moved with her husband, Wing, into a condo in the Glassell Park section of Los Angeles. The following week, she was walking to the community's mailroom. The complex's dog run was along her route.

There, one of Deanna's new neighbors had two small dogs, both leashed. He gave her a warm smile, and Deanna, being new to the complex, stopped to introduce herself. Then, for no apparent reason, one of the dogs leapt at her and chomped down on her calf. This was no mere nip.

"He clamped down hard," she recalls, wincing a bit. "He took out a chunk." The other dog joined the fracas, gnashing and lunging at Deanna. To that, the owner did…

… pretty much nothing. Whether momentarily dumbfounded or just plain dumb, he was, per Deanna, "sort of stuck on stupid."

Deanna is a very polished person—a fortysomething, educated, well-spoken woman. The only time she even approached profanity during our discussion was in relaying her reaction.

"I said something to the effect of 'Get your *fucking* dogs the *fuck* off me!'" she exclaims. It was the last thing someone already fearful of dogs needed.

The damage was far more than emotional. The small dog's big bite required a wound care specialist, and left Deanna dangling a leg out of the tub while bathing all summer. No pool, no ocean, no water-related anything.

And definitely no more dogs. It got to the point where she was beginning to panic simply passing leashed dogs in the park. And if they weren't leashed, the owner would hear it from her in no uncertain terms.

"The fear was heightening," she admits. "I was now at a fever pitch with dogs."

Shortly thereafter, pretty much everything else was at a fever pitch. It was March 2020, and Covid-19 was starting to inundate its first three U.S. outbreak zones: New York City, the Seattle area, and Deanna's Los Angeles.

On March 4 a state of emergency was declared. Two weeks later, a stay-at-home order was issued that remained in place for over 10 months—and even then, the country was still three months shy of widescale vaccine availability. Covid has killed nearly 100,000 Californians, which comprises some 12 percent of the population in a nation that has lost north of a million people to the protracted pandemic.

Along with the whole of white-collar America, Deanna began working exclusively from home. She has a company that creates montage videos for celebratory gatherings—something she was, in fact, already doing mostly from home. But her husband was in a different boat. Or rather, on one.

"Wing is in the merchant marines," she said. "He's five weeks here, five weeks gone, repeat."

Wing was on duty when the lockdowns commenced. The couple was childless. Deanna had a sister nearby but, other than that, was facing what so many endured throughout the public health crisis. Loneliness. Isolation. Alienation.

Deanna was alone—and she wasn't alone. In the early weeks and months of Covid-19, depression in the United States tripled. Pre-pandemic, one in 12 Americans suffered with it. As it stretched on, that figure rose to more than one in four. By mid–2021, it approached one in three.[10]

Deanna was going stir crazy. Then she got an idea that, for her at least, was stone cold crazy. What if she could cure one mental malady while preventing another?

"What if I fostered a dog?" she relates, understanding full well the non sequitur.

At first pass, it seems like a strange statement. Someone afraid of snakes isn't going to rush out and bring a slithering death monster into her home at a time that mandated she … well, be in her home.

But dogs are different, and Deanna knew they were different. She didn't want to live in fear of a creature with the pedestaled moniker of "man's best friend." And she saw this as a chance to rescue, even temporarily, an animal that might return the favor. An animal that might, in turn, rescue Deanna from her hyperventilation-level dread of a species the vast majority of others viewed as lovable and life-affirming. Perhaps this was an opportunity for a silver lining during exceedingly dark times.

"I thought maybe I could do something good," she remembers, "and maybe change my relationship to dogs, because my fear had heightened so much and it just wasn't good."

But as she admits, that doesn't fully cover it. There was something inexplicable going on here.

"I really can't explain an element of it, because it was so out of character."

Her husband agreed. In fact, he was shocked by the suggestion. He was also all-in on the idea, since he was a dog lover.

Soon, though, Deanna and Wing would encounter the same circumstances that so many would-be canine foster parents faced during Covid: there were, simply, very few dogs to foster. As the effort drew out into weeks, Wing worked his magic.

"He said something like 'I don't know if I'm going to be able to give a dog back,'" Deanna said. "He was slowly moving the goalposts on this whole project." To editorialize briefly, it was clearly spousal manipulation—and clearly awesome.

As a compromise, Wing suggested adopting a puppy, which would naturally be less instantly intimidating to Deanna. They could train the young dog and allow it to bond with the couple while it was still relatively harmless.

Following some false starts, they got lucky. After waiting for several hours at a local shelter, they were down to just a few folks ahead of them when the facility's last dog was adopted. As they turned to leave, though, they noticed a rescue organization drop off four black puppies. "They looked like little bears," she recalls. She learned later the litter of siblings was a mix of Golden Retriever, Labrador Retriever and Australian Shepherd.

They woke at 4:30 a.m. the next morning, arriving at the shelter, which opened at 7:00, by 5:00. The first dog available was skittish. Wing made a quick calculation and passed.

Then the dog's brother was brought out. It was love at first sight … for Wing, anyway. Deanna remained simultaneously all-in and reluctant. But a few weeks later, on April 28, Otto officially entered their lives.

Or rather, Deanna's life—because Wing had shipped out two days prior.

That was how the antithesis of a dog person found herself with a dog, alone in her condo, at the inception of the most isolating event in modern history. It was the combination of a commitment to personal progress, spousal cajoling, exceptional circumstance and…

… what exactly? There's a gap in the pie chart—a small but significant "other" amid the reasons Otto came to be a Cheng. There is something about dogs, and about us humans' symbiotic relationship with them, that defies categorization.

Deanna can't put her finger on it. And after countless hours of research, interviews and writing toward developing this 200-something-page book, nor can I. Science might call it the confluence of human evolution and canine domestication. But even that leaves a little sliver of inexplicability, and there is beauty in this mysteriousness. It took that extra something to make Deanna a dog owner.

"I didn't even think I could get him from the shelter to the car without dropping him," she confesses. Otto was about eight weeks old. "I was just completely out of my depth."

A friend who happened to be a dog trainer advised Deanna not to dote too much over the puppy, to give him his space to acclimate to the new environment. Deanna had no trouble doing that.

"I really just kept my distance for a while," she remembers. Still, she spent a considerable amount of time training Otto. Here, we start to witness Deanna's "two birds with one stone" plan come to fruition. She was slowly starting to understand a dog—a prerequisite for accepting and, eventually, loving it—while filling the lonely, monotonous glut of time so many of us suffered through during Covid lockdowns.

She also set boundaries—mostly, it seems, to provide her with a buffer between her and her budding yet imperfect acceptance of dog ownership. Otto wasn't allowed on the couch or upstairs. Deanna was getting there on her own terms—but she was getting there.

When her vet gave the all-clear for outside play (at first, Otto was exclusively inside due to fears of catching parvovirus, which kills 80 percent of puppies who contract it[11]), her sister's backyard became a several-times-a-day mainstay. Otto learned to sit, give paw, stay. They played treatsie hide and seek.

Deanna was both on a mission and still on guard. Her sister noted that she'd show up every day wearing the same "uniform"—hard jeans, boots, hair in a bun. Deanna recalls her retort.

"These things bite you," she told her sister. "I was in military mode. It was my only way through." Deanna was in the early stages of recovery from her fear of dogs, and wasn't letting her defenses down just yet. It was foreign, and frantic, and completely out of her comfort zone—and it gave her purpose during what for many seemed like an aimless purgatory.

In like fashion, Otto was becoming a double-trauma-drubbing dog. Deanna's obsession was shifting from her fear *of* dogs to caring *for* a dog. Among other endearing details, she gave her new family member a nickname that stuck.

"Otto Po-tah-to," she smiles.

For the first month, Deanna found herself sleeping not in her own bed but downstairs, next to Otto's crate. Wing put the kibosh on that when he returned, assuring Deanna that Otto would be fine for the night. Deanna's obsession pendulum, which had swung full range from deathly scared of dogs to scared to death of leaving one alone for a single moment, began to correct into something resembling normal.

And during the lengthy lockdown, Otto also was more than just a housemate to hunker down with. Her husband had a colleague who was working despite a cancer diagnosis, meaning he absolutely could not catch Covid. As a result, Deanna's pandemic pod consisted of her sister's family … and that's pretty much it.

Fortunately, Deanna had two young nephews, making the sojourns to her sister's backyard as much about existing family ties as they were about her newest family member. In bringing Otto there, she wasn't just alleviating her loneliness—she was delivering joy.

"My sister says Otto came at just the right time," she says. "Having Otto was such a ray of light for everyone—something fun and beautiful and brand new at a tough, uncertain time."

Then the kicker: "We needed him." In fact, her sister ended up adopting a dog the following year, making Otto influential in rescuing a fellow dog as well as a human.

Today, Deanna has zero fear of dogs. She goes to dog runs with Otto nearly every day. Otto is a big dog, and therefore in the big dog pen.

"Pit Bulls, Dobermans, whatever," she proudly reports. "There's no part of me that tenses up."

Deanna Cheng, her husband Wing, and Otto Po-tah-to (courtesy Deanna Cheng).

3. Trauma: Two Birds with One Bone

Otto spared Deanna the worst of Covid's emotional trauma. He didn't just alleviate the trauma her fear of dogs had caused, but completely eradicated it. It's gone—more than gone, actually. Deanna now finds herself on the other side of the Fido fence.

"I have no empathy now for people who *don't* love dogs," she shares. "If you're afraid of dogs, I don't get it. Nothing has carried over."

"I feel like he's opened up something in me. I feel like I have more love to give because of him." She turns around. Otto is upstairs, and up on the bed. Deanna doesn't order him down.

Deanna Cheng: from dog-averse to dog-avowed (courtesy Deanna Cheng).

Kyrah Altman was a young woman with her first apartment. Her new digs were dimly lit and in a dodgy area, but she fondly recalls it as a "mansion," complete with a grand (albeit fake) fireplace and broad windows providing upscale views of a downtrodden neighborhood.

It was something she'd been building toward for quite some time. Her own place—just her and her Beagle, Bambi. Kyrah was at peace.

Bambi not so much.

"Bambi would hear people walking outside, or on the apartment building stairs, and start barking," Kyrah recalls. "And it wasn't a bark for attention—it was more urgent, more fear-based."

Knowing it was nothing, other folks may have hushed the dog over a false alarm. Perhaps lovingly called the pooch silly. Maybe distracted it with a treat or chew toy.

This was the easiest path. But it wasn't the wisest—and despite being barely an adult, Kyrah Altman knew that intimately.

"I realized Bambi was reacting to some trigger that felt very real to her, so me telling her to stop barking—me dismissing her, saying 'it's nothing'—just doesn't work." Instead, she took a different tack.

"I found myself saying, 'I can understand why you're scared. You're safe, and we'll get through this together.'"

Kyrah knew that Bambi needed validation rather than repudiation, hugs rather than hushes. And in comforting her frightened canine friend, Kyrah Altman also was sending a message to the one being in the room that fully understood her.

Herself.

Bambi had brought a garbled inner monologue into a clear, outward dialogue. The barking Beagle played an integral role in helping Kyrah cogently formulate words that hadn't completely coagulated in her head. Bambi was a canine catalyst to sounder mental health practices for a young woman who'd already experienced a lifetime of trauma. As we'll see, it was by no means Kyrah's first breakthrough, nor would it be her last.

Bambi helped recall this wisdom from Kyrah's psyche because, while the threats Bambi perceived weren't real, the dog's trauma certainly was. Several years earlier, when Kyrah was still in junior high school, Bambi entered her life as a rescue from Tennessee. Life on the streets had been rough. Most of her tail had been cut off—a sick, Southern U.S. practice meant to show that, despite her well-suited breed, this Beagle wasn't a worthy hunting companion.

If possible, life in the ensuing decrepit shelter was even worse. Parvovirus ran rampant, and had killed a number of dogs. She was caged outside and fed just once daily. Bambi had survived, but faced another unacceptable outcome: due to their docility, Beagles are the most common breed used for medical experiments, particularly by the pharmaceutical industry.[12]

In 2022, the Humane Society conducted an undercover investigation that found Beagles subjected to tests for harsh cancer drugs, powerful painkillers and potent Hepatitis B medications.[13] Notably, the drugs weren't being tested for efficacy but rather toxicity; researchers basically wanted to determine whether the drugs were harmful or even deadly.

Bambi's breed is the first in the firing line of this disgusting practice. Because of this, Beagles are often bred in slapdash, slovenly fashion with the sole purpose of selling them to researchers. In 2022, a particularly putrid Beagle breeding facility in Virginia was shuttered and, fortunately, its dogs earmarked for adoption rather than pharmacological torture.[14]

Notably, the issue led Kyrah to support her first nonprofit. The Beagle Freedom Project is an organization that lobbies testing facilities to release their beleaguered Beagles directly to them rather than killing them post-experimentation. Shamefully, online videos show rescued Beagles experiencing sunlight and grass for the very first time, as many had never seen so much as the outside of a cramped cage.[15]

Luckily, Bambi avoided that particular fate. Still, when Kyrah met her, at the waiting room in that rundown shelter, her coat was tainted with feces. She stunk of urine, and had difficulty making so much as eye contact. She was a trembling wreck.

But then Bambi—in a scene strikingly similar to a shaking Vector's instant, character-breaking embrace of my wife and I—tepidly trotted up to Kyrah's three-year-old sister. The poor pooch, who the shelter folks had been calling Tilly, began licking her neck. The girl giggled, the dog seemed to exhale, and Kyrah swooned. A few days and a Disney-derived name change later—one inspired by her tan fur with white speckled spots—Bambi was an Altman.

So clearly, Bambi was a trauma survivor. And as we'll learn, so was Kyrah. In comforting her distressed dog that night, Kyrah was giving herself permission to love herself in whatever state she was in on any given day.

Kyrah is still a young woman—very young, in fact. When I interviewed her, in August 2022, she was all of 25. That's only significant because Kyrah Altman is also a CEO with nearly 10 employees. And because her organization, LEAD, is about as linear an example of turning pain into gain as one can find.

LEAD—an acronym for Let's Empower, Advocate & Do—arose from trauma on a variety of fronts. One was Kyrah's personal story. She grew up in a home that involved physical, psychological and sexual abuse of a caregiver. Notably, the family's chocolate Lab, Guinness, was a safe space for Kyrah—until a caregiver presumably killed it. For Kyrah, the dog came to exemplify lost love and unprocessed harm. Kyrah never got to say goodbye to Guinness—a harm that echoes with her to this day.

The eldest girl among four siblings, out of necessity she'd already become a de facto mother to two younger siblings when, at age 12, home life became even less tenable. It was time to go—and abruptly at that. After a tumultuous week in a hotel, Kyrah and some additional family members found an apartment. It was better than before, but nowhere near good.

Then, on December 14, 2012, a disturbed young man named Adam Lanza entered Sandy Hook Elementary School in Newtown, Connecticut. Armed with two rifles and a Glock handgun, Lanza murdered 27 people—including 20 children between the ages of six and seven—before taking his own life.[16] It is the second-deadliest school shooting in American history, surpassed only by the 2007 slaying of 32 at Virginia Tech University.

A nation with more guns than people mourned.[17] The president openly wept on national television. And eight sophomores at Leominster High School in Massachusetts founded an advocacy organization. Kyrah Altman was their leader.

Initially a means of raising awareness for gun violence and mental illness, by 2014 LEAD's scope had expanded to touch substance abuse and poverty, as well as two issues near and dear to Kyrah: domestic abuse and homelessness.

At its core, though, LEAD was focused on mental health—especially youth mental health—because Kyrah and her associates felt strongly that untreated mental illness was at the root of nearly all social issues they sought to influence. Among other initiatives, LEAD devised an in-depth mental health program to complement the course Massachusetts high schoolers already took. Titled "Mental Health Promotion," the 900-page tome met standards for PreK–12 health education, and suggested novel ways to incorporate mental health into existing curricula.

In 2016, now a student at George Washington University in Washington, D.C., Kyrah competed in the institution's new venture competition. Despite being among the only freshman and female finalists—and the only non-business undergraduate—she was awarded over $30,000 to incorporate LEAD as a nonprofit corporation. Three months later, Kyrah and co-founder Lauren Wilkins became credentialed as the youngest Youth Mental Health First Aid instructors in the country for the National Council for Behavioral Health. They were taking LEAD national—from their dorm rooms.

LEAD was highlighted on national television and highlighted in *The New York Times*' "The Edit," a newsletter targeted to college students.[18] Almost as an afterthought, Kyrah graduated in 2019 with a degree in human services, social justice, public health, and entrepreneurship. Lauren graduated from Northwestern University that same year, and the two launched LEAD as a full-time venture before their tossed mortarboard caps hit the ground.

LEAD expanded its program to provide programming and training for adults who work with underserved and high-risk youths in settings like summer camps, sports teams and athletic departments. To subsidize the cost, it also began working with corporations, to help companies craft their own mental health certification programs. That fall, its official train-the-trainer program, LEAD Academy, was launched, expanding the organization's reach to 20 states, which has since grown to 45.

The Covid-19 pandemic hit. Camps closed, schools went remote, youth sports were suspended. LEAD stumbled before pivoting to an online format. But it survived, led by its twentysomething survivor-in-chief.

Kyrah did all this without firm roots, without stability, without the reliable support a young person deserves. In fact, she did all this for lack of such nurturing. She admits that channeling her energy into building LEAD was an attempt to harness control from a life consistently devoid of it.

But she didn't do it alone. Her effort included more than a decade of various forms of therapy and coaching to deal with depression and PTSD anxiety. And throughout her healing journey, Kyrah had one constant at her side while she simultaneously tried to heal herself and launch a nationwide nonprofit.

Kyrah had Bambi. She had a dog healing from trauma for a life steeped in her own recovery from trauma. This wasn't dog ownership; it was dog partnership.

"I felt like I was her human rather than her being my dog," she says. "Bambi was with me through so many traumatic experiences. After difficult days and sobs in my car or in the bathroom, I'd look forward to returning to her for hugs, and to give her full-body massages and belly rubs. Despite her trauma, she was *confident* I was there to show her unconditional and limitless love, affection, and attention."

This was crucial, because times were exceptionally tough. In high school, Kyrah sometimes had to leave Bambi in the car on cold New England winter days, running out to the parking lot between classes to throw another blanket on her precious pooch. Despite the hardships, Kyrah was determined not to let Bambi experience any unnecessary pain or discomfort—because that was one of the few things in her control.

It was a labor of love—and of sanity. Bambi kept Kyrah's unraveled life tethered to something pure and wholesome. Here as elsewhere in this book, we find a dog with a bad past filling a void for a human with a bad present. A teenager from a broken home couldn't control much. But she *could* control whether Bambi's remaining years would be far better than her first few. And since animals are entirely innocent beings, she could do so without reservations or resentments—a mental salve with no emotional hangover.

"I also appreciated her honesty," Kyrah conveys. "If she was irritated with me, she would make silly groans and give me expressive looks. If she was hungry, she would 'tongue swoop' food directly off my plate."

This unencumbered honesty, she contends, is something she rarely finds in humans—or, she admits, herself. Bambi's faux-pas-be-damned candor gave Kyrah permission to be honest with her beastie bestie in ways she could never be with others.

Bambi was with Kyrah through abrupt, disruptive moves, through uncertainty and unfairness, through continued traumas that compounded existing scars. Kyrah's current life—her CEO life—showcases her resilience, strength, and ability to parlay pain into productivity. But whether she could have endured her volatile teenage years without her post-traumatic pal is an open question, one made moot only by Bambi's perpetual presence and unconditional love.

She couldn't, however, take Bambi to college in Washington, D.C.

Instead, while Kyrah was away, Bambi stayed with one of her high school teachers, who also had a Beagle.

"Bambi would go stay with her boyfriend, Odie," Kyrah jokes. In her DC dorm room, she kept a scrapbook full of Bambi photos and musings. She'd take Bambi back on breaks and during summers, piecing their lives together the best anyone in her position could. She remembers joyfully anticipating and craving their reunions.

By 2019 Kyrah was a full-blown dichotomy. Professionally, she'd achieved in less than a quarter-century what most people don't accomplish in a full one. But personally, she was still yearning for the very foundations of a healthy home life. Now, Kyrah was driven to change that.

"When I graduated from college, I was determined to give Bambi the life I always wanted for her throughout my adolescence." She pauses, then adds: "As well as for me."

"So when people asked me what my goal was in life," she continues, "my answer was always 'to be happy and safe.' I wanted a safe home where Bambi and I could live comfortably."

That Kyrah achieved this is as astounding as a sophomore in high school founding a nonprofit organization. Their modest apartment—the scene of this section's opening anecdote—was both *for* Bambi and *because of* Bambi. Their residence, like their rescue, was reciprocal. Kyrah and Bambi were in a peaceful home of both their making, lightyears from where each began.

Unfortunately, their newfound domestic bliss was short-lived. In late 2019, Bambi developed bladder cancer. It was aggressive. Kyrah depleted her meager savings to afford the medication that allowed Bambi to pass where Vector and, we can safely assume, the other rescues in this collection will pass: at home, surrounded by love. Bambi died in early 2020.

"She was the first being to show me unconditional love," Kyrah says. "Or maybe she taught it to me."

She didn't wait to pay that love forward.

"I was shocked by how ready I was to adopt again," she remembers, "but I think it was because of how much Bambi gave me. She gave me so much love and so much hope that of course I wanted to do this again."

Just a month after Bambi's death, Kyrah adopted Ollie from the Sato Project—Vector's alma mater. Bambi had helped create a life for Kyrah. Now Bambi had created a legacy that benefited both her trauma-surviving best friend and her trauma-surviving successor.

And it's a good thing Bambi did, because Ollie needed someone with both a heart and … well, patience. And stamina. And perhaps a good pair of running shoes.

Ollie—originally Pilgrim, because he was taken in by the Sato Project

Boating Beagle: Kyrah Altman and Bambi on a kayaking excursion (courtesy Kyrah Altman).

on Thanksgiving Day—was a tough nut to crack. Or rather, to catch and contain. While it's common for the Sato Project team to need some time to earn a prospective rescue's trust (to get close enough to scoop up), this pooch evaded them for a full week and a half leading up to his most fortunate Turkey Day feast.

His elusiveness was a preview of things to come.

"I quickly learned that he likes to run—and likes to run away," Kyrah says. "And he doesn't like to get caught." She swears Ollie sprints with a smile on his face.

Ollie has either broken or Houdini-ed his way out of multiple collars, leashes and harnesses. Once, he ran for miles through Worcester, Massachusetts' second-largest city. The incident ended with Ollie's cameo on a newscast and, shortly thereafter, reunion with his mortified mom.

"Me chasing him through traffic, and him loving it." For Ollie's own safety, Kyrah hired a trainer to teach him recall—commands like come, heel, here. After several months, the trainer gave up. Ollie was one stubborn sato, a proclivity with which I'm quite familiar.

Still, his troublemaking—and his eccentricities, like nuzzling into Kyrah's armpit, an oddity she calls "crevice time"—came in handy. The Covid-19 crisis commenced just a month after his adoption. Kyrah, like so many otherwise isolated folks during the pandemic, gives her dog a sizable sanity-saving assist.

"He was constantly making me laugh," she shares, "versus Bambi constantly giving me peace and love. Both are so important. I didn't realize how much I needed an Ollie kind of dog until I had already fallen in love with him. That laughter, that reminder of being present. That's important, especially with my past, and my issues."

Still, there was the runaway worry. Often, the impetus for Ollie's wanderlust was his desire to play with other dogs. Usually bigger dogs. So…

… Kyrah got a bigger dog. She adopted Daisy from Luving Paws Foundation, an affiliate of the Sato Project.

Daisy—a.k.a. Daisy Lu and Daisydoodle—is a big ball of love. She is calmer than her brother, and decidedly more attention-hoarding. Like Vector, she was all alone on that island for too long, and is really just done with lonely. She's a shadow through and through.

Kyrah surmises that Daisy would have been fine as an "only child."

Ollie (foreground) snoozing with his sister, Daisy (courtesy Kyrah Altman).

3. Trauma: Two Birds with One Bone

But of course, a huge reason for her adoption was her now-brother's excessive social streak. "With Ollie, I'm just so glad he's mine because I love him endlessly and I don't think he'd do too well with most people. And I think he's done so well with me because I'm able to provide trauma-informed love."

Kyrah Altman had a traumatic childhood. But while her young adulthood is shaped by trauma, it is by no means controlled by it.

The mid–20s are a transitory time, and listening to Kyrah's story leaves little doubt that the traumatic wounds of her youth will not metastasize in adulthood. Kyrah's four-legged children both benefit from her recovery and further it.

Of course, life is still … life. And death. In late 2022, Kyrah had to say goodbye to her mother, who died of addiction-related organ failure and physical injuries due to alcoholism. She was just 49. It was a bitter end to a lifetime of not seeking help for herself. In a follow-up to our interview, Kyrah admitted she was still nowhere near OK.

But she is … well, OK. When she came home from the hospital where her hopelessly comatose mother lay dying, her newer family members were waiting. Kyrah collapsed, crying, on the couch, clutching Daisy as Ollie perched over them. She was safe, and loved, and home. She was not OK, but had all the ingredients for OK right there with her.

There will be no cycle of trauma here. It ends with Kyrah—and began with a Beagle that gave her reason to push through to a time when the narrative was in her hands alone. It is a conscious choice that began unconsciously—with the simple act of loving and living for a fellow trauma survivor. A fellow rescue.

"It's rewriting your story, and deciding that from this point on, these are the values that we abide by, and this is the home we're going to have. Fuzzy blankets and candles. We live a simple, safe, good life."

4

Addiction

A Hopeless Drug Addict and a Doomed Dog Walk into a Bar...

Each September 25, Vector celebrates another birthday—or rather, another "gotcha day," the anniversary of his adoption into our family. The festivities have become a tradition centering around something that solidified his salvation with us.

Meatloaf.

As mentioned in Chapter 1, among the first things Vector did upon reaching his forever home was flee from it. On our inaugural walk the evening of his arrival, he wriggled free from his harness and sped off into the night. Patty and I scoured the neighborhood fruitlessly and returned home, distraught. He was gone for the longest 90 minutes of our lives.

Luckily, Patty had prepared a meatloaf the night before, and left a slice on our porch in an attempt to lure him back from wherever he was cowering. It worked. Not only did Vector take the bait, but he also pawed at the front door immediately afterward. Seconds, please.

At the time, all that mattered was the return of a scarred, scrappy sato from Puerto Rico who nearly became a scared suburban stray in northern New Jersey. We could care less how he got back to us; no use looking a gift meatloaf in the mouth, or in Vector's. What we hadn't yet realized, per Chapter 2's exploration of his trauma-born inability to pass up food, is how crucial that hastily heated hunk of hearty goodness truly was. In Vector's disoriented and distrusting state, swallowing a meal might have been the only invitation capable of coercing him to swallow his fear, however temporarily.

So each September 25, we celebrate this happiest of happenstances with a candle in a fresh piece of meatloaf. Hugs pulling double duty to restrain Vector from hopping atop the table before the last notes of "Happy Birthday!" are belted. Beaming smiles as he consumes his special-day dinner in all of 15 seconds. My overdone, snooty impression of a restaurant

4. Addiction: A Hopeless Drug Addict and a Doomed Dog ...

manager telling Vector that *Chez Dale* can squeeze him into the doggie dining room between the 7:30 and 7:31 reservations—a recurring daddams joke lovingly teasing the hound of the hour.

We celebrate all that Vector is, even the trauma staining his soul from his nightmarish first few years of scavenging subsistence. We honor the long-obvious reality that while we took the sato off the streets, the streets have never left the sato. We commemorate the beginning of his recovery from a near-death experience, however imperfect and incomplete this now-decade-long journey has proven.

Less than three weeks later, another milestone date warrants celebrating. Each October 11 marks another year of continuous sobriety for me—a

Vector's annual birthday meatloaf, with Patty and me in September 2018.

development that, as much as anything, is the genesis and cornerstone of our family. Had I not gotten clean and sober, Patty and Chris would go from having a history to being history. From there, two unfathomable consequences: Nicholas, our son, would not exist, and Vector would reside with someone else.

I do not believe in a god, or in fate, or in destiny. The advent of my 4,000-plus days without an alcoholic drink or inebriating drug was, before its sudden start, an extreme unlikelihood, the polar opposite of preordained. It was far from a foregone conclusion; it just happened to be the best possible one.

The same goes for Vector. A dog once earmarked for an early, anonymous and undignified death was not destined to reach old age in peace and love, in cuddles and kisses. Our humble ranch-style house was not fated to be Vector's forever home. It hinged on a series of improbabilities that began well outside each of our abilities to control, contain, or even indefinitely survive.

But we both beat the odds. We both did it. We both won.

My salvaged sato is a ripple effect of my salvaged life. And now that we have this—now that we have safety, security, each other—the very least I can do is commit to not picking up a drink or drug for another 24-hour period. To not sliding down the slippery slope of a relapsed addict grasping defeat from the jaws of victory. To remaining free of it one day at a time, preferably in perpetuity.

It is easy to label Vector and everything else good and gratifying in my life as a gift of my recovery from addiction; indeed, Alcoholics Anonymous certainly ascribes to this sentiment, one of many oversimplifications I find unattractive about an otherwise exceptional path to longstanding abstinence. What's more, I've already declared my sobriety the foundation upon which my house and household were built.

However, few things—not even a recovering pooch paired with a recovering person—are that simple. Recovery has too many mini-failures and mega-frustrations to paint with so broad a brush, or attempt to draw with straight lines. It is not a linear process but rather a living one, with the wrapped curves of symbiosis revealing Vector and I equal parts benefactor and beneficiary.

But let's back up. Before it got so very awesome, it got very, very awful.

"Are you *sure* about this?"

Mark, the office accountant, was doing his due diligence handling an exceptionally stupid demand.

In March 2010, I was "let go" from my executive-level position at a Manhattan public relations firm. But this was no downsizing: I was fired

4. Addiction: A Hopeless Drug Addict and a Doomed Dog ...

for being a drug addict. Weeks later, I was just a junkie needing cash, even if that meant "retirement" was coming three decades early.

"Yes," I replied. "Send it." Uncle Sam got a hefty tax penalty from the $30,000 check. The rest went up my nose. My bottom? Far from it. Another year would pass before I worked again and, from there, another six months before sobriety would finally commence.

My 401(k) caper was another step down addiction's steep spiral staircase. I was completely broke, and entirely unable to break a $1,000-per-week cocaine habit. I'd pilfered all I could from the joint account shared with my wife. My credit cards, courtesy of cash advances, were maxed.

This wasn't desperation, but rather resignation. Powerless against addiction's stranglehold, I was doomed. And since I was doomed, why not get high, ferociously and frequently, until the final curtain fell?

Alcoholics Anonymous and its program-adjacent Narcotics Anonymous cite the likeliest destinations for active addicts as jails, institutions (i.e., rehabs) and death.[1] Physically, this is true—and I would experience two of these three before getting clean. Emotionally, though, addiction is more like a road to nowhere. As the condition progresses and its sufferer deteriorates, priorities shift and narrow. Matters of importance—relationships, career, long-term plans—become compromised and, eventually, consumed by the need to imbibe ever-growing quantities of drugs and alcohol. Substance abuse has a winnowing effect—a one-way, single-lane street.

My road wasn't particularly long. By mid-2010, I'd been a full-blown addict for about three years. While that may seem an eternity to non-addicts, most people in recovery report lengthier battles. That my active addiction lasted "only" three years likely saved my life, and certainly saved my marriage and second (and current) well-paying job.

So there I was, stuck in addiction's rinse-and-repeat cycle. The only thing separating me from homelessness was my marriage, which was fraying in parallel with my health and sanity. If I'd used the previous night—about a 50/50 proposition—the day started on the living room couch, a few toots' worth of overnight debauchery hidden sloppily nearby.

I got up and dressed, a wary eye on my hasty hiding place. Meanwhile Patty showered, ate, dawdled. If she didn't know for certain what would occur once she departed our Brooklyn apartment for her Manhattan office, she sure as hell suspected it.

By 10 a.m., any remaining cocaine was gone; by 10:30, cheap beer from the corner store. I sat, sipped, and waited for my dealer to start his day, usually around 1 p.m. Sometimes I'd halfheartedly apply for a job online. But usually not, because unemployment meant unaccountability—expedited addiction with reckless abandon.

Call the guy, drive half-drunk to our meetup spot. Small bumps in the car, then large lines at home. A few minutes of euphoria followed by a few hours of oblivion. And inevitably, panic as evening—and therefore Patty—approached. An unconvincing cleanup, a useless airing out of our smoke-filled apartment. A rushed shower to drown, unsuccessfully, the stench of sweat from a drug that significantly raises body temperature.

A disappointed look, a disbelieving wife convinced of my guilt but lacking concrete evidence. Choking down dinner despite an eradicated appetite. Watching television in silence, conscious of my cocaine-clogged nose and artificially nasally voice.

It just went on like this, blow by blow, day after day. A road to nowhere. But an addict can't continue down this precarious path indefinitely. Eventually, he will either change for the better or have change for the worse—jail, institutions, death—thrust upon him. With my addiction unconstrained and steadily progressing, I'd become incapable of determining my own destiny.

Meanwhile, in Puerto Rico, Vector was entering the world. We will never know precisely when or where, but it was likely sometime in 2010, and certainly somewhere on that doggie deathtrap of an island.

Regardless, it's safe to say that Vector's prospects were even less hopeful than mine. And since he had zero say in his poor fortune, it's fair to say they also were less deserved. Whereas my downfall was my own doing, Vector seemed slated for innocent victimhood in a place as inundated with his sort as any on Earth.

In Chapter 1, I detailed how high the deck is stacked against Puerto Rico's satos. To recap: an island of 3.2 million people has upwards of half a million strays—an unworkable and ever-worsening human-to-stray ratio. Only a handful of shelters dot an area the size of Connecticut, with predictably ungodly kill rates as high as 97 percent.[2]

Poverty, natural disasters and pandemic all have exacerbated the island's problems—as has a "brain drain" in which educated and well-off Puerto Ricans, as American citizens, leave for the U.S. mainland. Puerto Rico is in deep debt and deeper despair, and it wasn't a hell of a lot better back in 2010.

Enter a newborn mutt that, judging by the size of most satos who share his features, was likely the runt of his litter. Enter a puppy with little to no chance of survival, let alone of becoming one of the loves of my life. Enter Vector, who for completely disparate reasons would share the same prognosis—disaster—as I did at that moment in 2010. Two beings, same hopelessness, 1,500 miles apart.

4. Addiction: A Hopeless Drug Addict and a Doomed Dog ... 61

Was he born into a human family? Possibly, but that doesn't mean much in Puerto Rico, where everyone who wants a dog already has one since they're literally everywhere. They might keep one of the new pups ... but all five? Six? And a runt no less? Highly doubtful.

The details are uncertain, but what we can state confidently is that Vector spent at least some time—and probably an extended amount of it—on the streets. Again per Chapter 1, we can surmise this largely because of his injuries and ailments.

For starters, Vector is missing a toe, and a deep, sizable scar adorns his snout. While those type of injuries could have occurred, for instance, in a crowded shelter, his tail—or lack thereof—says otherwise. Per our vet's assessment, Vector's tail was either bitten off by another dog or, equally gruesome, gnawed off by Vector himself after it sustained an unsalvageable injury—for example, getting crushed by a car. Two other health issues that point toward a life on the street are heartworm and ehrlichia. The former is spread by mosquitos, the latter by ticks.

Vector, then, clearly spent a significant amount of time in the elements of a humid, poor, stray-infested Caribbean island. He begged and scrounged for food. He drank fetid water. He hid from the blaring sun and teeming rain.

He was completely alone, and completely hopeless. He was on a road to nowhere that, like mine, had to end sooner or later. The chances of it ending well for Vector were near nil.

In describing the urgency of a street dog in Puerto Rico, the word "desperation" doesn't cut it. Vector's plight was beyond that. If he wasn't mauled to death by a bigger dog or run over by a car, he'd be done in by his heartworms or crippled by ehrlichia. Vector wasn't desperate; he was doomed. Survival was impossible. He was a dead dog walking, and he wouldn't be walking for long.

A thousand days. A *thousand* days. That's approximately how long Vector survived in Puerto Rico before stumbling upon a group of air traffic controllers at San Juan airport, gaining their sympathy and concern, and being handed over to his saviors at the Sato Project.

One salvation down, one to go.

By the time Vector was rescued by the Sato Project, another extreme unlikelihood had occurred: I was approaching two years of sobriety.

In 2011, I landed in rehab. While I relapsed afterward, my substance abuse went from chronic to episodic. Using every few weeks instead of every few days may seem trivial, but yielded tangible results—most importantly, the well-paying job I still hold today. Still, perpetual abstinence eluded me for a few more months.

Finally, the unceremonious conclusion. On October 10, 2011, I got drunk, and wanted what I always wanted when alcohol lit my fuse. Off I drove to Manhattan...

... where I sideswiped a taxi and was arrested for drunk driving. Night in jail, lost license, court date. Bullshitting a new employer with old excuses. Patty researching divorce attorneys.

Game over.

I regret an awful lot about active addiction. But not that night, because it scared me enough to give recovery a proper go. I needed those consequences—legal fees, suspended license, near divorce—and was fortunate not to incur others: dying, maiming someone, actual divorce.

Fast forward to 2013. Vector is in the loving care of the Sato Project; I'm in promising yet still-nascent recovery. Early sobriety was grueling, but no acceptable alternative existed. Addicts get better, or else. To do that, we must not only stop drinking and drugging but discover and diminish the emotional root causes that fueled our physical addictions. Alcoholics Anonymous calls them "character defects," but "shortcomings" also works.

This concept isn't exclusive to AA, which gets simultaneously praised and pilloried simply for being the most prolific recovery organization. Few achieve long-term sobriety without dampening their anger, jealousy, inferiority complexes or other issues. Fear gets addicts into recovery; personal progress *keeps* them there.

This digression is in the interest of universality. Soon, I'll be asking recovering or aspiring-to-recover alcoholics and addicts to identify with the ways Vector bolsters my recovery. To that end, my intention is to demonstrate how the tenets of recovery are similar regardless of the program. Indeed, the principles behind AA's 12 Steps—often criticized for rigidity and religiosity—translate to most non–AA recovery settings. Its 12 Steps, briefly:

In Steps 1 and 2, we admit our substance use is adversely affecting our lives, and that we're unable to stop by ourselves. Step 3 asks us to "turn our will and our lives over to the care of God as we understood Him." Fortunately, we're allowed broad interpretations of "God." The takeaway is whatever good exists in the universe would rather us recover than die.

In Steps 4 and 5, we list our shortcomings and how they propelled our addiction, then discuss our catalog with someone who has worked the Steps. The goal is finding personality patterns that fueled addiction.

Steps 6 and 7: (6) "Were entirely ready to have God remove all these defects of character" and (7) "Humbly asked Him to remove our shortcomings." God or no god, move toward diminishing the shortcomings that fueled addiction.

4. Addiction: A Hopeless Drug Addict and a Doomed Dog ...   63

Step 8 instructs us to build a list of the people we've harmed during active addiction, Step 9 to make amends to these folks whenever possible. Elementary stuff: alcoholics and addicts hurt people and need to take steps toward restitution. Confronting old grudges and humiliations helps us solidify a sober foundation.

Step 10 tells us to continue taking stock of our behavior, and promptly admit when we're wrong. Honestly policing our actions helps replace bad habits with good ones, yielding incremental improvement that gradually diminishes our shortcomings.

Next comes the most "God-y" entry: Sought through prayer and meditation to improve our conscious contact with God ... praying only for knowledge of His will for us and the power to carry that out. As a nonbeliever it's admittedly not my favorite Step. But meditation never hurt anyone, religious or otherwise. Just stay focused—a non-denominational "keep it up."

Finally, Step 12 suggests that those who've achieved sobriety through AA pay it forward by assisting others still struggling to recover.[3]

Despite ignorant attempts to portray AA as cultish, these are commonsense guidelines applicable to anyone in my once-desperate condition. Of course, no one performs them perfectly—especially newcomers. In 2013, I was in the relatively early stages of processing everything that happened, and all I still needed to do.

Addiction is lonely. Like depression, it convinces sufferers that their situation is tragically unique—that no one else could understand. In group-centric recovery, we find folks who drank and drugged in the same obscene fashions as us. This brings relief, comfort, hope.

But for me, something was incomplete. While I gratefully identified with new sober friends at meetings, the spark faded outside the church basements. Home life was ... OK. Patty and I were straining to find our marriage's mutual recovery—a trying, tenuous time for our union. I mentioned in Chapter 1 that we could use an uncomplicated distraction, something to rally around.

Correspondingly, I needed a recovering companion to comfort and inspire me for more than an hour an evening. I needed mornings, weekends, holidays. I needed a live-in recovery buddy.

I needed Vector.

The roles Vector plays in my recovery stretch well beyond our obvious parallels. His value is far more than the understandable attractiveness a now-sober drunk feels toward a fellow redemption story, four-legged or otherwise.

This is deeper than a rags-to-riches tale of two lost souls spared from the trash heap of existence. Vector doesn't just exemplify my past; he plays an active part in my ongoing recovery in tangible ways.

For starters, Vector helps give me a faith that works. For addicts, this is no small thing.

For me and countless others in AA and other group-centric recovery programs, a key tenet of overcoming addiction was finding something greater than myself that could help keep me physically sober and emotionally sound. Now more than a decade clean, my recovery is mature enough to realize that this doesn't necessarily mean developing a clear-cut concept of God.

But back then, I didn't know what I didn't know—and in early recovery, what you don't know can kill you. Early on, my agnosticism gave me a spiritual inferiority complex compared to many others in AA. Could my recovery be sustainable without an ironclad, capital-G God in my life?

These are the ecclesiastical-turned-existential questions that can make a recovery newcomer stumble. Indeed, the search for a higher power is a common sticking point for addicts—and costs too many their hard-fought sobriety.

I for one will never believe in an interventionist deity who, for some arbitrary reason, chose to save me while leaving the drunk on the next barstool to drink himself to death. Recovery requires honesty, and trying to "fake it 'til you make it"—another AA-ism that makes me cringe—with something as fundamental as spirituality is disingenuous and counterproductive.

Vector helped me overcome my spiritual inferiority complex. He did this with a duality that, I believe, only a rescue dog can embody.

First, of course, there is his very existence. Given the brutal environment and his diminutive size, it seems impossible that Vector survived three years before being rescued. That island is a doggie death sentence; that Vector ran this gauntlet losing only a tail and a toe is living proof that life finds a way.

Vector showed me that life is so resilient that ascribing to some Essence of the Universe becomes more logic than leap of faith. There are inexplicable microbes under the Antarctic ice shelf. There are blind fish thriving in the lightless ocean depths. And there is Vector, who spent 1,000 days in a figurative war zone and lived to bark about it.

But it was Vector's rapid rise from frightened to frolicking that placed this newfound faith into action. Understandably given his past, when we first adopted Vector he was a shaking nervous wreck, too shell-shocked to so much as relieve himself outdoors. He spent hours on end curled up and trembling, my wife and I petting him while whispering gentle encouragement.

4. Addiction: A Hopeless Drug Addict and a Doomed Dog ...   65

Two weeks later Vector was a nub-wagging, fetch-playing, full-fledged dog. He had assessed the situation and decided that these new circumstances had real potential. He was safe, fed, sheltered, loved. He was home.

Vector's faith—ironically, his faith in me—taught me to stop intellectually fighting recovery and just recover. The same as rescue families everywhere have been privileged to witness their frightened former strays become carefree, life-loving dogs, group-centric recovery has gotten millions clean and sober. Vector taught me to trust the process and the good people I'd met through it, and to move forward one day at a time. His uncomplicated spirit showed me I was overcomplicating spirituality—and therefore recovery.

Vector also helped take the emotional edge off early sobriety, a time when experiences are new, edges are rough and failure can be fatal. Early recovery is a prolonged stress test, with newly clean addicts thrust out of the frying pan and into the pressure cooker. Abstinent but by no means free, we become piles of rubbed-raw nerve endings suddenly robbed of our anesthetics of choice. It is a period of dizzying, even dangerous hypersensitivity.

Compounding this, alcoholics and addicts are—by both nature and nurture—an emotionally unstable set. All of us have fears, insecurities, and trauma that led us to drink and drug to excess and, from there, fueled that excess into obligatory obsession. Our physical addictions are, at their root, mere symptoms of deeper emotional affliction. And when we stop blotting out these bad tidings with booze and drugs, those emotional issues tend to come rip-roaring back.

I was no exception. Back then, I often found myself on the brink of letting my feelings get the better of me. And if they had, I would have felt my way to a bar or a drug dealer. Addiction wants its sufferers discouraged and disaffected. Emotional sobriety comes with patience and practice, and serves to buttress physical sobriety. The less we let life rattle us, the less likely we are to relapse.

During this delicate dance, Vector became Exhibit A for being unaffected—the emotionally mature yin to disaffected's yang. Blessed with an animal's amnesia, rescue dogs live in the treasured present rather than the troubled past.

Of course, Vector has some PTSD of his own. As we discussed in Chapter 2, to this day he doesn't like other dogs, the result of fighting for his life against fellow canines. He simply *cannot* behave himself around food, and also disdains being left alone, hinting at potential abandonment in his past. But beyond that, Vector, like all dogs, is a creature of the current. And his current situation, like mine, is very, very good.

I wonder if Vector remembers any of his harrowing history. I'm unsure whether or not I would want him to. I'm not certain which is preferable: a survivor's gratitude for the plenty of today, or the eternal sunshine of a spotless mind.

Regardless, Vector is an unknowing teacher of what, for us humans, is easier said than done: living in the now. This simple message is invaluable to a set of people for whom dwelling on the past can mean succumbing to it.

"We're here now," his tongue-out doggie smile says, "so whatever remorse or resentment you're harboring, let it go. Give yourself a break, and give me a treat." Over the years, Vector's suffering-turned-simplicity has spared me countless complications and, unsurprisingly, scored him countless dog biscuits.

There's a reason for this. When addicts and alcoholics get clean and sober, our own fledgling normalcy brings a culture shock that no one around us shares. Most people are accustomed to being reasonably decent, productive members of society. We are not; and once the initial oddity of it all fades, what emerges is an appreciation for the routine rhythms of civility.

It is difficult to explain to any non-addict, not even my wife of 15 years, how I can be so enthusiastic about ennui, so blissful about blasé. How totally exhilarating boredom can be after years of living life on a razor's edge.

But considering his past, Vector emits a calmness that is both attractive and contagious. Watching him casually sniff around in the backyard, I'm left to believe that he, more than any non-addict I know, understands the miracle of the mundane. His extraordinary salvation now affords him the privilege of being an ordinary dog. Cognitively, of course, he is aware of very little of this.

Vector in summer 2021: from Dead Dog Beach to life's a beach.

But there's a feeling in there somewhere—a hint, a notion, a "this is better" aura—that encapsulates how weirdly wonderful the everyday is for a recovered drug addict or alcoholic.

And as recovery slowly restores us to sanity—as normalcy slowly becomes ... well, normal—we incrementally accrue an authentic sense of self. Once we learn what made us use, we get to learn what truly makes us tick. Interests, talents, proclivities and penchants. Likes and dislikes, turn-ons and turnoffs. The stuff that makes us *us*.

In Vector's case, this allowance to develop into his true self is magnified all the more. Because while there was a pre-addiction Chris, there was no pre-desperation Vector. I had an opportunity to develop before my descension; Vector was born at the bottom. His life was a perpetual emergency. From the day he entered the world, Vector was not living but rather merely surviving.

In our home, Vector became an actual dog rather than a shell of one. He grew to love playing fetch in the backyard, to enjoy a spirited game of rope-toy tug of war, and to become a safe bet to sniff and mark seemingly every tree in the park. He developed a *personality*—quirks and subtleties that make him unique, make him ours, make him *him*.

And he only has these things because he has an environment in which those personal attributes could emerge. Vector has peace, love, assurance. He doesn't have to worry where he's going to sleep tonight, or where his next meal is coming from.

For me, Vector is a living reminder that desperation trumps development and suppresses individuality. Giving him a forever home saved not only Vector's life, but his sense of self.

Witnessing this helped me realize that true recovery leads to far more than physical sobriety: It provides the safety and space to discover and embrace, little by little, my individuality. Calamity may test one's character, but stability helps one build it. Only by fully understanding this could I commit to continued recovery above and beyond mere abstinence. I don't want to just survive addiction; I want to *live* in its aftermath.

Recovery from addiction has no graduation ceremony. There's no cap and gown, no diploma formalizing my final victory over cocaine and alcohol. I will always be an addict—and will always possess, to varying degrees, the character defects that drove me to obsessively drink and drug.

For example, to this day I have an unhealthy romance with justified anger. The obscene amount of idiots and assholes I come across on a daily basis certainly don't he...

There I go again. I'm in love with loathing. It makes a person with an ingrained inferiority complex feel superior—more intelligent, more sophisticated, more moral. It makes me feel better to feel better than you.

For about 10 minutes, anyway. Then it feels like shit. Because today I know better, and should therefore behave better.

Regardless of the circumstances—ranging from being cut off on the highway to trolled on the internet—all justified anger does for me is turn being wronged into being ... well, wrong. Despite being a sign of the more polarized and less civil times in which we live, my hot-headed revenge fantasies are infantile and unhealthy.

And despite damn well knowing it, too frequently I take the bait anyway. Today my drugs of choice are adrenaline and testosterone, and my hangovers are emotional. While I've certainly made a lot of progress, I just as certainly have a long way to go.

By contrast, Vector ... doesn't. He's as good as he's going to be, which—save for occasionally mugging my young son for some low-hanging food—is pretty much perfect in my proud-papa opinion.

I am amazed by this. While I'm frothing at the mouth over some stupid comment some stupid person posted under my latest article, Vector is letting my one-year-old niece tug his ehrlichia-ravaged ears. He's not thrilled about it, but neither is he snarling, nipping or even running away. He's just being Vector. A good dog. A great family member.

What's more, this is nothing new. With very few exceptions, Vector has been this kind, this docile (toward humans anyway) for as long as I can remember. I strive to be as recovered in more than a decade as Vector was in less than a year. Some people have parents or priests or politicians as role models. I have a dog.

And like this dog, I don't ever—*ever*—want to go back to before. Back to drugs. Back to despair. Back to hopelessness. Back to doom.

I can't. I'll die, and I know it.

Fortunately, in long-term recovery I no longer get urges to drink or drug much anymore. What I do get are urges to become complacent. To fade away from AA meetings. To stop helping newly-sober alcoholics and addicts recover. To declare myself cured from an affliction that has no cure.

With a healthy marriage, a terrific son, a comfortable suburban house and a well-paying career, I can easily start convincing myself that I'm good enough now. I have a full and fulfilling life; the only thing I'm short on is enough time to give each of my life-affirming responsibilities due attention. So yes, it's tempting to stop investing precious hours in a process whose ultimate goal, after all, I've accomplished for a decade running: abstinence from drugs and alcohol.

Vector sneers at this notion. Or rather, he sniffs at it—because it smells like the bullshit it is. Snoozing on the sofa. Chomping on a rawhide. Soaking up the afternoon sun in my backyard. The message is clear: "You're absolutely nuts, dad."

In addiction I was insane, because I made the same poor choices and expected better outcomes. Abandoning the tools that strengthen my recovery—*not* doing the things that led to my salvation—would be equally insane.

I have been restored to sanity. I will continue to do what got me—got *us*, got Vector and I—to this remarkable time and place. My recovery depends upon it, and my recovery buddy deserves it.

5

Addiction

Johnny, Be Good

"Drop it," I said, gently.

The energetic German Shepherd, who seconds before had determinedly tracked down the tossed ball as if life itself depended on it, now casually laid her favorite toy at my feet.

"Amber, sit," said her owner, John W. The dog's sloping Shepherd haunches descended, rump meeting grass. "Paw." Check. "Lie down." Sure, here you go. "Roll over." No sweat, dad—why the pop quiz?

John drops the ball near Amber. The dog briefly glances at it, then back at John. Her head lowers toward the ball…

"Wait," commands John.

Amber's head jerks back up, the whites of her big Shepherd eyes showing the slightest hint of impatience. She sat attentively, sensing she was on display—a brainy, barking boast from her proud papa. She was right. And it worked.

"Wow," I said. "She's *really* sharp."

John picks the ball up, pauses, pretends to throw it. Amber glances over her shoulder, but doesn't dart. Most dogs—mine included—would have followed the false trajectory into confused nothingness. Amber's mouth opens in a tongue-out doggie smile. Nice try, dad.

John's arm moves forward once more. The ball takes flight—for real this time—and so does Amber, bounding between socializing adults, children at play, and tables full of food and beverages. She deftly avoids them all, pounces on her rubber prey, and gleefully trots back to John.

Most of the folks featured in this collection reside nowhere near my northern New Jersey home. I got to know them and their pooches largely through Zoom and Microsoft Teams. John, though, lives just over the border in New York State—and has family in the town adjacent to mine. I had the pleasure of meeting him, and of course Amber, at a backyard party for his nephew's birthday.

5. Addiction: Johnny, Be Good

I also met Joni, whose slenderness was made more pronounced by her bulging baby bump. Joni and John had married in 2019, and were about to transition from newlyweds to new parents. A compatible young couple accruing the milestones of their lifelong commitment. Commonplace, but special.

John excuses himself to get a soda. It may or may not have been an excuse to keep showing off his wunder-canine.

"Heel," he dictates. Amber snaps to attention and positions herself to John's left. She waits for him to start walking, then keeps pace a foot or so beside him.

"Rub it in, Johnny," I joke, before stating the obvious. "She's impressive." She had the easy obedience of a K9 officer—a pleasure-to-serve similarity no doubt reinforced by her breed. She looks happy to work, happy to play, happy in general.

So does John. He looks sturdy, solid, healthy. Most importantly, to someone like me who can damn well spot the difference, John looks fully unencumbered. John looks free—a look distinct to those who've experienced freedom's agonizing alternative. Who've been caged, figuratively or literally.

Addicts lie, and fail, and lie about failing. But John's triumphant truth is evident to me. He is clean—even my damaged eyes can see that. Recovering addicts can sniff out faux-clean phonies, a sort of recovery radar whose precision is honed by staying sober and, conversely, witnessing others relapse. John might get away with it around a normie; I am anything but normal.

My radar stays silent. This is the real deal. This is a man in the clear and out of danger—which, knowing his history, is nothing short of miraculous. John is confident but not cocky; fearless. but with a healthy dose of respect for his narcotic Kryptonite.

John is done. And Amber, arguably the most thoroughly trained dog I've ever met, has done it.

All of the dogs profiled in this book helped their humans significantly, even immeasurably. But while many salved psyches, Amber—a German Shepherd who changed hands from an abuser to an addict at just the right time—saved her human's life.

Without John's opportune intervention, Amber faced a life of abuse, disability, or both. But without Amber, John W. would almost certainly be dead. Their relationship is not merely extraordinary. It is existential.

In 2021, the United States crowned a new king killer. Over the previous 12 months, it had taken more Americans ages 18–45—more people in their prime—than anything else.

The answer seems obvious: 2021 was the height of the Covid-19 pandemic, whose death toll now eclipses 1.1 million Americans.[1] Vaccines were adopted inconsistently, and an economically depressed nation was haltingly reopening despite repeated regional outbreaks. Though most killed by Covid were older, the toll of 18- to 45-year-olds had to be over 50,000, right?

Right. But that's not nearly the body count drugs racked up. Actually, not even drugs. *Drug*—in the singular.

In the same period between 2020 and 2021 that Covid killed 53,000 Americans ages 18–45, one ultra-lethal narcotic killed nearly 79,000. Its name is fentanyl, and it's fueling the latest wave of America's protracted opioid epidemic.[2]

That's right: amid the deadliest pandemic in a century, *one narcotic* outpaced the death toll among younger adults by almost 50 percent. We didn't hear much about fentanyl during Covid, because dying patients on respirators boost TV ratings. No studies exist examining how much more publicity Covid has received than fentanyl, but "Fentanyl × 1,000,000 = COV-19" seems like an apt equation.

Fentanyl is a synthetic opioid 50 times stronger than heroin.[3] It is cheaply made and overpoweringly potent, a killer combo leading to its rapid proliferation in the illicit narcotics stream.

The opioid epidemic's origin story is well known: uncaring pharmaceutical companies, most infamously the Sackler family-owned Purdue Pharma, flooded the market with painkillers like OxyContin, Percocet and Vicodin. They misrepresented how addictive their lucrative products were, converting countless patients and pain sufferers into addicts.[4] The phrase "pain clinic" became code for "pill mill," allowing shady doctors to peddle legal heroin in wink-wink arrangements often funded by America's complex, easily defrauded health insurance system.

While those days are waning, the epidemic has reverted to the streets, where fentanyl poisons often unsuspecting users who believe they're buying "only" heroin, cocaine or methamphetamine. They go home, shoot, smoke or snort their usual score…

… and die from the product's often minuscule amount of fentanyl. Fentanyl accomplishes this deadly deceit once every eight and a half minutes, killing an average of 175 Americans daily.[5]

Like Covid, fentanyl came on fast and hit hard. In 2020, drug-related deaths jumped 30 percent from 2019,[6] with the rate for synthetic opioid overdoses—fentanyl's category—spiking an horrific 56 percent.[7] In 2021, nearly 108,000 Americans died from drugs, with nearly 71,000 linked to fentanyl.[8] In 2022 alone, the U.S. Drug Enforcement Administration seized enough fentanyl to kill each of America's 333 million residents, including five tons of fentanyl powder.[9]

5. Addiction: Johnny, Be Good

Fentanyl's mixability with other narcotics to boost potency, therefore stretching supply, is a drug dealer's dream and a drug addict's worst nightmare. It is the hot dose potentially lurking in every baggie a substance abuser buys.

It is a frightening fate—a blue, bloated death. And it was waiting for John W.

John W. grew up in Westchester, north of New York City, in a comfortably middle-class environment. Two parents, safe streets, well-funded schools. Engaging and unpretentiously intelligent, John shines in group settings—school, work, social gatherings. Strong and stocky, he wrestled in high school.

Teenage John was no teetotaler—he drank and smoked pot because … well, he was a normal teenager. None of it was "red flag" stuff. But one day, a teammate offered him something new: Xanax. There was peace in the muted state the benzodiazepine provided. Then, John's budding affinity for downers intersected with the already-raging synthetic opioid epidemic.

"Hey, John," said a classmate, "if you like Xanax, you'll love Oxy." That was that: a cliché, *ABC Afterschool Special*-worthy scene fomented a decade-long opioid addiction.

John became a stereotypical statistic: another pinned-eyed, privileged white kid forfeiting his clear path to a successful adulthood for the next fix. If you don't mourn his derailment, you're one of an ever-decreasing number of people unimpacted by addiction. Who haven't seen family and friends suffer and die in a four-alarm fire fanned by corporate greed and medical malfeasance. Unsuspecting teenagers like John were the perfect patsies for the perfect painkillers.

Soon, Oxycontin met oxymoron. Hooked on illegally purchased painkillers, John W. the addict entered John Jay the college, studying the school's specialty: criminal justice. His addiction progressed, mandating ever-increasing amounts to get high and avoid debilitating opiate withdrawal. He was also going broke.

"The price started creeping up—$35, even $40 a pill," he recalls. Worse, connections were drying up. Some got busted, others quit while still ahead of the law. For the price of four hits of synthetic heroin, John could purchase a full gram—about 20 hits—of *real* heroin.[10] Suddenly, he'd gone from popping pharma facility pills to shooting street narcotics.

College doesn't mix with track marks, paraphernalia and jonesing; John didn't flunk out, he just flamed out. All of 20, he had no promising prospects and a vicious drug addiction. In hindsight, his next decision seems logical.

"I joined the Navy," he recalls.

Moving from mid-college to midshipman represented an extreme "geographical"—addiction terminology for a fresh setting meant to jump-start recovery through healthier routines. John was shipping out to shape up, and to clean up.

The ship almost didn't set sail. The same day John was sworn in, he overdosed. His quick-thinking sister saved his life. Unhealthy but undaunted, he entered bootcamp.

John's gregariousness served him well in the Navy. Addicts are often chameleonic, because we struggle with a true sense of self. John meshed well with both the ramrod-straight go-getters and bottom-feeding stragglers.

But geographicals rarely work. Five months in, John was posted near Seattle. He ran into someone from training—someone John knew could get pills.

"That was all it took," he said, echoing countless relapsed addicts. Soon, he was spending his entire paycheck on opioid painkillers and, inevitably, street heroin.

It wasn't long before John was done. Not done using; done as in shot. Exhausted. Despondent.

And finally, fed up. On kitchen detail, John repeatedly punched a heavy box of food, prompting an officer to ask what his major malfunction was. John's flash of rage sparked a flash of honesty. He had a drug problem. He needed help.

A requisite urinalysis ensued. Unfortunately for John, heroin's brief half-life meant it had already left his system. What remained was the marijuana he'd recently smoked. For the Navy, weed wasn't rehab-worthy. But it *was* expulsion-worthy. Instead of in rehab, John was out on his ass.

In the ensuing year, John was hired and fired from several jobs, embraced and estranged from several friends and family members, in and out of short-term relationships. The only constant was heroin. He went to rehab. Like me, he got high shortly afterward.

He overdosed again. Not once, not twice. *Six* more times. Were it not for the instant overdose-reversing drug naloxone—better known as Narcan—John would be dead. He recalls his final OD vividly.

"I was alone in the house—my girlfriend at the time was at work. I got my stuff and went into the bathroom. I locked the door."

Then some lifesaving self-awareness kicked in.

"Something told me to unlock the door, so I did."

John shot up, passed out ... and came to on the bathroom floor. His girlfriend had performed CPR and called 911. A man on death's door was saved by the bathroom door.

5. Addiction: Johnny, Be Good

I'd love to report that John had finally flirted with death enough to quit and stay quit. Unfortunately, that didn't happen. But what *did* happen was another lifesaving hunch.

"Out of the blue, I decided I wanted a dog."

There was no rational reason in John's fried mind. It's tempting to deem this another random straw grasped by a desperate addict. A junkie trying to exchange a monkey on his back for a canine on his couch.

But it wasn't. It wasn't tethered to salvation, or even hope. It was just something he … well, *wanted*. It was, he insists, "just a feeling."

Sometimes you can't explain why a decision is right. Sometimes its intractable staying power in your mind only reinforces its rightness. And as dangerous as it is for an addict to follow an impulse-turned-yearning, this wasn't John's addiction goading him.

It was his higher power guiding him.

When I adopted Vector, I had nearly two years clean—by no means a recovery veteran, but no longer a newcomer, either. The value Vector provided then, and continues to offer now, dealt more with emotional progress than physical sobriety.

However, the benefits of dog ownership in ultra-early sobriety, a time when physical relapse is an outsized, daily danger, are several. Many rehabilitation centers incorporate animal therapy into their group-centric recovery programs. This is in line with evidence that "good distractions"—music therapy and art classes, to name two others—lead to deeper participation in recovery-specific environments like group meetings and one-on-one therapy.[11] Such healthy activities help train our warped brains to release dopamine in situations that actually warrant it. They are tools to help wean us off our learned, defective mental response to drugs and booze—the genesis of the addict-unique phenomenon of obsessive craving.

It's an easy equation: dog=happy > dope=happy. "Here boy" is greater than heroin.

Of course, the real test of fledgling sobriety is the weeks and months *after* formal treatment. This is what separates the men from the boys—and where man's best friend can earn this lofty distinction.

For starters, dogs encourage exercise. Most dogs require walking at least once a day, even if you have a fenced-in yard—which many newly sober folks don't, since addicts are typically closer to the gutter than picket fences and two-car garages. One study, published by the National Institutes of Health, found dog owners 57–77 percent more likely than non-dog owners to get enough physical activity every week.[12]

At a crucial time when life-affirming commitments are good (walk into any AA meeting and the person making coffee is likely a newcomer, because the chore helps keep them accountable), walking a dog is a terrific obligation. Rain or shine, hot or cold, dogs have a basic bodily need that is our duty to facilitate, pun intended.

And for the trouble, we get far more than a full poop bag. Exercise is particularly important for people recovering from addiction, especially early on. Mood, memory, concentration, discipline—all assets addicts need to build, and all bolstered by regular exercise. There is also spirituality in exercise; regardless of your belief system, it is safe to say that whatever higher power you hold dear granted us a mind and a body, and it is our responsibility to maintain each of these precious gifts.

Dogs also help us establish routine. In addition to walking, dogs must be fed several times daily, and bathed and groomed regularly. Crucially, dogs also need to develop a special attachment with their owners, a bond-building that requires our attention and, most of all, our physical presence. At a time when recovering addicts are best served sticking to rigid routines—work, group-centric recovery meeting, home, repeat—dogs give us yet another reason to stay on schedule as we gradually build a foundation of durable sobriety.

But how much is *too* much? Some argue that, for a newly sober person reintegrating into society, lower-maintenance pets like fish, hamsters or cats are the way to go. Many who *do* recommend getting a dog believe a housebroken adult is preferable to a puppy, due to the workload the latter involves.

"A puppy is work," says a post on *I Am Sober*, a website and sobriety-tracking app with over 50 million users. "It's bombastic, needs training, whines incessantly and many people struggle more with a puppy than a baby. Do not adopt a puppy in your first year sober."[13]

As a father, I find it doubtful that anyone who thinks a puppy is more work than a baby has ever actually had the latter. And as someone who has had the pleasure to meet John W., I have strong anecdotal evidence that the outsized care and effort a puppy requires can be a benefit rather than a drawback.

In 2015, John W. was broken, and needed to be put back together. He was hopelessly mired in addiction's unforgiving binge-remorse-repeat cycle, and too ashamed to admit how befuddlingly stuck he was. He needed help, yes. But before that could happen he needed to be able to look someone, anyone, in the eyes again.

It is a low-bottom addict's conundrum: John needed someone to meet him where he was, but wasn't able to fully confide in anyone. He needed someone—or some*thing*—to help him start his road back to humanity, let alone sobriety.

John felt less than human. And so it was that, in September 2015, he went looking for a non-human.

"It was a really shitty pet store," John remembers. The date was September 20, 2015.

He walked in with his then-girlfriend. Among a pen of playful pooches was a lone German Shepherd pup, self-segregated into a corner. She seemed scared and alone. That she resonated with an alienated addict like John is only natural.

"That was the one," John said. He took her home, and named her Amber.

I know what you're thinking: isn't this a book about rescue dogs? Yes, it is. But Amber counts, because John was completely right about that pet store being a shithole. The following spring, it would become the last of three sister stores to close shop forever.

The store's name was American Breeders: Puppies & Kittens in Mohegan Lake, New York. Its owner, Richard Doyle of nearby Mahopac, New York, was abusing the animals and even performing unlicensed surgeries on them, possibly "pre-harming" them in a kickback deal with a local veterinarian.

The charges against Doyle were the result of two separate arrests, including one for "maliciously and intentionally torturing and causing wounds" to a St. Bernard puppy. Doyle plead guilty to five counts of animal cruelty in January 2017.[14] As is too often the case, he avoided jail time, getting off with three years' probation and a $5,000 fine. Amber would have ended up in a shelter within weeks had John not rescued her. And Amber, of course, had her own rescuing to do.

After all, John W. was still an active addict. He was honestly trying to stay straight but relapsing frequently. With everyone—his girlfriend, family, friends—all in the know about his addiction, relapse was an exercise in avoiding others long enough to use unnoticed.

Only now, John had someone he couldn't avoid. And she wouldn't stop staring at him.

"Those eyes," John said. "Those German Shepherd eyes."

Anyone familiar with dogs instantly understands that statement. Shepherds and similar breeds have large eyes with piercing pupils and gaping white spots. Their gazes seem simultaneously searching, knowing and revealing.

"I didn't want to keep letting her down. I couldn't go out, get the skag, come home, bang up and not be awake to feed her. Or not wake up again at all and leave her alone forever."

That's how a dog whose life was nearly ruined by animal abuse ruined heroin for John W. Opiates are downers, but it took Amber's eyes to make John feel lower than low. Low enough to quit.

There's a distinct difference between guilt and shame. Guilt is when a person believes he *did* something bad; shame is when a person believes he *is* bad. Unable to shake dope for nearly a decade, John, like so many addicts before him, came to believe he was a completely defective person. That he was worthless—not just unable to recover, but undeserving of recovery.

Shame pushes addicts like John and me deeper into a hole. If we're bad, and bad people don't deserve good things, then recovery—already an intangible, difficult-to-obtain destination—seems all the more distant, even foreign. Shame zaps whatever fleeting motivation we can muster toward beginning our lifesaving journey.

But Amber did not bring shame. Amber brought guilt. And considering where John was, guilt was a very useful thing.

Adopting Amber was, John knew, something that spoke well of him. Even if bringing Amber home wasn't a completely selfless act—as we've seen, John had a strong, albeit incoherent, notion that a dog would help him—she gave him the first concrete example in quite some time that he was not, in fact, a despicable person.

For a struggling addict like John, Amber was a happy aberration. She was a ripple of success in a sea of failure. And after a few times staring into those eyes while high on heroin, John W. decided that he'd be damned if he'd fuck this up, too.

If he couldn't get clean for himself, he'd get clean for her—an innocent being who'd never harmed a soul. Amber was deserving of a recovery, and John was dutybound to provide that for her. The only way to do that, John knew, was to recover himself.

Of course, addicts have sudden epiphanies and solemn vows all the time. I had them almost every morning, and was typically high by mid-afternoon.

But for John, this time was different. The thousandth time was a charm—and that charm was begging for a treat. This time, the catalyst lighting a fire under John W.'s ass was a constant. She was there in the morning, and would be there every morning, indefinitely. John's foxhole compassion clung rather than faded, because Amber was difficult to dodge and easy to love. His sense of obligation remained steadfast, because she was a blameless dependent against whom generating angst or resentment was unfathomable.

And his fledgling abstinence from heroin stuck because ... well, mainly because of those eyes. John had seen enough of the sad Shepherd face.

5. Addiction: Johnny, Be Good

In John W., Amber had a mountain to climb (courtesy John W.).

John and Amber were starting their recovery together, and it was time to get to work.

The alarm went off at 7 o'clock most mornings. But John W. didn't have a 9-to-5 job. It was more like a 3 to 11, as an MRI technician aide. That left a lot of time to kill—a dangerous proposition for newly clean addicts.

What John had was Amber. Rising early each morning, he fed, leashed and walked her. That was the first half hour of his day.

The next six or so were spent training her.

Amber did not need six hours of training each day. John did. In running, jumping, teaching, rewarding and just plain doting upon his new family member, John was accomplishing a complicated personal feat—arresting addiction—in a wonderfully uncomplicated manner.

Other methods, however proven to help those trying to get clean and sober, just weren't working for John. He tried intensive outpatient treatment (IOP), a multi-hour-a-day, counselor-led group recovery arrangement that, among other benefits, keeps addicts honest via regular drug screenings. He tried Alcoholics Anonymous and its sister program, Narcotics Anonymous.

Admittedly, those tools helped me and millions of others. But addiction is too customized an affliction for a one-size-fits-all panacea. John didn't *hate* IOP and meetings, he just had mixed feelings toward them that ultimately compelled him to omit them from his personal recovery journey.

While he identified with others in group sobriety settings—helpful insomuch as it confirmed for John that he was, without a doubt, an addict—for him group recovery's usefulness ended there. Because when it came to his addiction, John just wasn't ready to talk about it.

"I found the programs and meetings triggering," he recalls. He was grateful to learn he wasn't alone in his predicament but, unlike myself and many other addicts, found no therapeutic assistance in opening up old wounds. He wasn't ready for introspection—not yet, anyway.

But he *was* ready to recover. The self-imposed daily 7 a.m. start said as much, as did the ensuing six hours spent training Amber to sit, give paw, roll over, heel. In exchange, Amber trained John to rise every day with a goal that didn't involve a needle in his veins. From there, Amber instilled in John what the U.S. Navy could not: a discipline capable of weathering the powerful, inevitable temptations to use again. Amber's training won out, albeit barely at times, because it was rooted in the trust and love of a faithful, nonjudgmental, four-legged family member.

Amber was the only being capable of pulling this off, because John wasn't ready to bear his soul to his fellow humans. It was too raw, too new, too tenuous. For John, Amber was a time killer, an energy drainer, a schedule setter. Train Amber, work a boring job, return home, repeat. She was a safeguard against his worst proclivities at a time when he was still too embarrassed to open up. A loved one for whom he felt a deep fealty but who, all eye-daggers aside, he knew wasn't judging him. No humans fit that bill—at least none John or I know.

"The woods near my house became my church," he said, acknowledging his lack of religiosity. In that metaphor, Amber became his altar girl. The spark of a nascent spirituality was lit, however lukewarmly. It was a good start.

In exchange, John helped Amber deal with her own damage. Part of this was the certainty of his kindness. The other part was the circumstance of his gender.

"Amber really hated men," John remembers. Given that she spent her first six months with a convicted animal abuser, it's not difficult to understand why. John isn't sure exactly what Richard Doyle did to her—Beat her? Cut her open to cause future, palm-greasing vet visits?—but he clearly did something.

God only knows what went through Amber's head when another man scooped her up and brought her to a strange place. And what she thought when, initially, that same guy intermittently nodded off with a needle in his arm. Probably the dog equivalent of "men, who needs 'em?"

But in short order, John did for Amber what I could not for Vector: drastically improve a public-facing trauma, in Vector's case his utter hatred of other dogs. As a non-canine, I was ill-equipped to help Vector equate other dogs with love. But by happenstance of his dog's background and his own gender, John significantly tamped down Amber's fear and aggression toward men, simply by being a caring, involved male adopter.

5. Addiction: Johnny, Be Good

Amber the spiritual altar girl, October 2016 (courtesy John W.).

Addicts, though, are typically trickier to revive, to recover, to rescue. But unlike my experience—and true to the mantra that, so far as getting clean and sober goes, "whatever works" and "to each their own" are wise words—John didn't need complex from the get-go. He needed simplicity to build a bridge to complexity. He needed a beginning so basic that it basically omitted other humans.

And he needed discipline, healthy routine, purpose. Amber played essential roles in attaining these. And soon, John realized something profound: progress.

"I was ready for people again," he says.

By that, John means he was ready to see people not just as inconveniences to endure, but rather relationships to enjoy. Months after Amber's eyes pierced his soul—in so doing jolting him out of his sick addictive cycle—he was finally ready to look other humans in the eyes again.

"When you build that relationship with her, you start rebuilding relationships with people in your life, and you don't want to let them down again, either."

Amber couldn't make everything right with everyone else, of course. Her role was prerequisite: she got John back into life, so that he could start getting his life back. In Alcoholics Anonymous, a frequent phrase told to newcomers is "we'll love you until you can love yourself." Amber did that for John. He could look in the mirror again and see a struggling person who made some bad choices, rather than an irredeemably bad person whose decisions were as inevitable as they were damning.

John's reintegration into society draws parallels with addicts working conventional group-centric programs. Fully digesting the truth that he was a heroin addict and, as such, could never safely use again. Recognizing that a power greater than himself—for example, his relationship with Amber—could start bringing him back to sanity. Ascribing to some semblance of a higher power, even an ill-defined Spirit of the Universe communed with in the woods. And of course, beginning the process of righting wrongs made in the throes of addiction's grasp.

Not all of the amends came easy.

"My brother Joe and I had such a bad falling out," John recalls. John lived with Joe during some of the worst of his active addiction, and had subjected his brother to the falsehoods and false hopes inherent in addicts. "He wouldn't even talk to me. When I joined the Navy we started talking again, but as I continued to use and relapse he turned his back on me." John doesn't blame Joe for doing so.

In John's early sobriety, Amber would be an icebreaking stepping-stone back to brotherly love. When John first brought Amber home, Joe would interact with her but not his brother. It was part breadcrumb clue, part olive branch—as if Joe needed to simultaneously communicate his eventual willingness to forgive John, while also conveying that seeing him care for an innocent, welcome new family member was a "prove it" prerequisite. The way back to each other went through Amber.

Then one day, the conduit completed her duty.

"John!" John recalls his brother joking. "Amber's got her bags packed and is getting on the school bus!"

A brother-to-brother dad joke, facilitated by and featuring a dog, brought John and Joe fully back into each other's lives. They remain close as John remains clean.

I met John in summer 2022. He was going on seven years clean and, as an addict in long-term recovery myself, it was clear to me that he was out of danger. John W. is no longer a newcomer. His recovery is no longer tenuous. Amber got him back on his feet and, from there, he hit the ground running.

John was a registered nurse in training, working in the emergency room of a local hospital. A sign of the times, he sees too many people suffering from the same substance abuse problems he had. He sees people hitting their bottoms as fentanyl looms large, adding a lethal urgency to their hopeful recovery. And he sees addicts whose bottom is a pulled-up sheet and toe tag—a fate that was waiting for him until Amber interceded.

His job entails handling opioid painkillers every day. John is never tempted. John is free.

John's wife, Joni, is from the Caribbean—Vector's neck of the woods, where dogs are often seen as far less than family members. Amber taught her a thing or two, too. When I met her, Joni was a proud dog mom, about to become a human one.

John cannot relapse. An addict who overdosed seven times before the age of fentanyl is a dead man during it. If he goes back there, his wife is a widow and his child is fatherless. Those aren't end-of-chapter heartstring tugs. Those are facts.

John W.'s life was once vanishingly narrow. It is expansively wide today. There are too many loved ones to make proud, too many dependents who rely upon him. There are too many reasons not to die. Amber did not provide them all, but without her none of those blessings would have come to pass. Amber took a man who was barely existing and prepared him for a full, fulfilling life.

6

Mental Health
Guide, Dog

I pull into the driveway at dusk, the conclusion of a trying, taxing day. Successes felt minor and fleeting, failures magnified and affixed. From the moment I awoke that morning, the deck seemed stacked against me, each subsequent hand a loser. Beaten down and bone tired, I resign myself to repeating this uphill trudge daily for the foreseeable future.

A little head pops up, peering from a front window. Even with his fawn faded to a grandfatherly gray, he still resembles a deer startled from grazing. For the first time since kissing my son goodbye that morning, a smile cracks my lips—a sincere one, not the game-face grin of public courtesies or professional etiquette.

I turn off the engine, emerge from the car, close the driver's side door. My arms feel noticeably lighter, my feet a bit quicker.

Near the porch, ecstatic yips become audible, then the thud of an old dog leaping clunkily from couch to floor. A scramble of taps—claws on hardwood—and scratches on the opposite side of the front door. Two beings, only one of whom can tell time, anticipate a happy reunion.

Inside, Vector comes flying at me with an energy that, though diminished by age, has been pent-up and building as afternoon turned to early evening. I crouch over, and a dog that should have died a decade ago comes fully alive, planting his front paws into my chest, hurling all 20-something pounds of himself against me. I smooch his snout, his cheeks, his head.

The raucous ritual concludes. I get up, Vector sits down. His cocked-head deer gaze returns. His thoughts segue from greeting to eating. The most rhetorical of questions ensues.

"Want a treatsie?" I ask excitedly, hurrying toward the kitchen. I usually let him chomp his doggie biscuit in peace. Today, though, I follow his contented, can't-wait-to-devour-this trot into the living room. There, I soak in a sliver of comfort in a day woefully short on good tidings. Or so my disease wants me to believe.

My depression does not just sadden. It confuses, obfuscates, stupefies. It lies, convincing me of castigations greatly embellished or totally imagined. It thrives on isolation, driving a wedge between me and the rest of the world.

But there, watching my satisfied sato inhale his treat after enthusiastically welcoming me home, my depression is … dented. By no means eliminated, but discernibly mitigated.

He's been doing this for years. Regardless of how severely my depression has numbed, cowed or befuddled me, one certainty shines high-beams through my disease's dense mental fog.

Vector loves me. All the way, every day, and permanently.

I know what you're thinking: so does your wife, your son. But depression is complicated, and sometimes must be met with simplicity—by the unabashed adoration of a being whose honesty is unquestionable and whose inherent goodness is unimpeachable. A pure soul who purely cherishes me.

I helped save Vector but once. He has returned the favor perpetually and in myriad ways, none more tangible than his assistance combatting my depression.

I have it in me to kill myself.

It's in there, dormant but lurking. Per Chapter 1's five-story staredown, this assessment is rooted in lived experience. If you suffer from chronic, clinical depression, such autobiographical anecdotes likely align with something you've considered—or at least didn't rule out—in your darkest moments.

I am a man of many mental maladies. Addiction means I can never drink again. Depression erodes my ability to *think* again. Both stand ready to blot out my ability to reason, care, enjoy. Both want self-pity, self-destruction and self-harm. Both are treatable but incurable. Both play nice with each other, but hate me.

Before we continue, some guardrails: This chapter covers chronic depression rather than situational depression, a traumatic yet transitory condition induced by extraordinarily stressful or sad circumstances.[1] For example, most depression stemming from Covid-19's landscape of death, alienation and economic ruin falls into this circumstantial category.

By contrast, chronic depression is ingrained, potentially permanent, and largely independent of external stimuli. The World Health Organization estimates 5 percent of adults—1 in 20—meet these criteria.[2] In America, land of the free and home of the freaked out, figures are murkier. A 2019 Centers for Disease Control survey found 18.5 percent of U.S. adults had recently "experienced" depression. However, most reported "mild" symptoms, leaving the total for severe and moderate depression at 7 percent.[3]

A 2020 National Institute of Mental Health report supports these figures, finding 8.4 percent of American adults suffered a "major depressive episode" within the last year. Such an event was defined as "a period of at least two weeks when a person experienced a depressed mood or loss of interest or pleasure in daily activities … such as problems with sleep, eating, energy, concentration, or self-worth."[4] That's roughly 1 in 12 Americans—far fewer than the one-third who reported depression during our era's most dispiriting crisis, Covid-19.

The larger point: there's a subtle yet significant line between depression and … well, the blues. Between the melancholy humans experience as we journey through life and something requiring therapy and medication. Between sadness and suicidal tendencies.

In our increasingly hyperbolic, self-absorbed society, that line is getting blurrier as victimhood, often masked as "awareness," becomes in vogue. Inclusivity is wonderful until everybody has everything—when misfortune is mislabeled as disease. When feelings are misregistered and misrepresented as facts.

Were I luckier, my depression may have proven situational. I could have shaken off being raised by a well-intending yet overwhelmed single father, or my 18-month nightmare of eyesight loss. Instead, my depression stuck around, playing an integral role in my descent into alcoholism and drug addiction and, from there, delaying and deterring my subsequent recovery.

It runs in my blood. As we'll explore in Chapter 12, my father's brother, Stephen, struggled with lifelong depression whose symptoms were so eerily familiar I call him my depression doppelganger. Uncle Steve provided both reassurance that someone I love identified with me, and a reminder that, however far progress takes me, our hereditary proclivity will always reside within me.

My depression, then, is not circumstantial, but rather a light switch in my brain flipped on by adversity, fear, or mere DNA. While I can dampen that light to a glimmer, the fixture has no off position.

The good news: Despite sporadic flareups, my depression has faded to the glint of a dying star. It took plenty of help—family and friends, psychiatry and medication—to get here. I am determined, even desperate, never to revisit that rooftop. Nearly throw me off a five-story building once, shame on you. Nearly throw me off a five-story building twice, shame on me.

I will not belittle depression by suggesting Vector played the lead role in its marginalization. He did not. Nor could he save me from the worst of it, since he wasn't born yet.

But again, my depression is not dead but rather dormant. And sometimes, it pops up and bears down, a weight around an otherwise happy life as a fortysomething husband, father and professional with a picket-fence yard and a decade-plus clean and sober.

It is these times when, for me, Vector shows the value of rescue dogs in alleviating depression's intermittent yet undeniable grasp.

In March 2022, my wife Patty and I took a sun and fun trip to the Caribbean for a few days. The winter had been a second consecutive long and frightening one, dominated by the advent and proliferation of Covid-19's hyper-contagious Omicron variant.

We needed an adults-only break, so our son, Nicholas, remained home with Patty's parents. Nicholas was in kindergarten, so his grandparents stayed at our house and took him back and forth to school in our absence. We FaceTimed with him every evening. He was perfectly fine, a five-year-old who fully understood that mom and dad would be back in a few days, and that he was with family members whom he loved, and who loved him. He didn't skip a beat.

Meanwhile, Vector went to stay with my dad, his grandpaw. Patty's parents aren't really dog people, and my father adores Vector and regularly watches him when we're away. We FaceTimed with him and Veckie every night.

Vector was ... miserable. Like, despondent-level miserable.

The experience hammered home a dynamic that had been emerging as Nicholas grew from a wary toddler into a well-aware boy: our dog misses us far more than our son does.

Vector misses me more than any human could. He *needs* me. As someone who battles depression, there's an out-of-self blessing in that. When I saw him from my phone, cuddled up on my dad's couch confused, concerned and sullen, Vector provided a glimpse of what his life would look like were I to suddenly vanish forever.

No one has complete control over death, of course. Car accidents, cancer, and the uniquely American anomaly of gun violence could wipe me out without my say in the matter. But I do hold sway over what, for an otherwise healthy man in his mid–40s, is my easiest path to oblivion: a spiraling depressive crash, likely exacerbated by drugs and booze. I alone control whether I open the door to invite that outcome inside—whether it is ever more than a remote possibility.

As we've seen, I could justify this to myself, and potentially to my loved ones. However scarred it would leave them, at least they would come to understand the circumstances behind such a fate. In my darkest moments, I can imagine a deeply depressed Chris taking solace in—and therefore extracting justification from—that sentiment.

But I could not do that to Vector, for whom no explanation is understandable let alone palatable. I cannot banish him to spending his remaining time wallowing in a corner. And because of that, I cannot wallow, either. In this fashion, Vector is a living life-preserver—a safeguard against complacency in my unending effort to keep depression as minuscule a part of my existence as possible.

This does not, of course, mean that depression won't come. Despite my healthiest of habits, the beast is going to boil up every so often, flinging a weight around my neck and heart that makes me lethargic, pessimistic and, most concerningly, emotionally numb. I can pitch a perfect game in recovery from drug addiction, where success has a clear (and thin white) line of demarcation. You either snort cocaine and guzzle booze, or you don't.

Not so with depression. That game is played on a grayer, muddier field, where my opponent will inevitably score its share of points. The trick is limiting, and abbreviating, the damage. Over the years, I've accrued tools to doing just that—to lessening the severity and length of my inevitable depressive bouts. And that forlorn sato on his grandpaw's couch has played a larger part in that than he could ever understand.

Of course, my vacation anecdote could describe any dog—one attained via rescue or retail—and it's become common knowledge that *all* dogs, as well as other intimate pets such as cats, can boost their humans' mental health. Considering this, it is worth exploring the positives canines in general bring to the mental health mix and, from there, discussing the added value Vector's former street dog status has for me.

First, the surface-level benefits, some of which overlap with the positive impact of dogs on people recovering from addiction, as touched upon in Chapter 5.

For starters, dogs are generally energetic and require walking, or at least trips out to a backyard or park to play and relieve themselves. They force us to get up and move and, in the case of walks or jogs, exercise a bit. A variety of official sources, including the UK's National Health Service, attest to the benefits of regular exercise for people suffering from depression.[5]

Here, a key word is *regular*. Depression is a disease that promotes apathy, making it tougher to get motivated even for tasks we know can help mitigate it. Dogs are a consistent reason to get up and get out, regardless of our desire to do so. Sometimes depressives, myself included, need *musts* rather than *shoulds*; avoiding a rug-pissing-or-pooping incident typically places taking our dogs outside squarely in the mandatory category.

Further, pets can help counteract loneliness, and depression-centric loneliness in particular. While conventional loneliness craves interaction with fellow humans—something that, for example, taking a dog to the park or the dog run might promote—I speak from experience that depression-centric loneliness makes me *less* enthusiastic to seek out other people. When I'm depressed, the circle of places, things and especially people I find palatable shrinks precipitously. Depression is an "I just can't deal…" state—and that includes dealing with other humans.

But not, at least in my experience, Vector. And that anecdotal evidence is backed up both by the experiences of others and professional insight. In a piece on the topic published on WebMD in 2017, a woman suffering from depression discussed how her cats' cuddling with her in bed, and following her around the house, calmed her during an episode[6] (in this example, dogs and cats are somewhat interchangeable, as anyone whose dog is basically their four-legged shadow would attest).

Key to this is reminding us that we're *not* entirely isolated even when, so far as person-to-person contact is concerned, we *want to be* entirely isolated. "A pet can remind you that you're not alone," says Desiree Wiercyski, a life coach in Fort Wayne, Indiana, in the aforementioned WebMD article. "Pets offer unconditional love, which can be extraordinarily soothing when feeling isolated." Clinical psychologist Perpetua Neo, PhD, concurs. "Animals pick up on when their owners are distressed," she says.

The young woman with the cats goes on to proclaim the elusive specialness that animals sometimes have—a difficult-to-define uniqueness that humans lack. "Animals are very connected in ways that people aren't," she says.

I and myriad others have felt that special something too, and as Covid-19 piled a mental health crisis atop a medical one, some went searching for that secret. "What is it about animals?" Ann Robinson wrote in the UK's *The Guardian* on March 17, 2020, little more than a week into widespread lockdowns. "As the bad news about the coronavirus continues, 'send me dogs and cats' has become a regular cry on social media, an easy-to-grasp shorthand for 'I feel terrible, cheer me up.'"[7]

Robinson goes on to explain that an important facet of this is what the mental health community calls social recognition—the process of identifying another being as someone important and significant to you. One study of functional MRI (fMRI) responses, published by PLOS ONE, found the bond between owner and pet can be similar to the one a mother forms with her baby.[8]

"Pet care and self-care are linked," reports Dr. June McNicholas, a psychologist and academic, in the aforementioned piece in *The Guardian*. "When pet owners leave the house to buy pet food, they're more likely to buy food for themselves and, when they feed their pet, they'll sit down to eat too. People with disabilities often find that able-bodied people are socially awkward with them; if they have a dog it breaks down barriers and allows a more comfortable and natural interaction."

McNicholas is referring to folks with physical disabilities, but could just as well have been discussing depression. When in the throes of an episode, people with depression are decidedly *not* able-bodied. Depression is a mental illness that affects the body in well-documented ways. Where mental joylessness and fogginess stop and physical lethargy and disorientation begin is a line so blurry that it is, practically speaking, irrelevant.

And besides, many depressives *are* lacking something physical: proper brain chemistry. People with depression often suffer from a lack of one or more crucial brain chemicals. Two of these are the "feel-good" chemicals oxytocin and dopamine, and studies have shown that simply playing with our pooches increases each. In fact, the positive effects are likely mutual; as reported in *Scientific American*, a 2015 study at Japan's Azabu University contends that our dogs get a similar mood boost from their interactions with us as we do them.[9]

For depressives, then, our dogs can become a consistent, reliable source of a substance so closely associated with our mental malady that certain drugs prescribed to treat it, called Dopamine Reuptake Inhibitors, boost exactly that chemical. Meanwhile, another common class of anti-depressant medications, Selective Serotonin Reuptake Inhibitors (SSRIs), actually *reduces* dopamine while boosting mood-regulating serotonin.[10] It's the reason that one unfortunate side-effect to these lifesaving drugs can be impotence—and why many psychiatrists, mine included, encourage seeking out healthy forms of enjoyment to replace whatever dopamine decrease my SSRIs may induce.

While by no means a replacement for therapy and doctor-monitored medication, our dogs' assistance in treating depression isn't just theoretical. It's not just a feeling—it's backed by sound science, even if neither us nor medical experts fully understand the phenomenon.

For depressives, then, dogs can be a source of strength, a spotter to help us push back against our inner demons who, to take the metaphor further, seem perpetually waiting in the gym parking lot to mug us. Here, rescue dogs are a shot of steroids—or, if you're not into semi-legality and side effects, a strong protein shake. Scrappy, resourceful and formerly downtrodden, our rescues provide a powerful extra kick in the pants to suck it in, sweat it out, and keep going.

All dogs are good for depression. Rescue dogs are *great* for it. Here are some reasons why.

I have done well to keep my depression mostly at bay, to keep its flare-ups fewer and further between. But as a treatable yet ultimately incurable disease, it inevitably reemerges now and again despite my best efforts and healthiest choices.

When it comes, among the most stubborn and dangerous symptoms of a depressive episode is an unshakable sense of worthlessness. Depression does more than make me feel down; it promotes the sick mindset that I *belong* down—that I have no business picking myself back *up*. In other words, the affliction tries to convince sufferers that they don't deserve to feel happy.

There's a disease-centric difference between "I did a bad thing" and "I am a bad person." Depression dwells in the latter, more self-loathing sentiment: it decimates self-esteem, making self-deprecation and even self-harm seem not only viable but reasonable.

To paraphrase my psychiatrist, the surest path to building self-esteem is through estimable acts. That's where Vector comes in.

Rescuing a dog—or any pet—is about as clear-cut an act of good as possible. When I hit a dark stretch, Vector is a cute, cuddly reminder of my ability to bring some light to this world.

He is also *perpetual*. By contrast, acts of kindness like monetary philanthropy, while wonderful, are singular acts whose sense of satisfaction quickly fades—especially for someone in a depressive spell. The same goes for charity work: it's terrific in the moment, but afterward we go home to our demons.

Rescuing a pet hits a sweet spot—a manageable, indisputable and ceaseless act of kindness. Vector is a constant reminder that I can't possibly be a completely bad, worthless person. I did, at the very least, one thing right: an innocent, formerly homeless animal is currently curled up with me on the couch.

Of course, I've done plenty right in my life, especially in the decade-plus since getting clean and sober. I've become a reliable, thoughtful husband, and a father whose roles span from reading instructor and baseball coach to disciplinarian and, I hope, moral compass. I've become a more intimate loved one to extended family members, and a more open, accessible confidant to close friends.

I've built a career as a communications executive, becoming a key team member at an employer I've worked with for the entirely of my sobriety. My finances and physical health are both in reasonably good shape. So yes, I've accrued some tangible currency in the self-esteem bank.

But try telling that to me when I'm depressed. During bouts, depression finds any inkling of doubt and exploits it. It enters slender self-conscious cracks, then expands exponentially.

Has my wife really forgiven me for my past transgressions? Am I *actually* an admirable, attentive father? Do my friends and family enjoy my company as much as I do theirs, and am I as valuable a colleague as I'm led to believe?

But while my depression can exploit and exacerbate nagging thoughts, what it *can't* do is eradicate a self-evident fact. And that fact is this: with Vector, I've done something right. Something good, and pure, and undeniably positive. I can't be *all* bad, because … well, because Vector. Because of this innocent, infinitely loved being who cannot care for himself.

Vector's depression-piercing capabilities have only grown with age—specifically, *his* age. As I touched upon in Chapter 2, Veckie's senior status means we've already won with him. He could collapse tomorrow and his life would still be a lopsided victory, one in which I had the privilege to play a leading role. After all, I'm his alpha human, his bestie, his go-to. I'm his daddams, for God's sake.

As he slows down, Vector is in the final chapters of his life while my other household members are still unfinished scripts. My wife, like me, is in her mid-40s, and my son is still a young boy. If, God forbid, the worst happened to them, the story of their lives would be sad—exceptionally so in my son's case.

By contrast, Vector has already lived a full doggy life. Every day from this point forward is truly a bonus and a blessing. He could have died a decade ago as a non-entity; instead, his end will come in our embrace, and his legacy will live on both through us and, eventually, through subsequent rescue dogs we take into our loving home. Vector has enjoyed a full canine lifespan, with all but the first few years safe and happy and adored. I love *that* nearly as much as I love *him*.

Further, I helped author (or perhaps direct) Vector's life story with a reassuring and altogether appropriate authority that simply does not exist in our human relationships. I could not exert such exacting control over others—not even my son, not permanently anyway—nor would it be responsible or acceptable to do so.

The outsized positive influence we have on our rescue dogs leaves little room for depression's doubt-mongering. My disease can strip away neither his fantastic life nor my undeniable contribution to it. I could not take such credit for the accomplishments of other humans. Point: rescue dogs.

Vector's life has been objectively good; therefore, I have *done* good—unalterably, inarguably so. These are not emotional assessments, but rather logical ones. My depression eats emotions for breakfast; I need firm facts to combat it. Vector's rags to riches life—and its contentedness, and its prolongment—can be wielded against my depression's diseased doldrums like few other tools.

6. Mental Health: Guide, Dog

Of course, Vector's value in combatting my depression extends far past his age. While the forgone conclusion that he's lived a full, loved life with our family has become a permanent wellspring of self-esteem, Vector paid depression-fighting dividends right from the get-go.

Here again, we find motifs that intermingle with my other major mental malady, addiction, so some themes intersect and intertwine with the benefits explored in Chapter 2. Still, these similar scenarios branch off to battle two compatible yet distinct afflictions. Addiction and depression are a formidable combination because, while they often team up in their attempts to drag me down, they must be addressed and counteracted as individual entities. Therapy and medication aren't enough to move forward in my recovery from drugs and alcohol, while my progress in Alcoholics Anonymous isn't enough to sufficiently arrest depression.

The point is I need customized weapons to fight each battle. But sometimes Vector provides a Swiss Army knife—a multipronged tool that helps alleviate various ailments, addiction and depression included.

One of those multipurpose moments occurred within weeks of adopting him. In Chapter 2, I discussed how Vector went from a nervous wreck to a nub-wagging companion in short order, how he quickly emerged from his terrible past to embrace his terrific present. Doing so required some measure of faith that this situation—his placement with my family—would be drastically different from his previous experiences. This aided mightily my own stunted quest for some semblance of faith, generally seen as a higher power-instilling springboard to long-term recovery from addiction.

In those early days with Vector, what I had the privilege to witness and participate in was an innocent being transitioning from hopelessness to hope. His tremors quelled. His gait went from tenuous and lumbering to trusting and light-footed. His eyes went from glazed over to glistening.

I saw Vector's lights come on. I experienced his rebirth.

Depression literally depresses—it gets me down and tries to keep me there. It exhausts my body and clouds my brain with the lie that my diseased state is, suddenly, my new normal. That I'll never come out of it.

If you suffer from depression, you know precisely what I mean by this perceived permanence—this sinking feeling that you'll never resurface to experience love or joy again. If you do not suffer from depression, consider the scenario that opens this chapter. Consider suicide.

But don't consider my suicide. When I tiptoed toward the edge of that rooftop, my life was legitimately screwed up. My months-long spiral had dug holes with my fiancée, family and career that would have been intimidating even for a sane person.

No, consider the suicide of someone whose life was plainly

salvageable, if not altogether fantastic. Consider Anthony Bourdain. Or Kate Spade. One was a universally admired globetrotter whose life consisted of eating exotic foods and exploring exotic lands. The other was among the most successful fashion designers ever.

Bourdain and Spade are dead because of depression. Their established diagnoses and jealousy-inspiring lives combine to eliminate practically any other explanation. And while news outlets around the world reported shock, those of us with depression simply registered sadness, and perhaps some quiet resignation. Because if depression can kill two beloved multi-millionaires in the primes of their lives, it can kill anyone.

They got down and stayed down. They couldn't see a worthwhile path forward. The light faded to the end of a long tunnel, then disappeared forever.

Seeing that sudden sparkle in Vector's eyes does not eliminate depression's ability to do the same to me. But it sure as hell diminishes it. Depression sufferers like me benefit greatly from real-world reminders of notions others may take for granted. That there is hope. That we are loved. That life is worth living. As he emerged into a confident, rollicking playmate, Vector was an infectious hit of doggie dopamine.

Crucially, that life-affirming feeling has proven durable—a milestone memory I can tap into while depressed. Nothing, save for my son's birth, has brought me as much pure joy as watching Vector first recognize then run toward his newfound safety, security and love. A tough mutt with a tough past choosing life—a life with me, no less.

And if recalling Vector's awakening doesn't help boost my mood? Well ... then I just do what Vector did in his early days with us. I wait.

Plopped into disorienting surroundings, and after knowing nothing but terror nearly his entire life, Vector retreated—but did not resign. He cowered and shivered and sulked, but he did not hide. Nor did he make repeated efforts to flee. Quite the opposite, in fact: remember, after breaking free from his harness on his very first night with us, Vector returned to our home—a random house he'd known for all of two hours—all by himself after our search for him proved futile. Well, with a heavy assist from meatloaf, at least.

Eventually, what Vector found is that his misery had a cessation point, and that life was waiting for him on the other side of it. Likewise, sometimes my depression is stubborn, stagnant, unbudgeable. Sometimes I need to just put my head down, accomplish what I can accomplish ... and wait the damn thing out. Sometimes I just need to let the storm run its course before the sun can reemerge—albeit with my wife's watchful eye ensuring a depressive bout doesn't become a depressive emergency.

Of course, on an everyday basis Vector, like all dogs, embodies

6. Mental Health: Guide, Dog

Vector enjoying some sunshine. "Join me in the light, daddams."

the exact opposite of waiting. Dogs live in the now, and witnessing my once-lost companion experience the good life, moment by moment, also dents my depression.

In Chapter 2, I mentioned that Vector, as a dog, doesn't seem to have the capacity to mourn for himself—not for his unacceptable beginning nor his pending death. He contentedly sniffs one spot in the yard and, satisfied, moves on to the next. There's too much to see and explore to sulk and dwell.

When I'm depressed, Vector's happy, monotasking life reminds me to look at the bigger picture. Though currently in a depressive spell, a pleasant life is still right there in front of me. Here, Vector is more catalyst than cause; his casual, unconcerned privilege to live each moment to the fullest mirrors mine, as well as reflects upon my indisputable hand in that outcome. The stable, reasonably affluent life I've built in recovery affords me such peace, and allows for my loved ones—including Vector—to enjoy the same. It's no panacea, for sure. But it helps.

And if all else fails, Vector has one last trick up his sato sleeve: good old-fashioned guilt.

Again, my depression can manipulate feelings, but facts are stubborn things. And the fact of the matter is my mutt survived three years in a killing field to join me and my family. My partial blindness, addiction and depression issues pale in comparison to whatever hell he went through in Puerto Rico.

Vector has this adorable way of approaching me, sitting on his haunches, then cocking his head and staring at me. Usually it means he wants a treat, or maybe wants me to move over so he can jump up on my chair, or the couch.

When I'm depressed, that look makes me feel … silly.

Humans, of course, are not advised to make a depressed person feel guilty—or flat-out stupid—for being depressed. We rightfully admonish them for it. Depression is a condition, not a feeling.

But dogs know no such social graces or medical differentiators. Vector is just moving forward with his life while I'm stuck in a foggy, sludgy pause. And his status as a tough-as-nails scrapper with battle scars galore gives him the street cred to mete out what, to me, has become good guilt.

Of course, some mental malleability is involved. In Vector's mind, that look means "fetch me a treat," or perhaps "move your big butt over a bit, daddams." In mine, it means "I won my war, so fight harder to win yours, asshole."

He is the only being in my life allowed to "speak" to me like that, all anthropomorphism aside. Hell, an innocent being incapable of inspiring animus can "say" pretty much whatever he wants. Vector makes himself heard through what he represents, and I hear his messages loud and clear, depression be damned.

7

Mental Health
Rx Rescue

Nadja Caban Lopez was adopting a dog. Or else.
This was no bluff, because Nadja had options. No dog? No problem. We move.
Nadja's family migrated to the United States from Puerto Rico in her childhood—another household that saw more opportunities on the U.S. mainland than its Caribbean homeland. Since then, she'd built a comfortable life with a loving husband, Stalin Guzman, and three beautiful children.
Still, they had more than their fair share of setbacks. Nadja's children each struggle with mental health issues, each with winding journeys and unique challenges.
Among mental health's most frustrating, frightening facets is that, to adequately address a problem, it must first be accurately assessed. Mental maladies often require protracted periods of displayed abnormal behaviors and trial-and-error therapy to correctly diagnose. Children and teenagers bring another layer of difficulty, as even those with sound mental health can exhibit hormone-inspired moodiness. Adolescents are, generally, about as consistent as the weather, creating conditions counter to exacting clinical analysis.
Nadja's oldest son, Tilson,* was no exception. Prone to depressive episodes, he'd shown signs worrisome enough to occasionally require inpatient treatment. Fortunately, Tilson had a reliable salve: sports. The exercise and team-oriented structure helped alleviate his depression.
Then came March 2020. Amid Covid-19 lockdowns, schools and extracurriculars were suspended indefinitely. Youth sports came to a crashing halt. So did Tilson.
"He went from having this crazy sports schedule to just nothing,"

---

* The names of Nadja's three children have been changed, as they are minors and the narrative covers medical conditions.

Nadja recalls. "Sports had been a really helpful outlet for him, and when they shut down, he did too."

On the downside, Tilson was ... down. Really down. But the emerging emergency finally led to an accurate diagnosis: Tilson had bipolar disorder. Today, he takes medication that helps regulate his mood swings more effectively. Still, he remains susceptible to exaggerated, condition-specific highs and lows.

The Guzman-Cabans' middle child, 12-year-old Alexandra, presented another hard-to-come-by diagnosis: a rare mood-altering condition called cyclothymia.[1] A sort of "bipolar lite," cyclothymia's emotional peaks and valleys are less pronounced, though still abnormal and alarming. Like bipolar disorder, cyclothymia presents a medical moving target: symptoms sandwich between extended stretches of baseline stability, making diagnosis a wait-and-witness, cat-and-mouse game. Also like bipolar, no blood or marker tests exist, so diagnosis involves an arduous, often lengthy process of elimination and educated conclusion.

Fortunately, doctors diagnosed Alexandra before her cyclothymia could do what it often does: devolve into its more serious cousin, bipolar disorder. Today Alexandra is properly medicated and, like Tilson, has displayed substantial improvement despite periodic struggles.

Nadja's youngest, seven-year-old Marie, is likely too young for any issues related to her siblings' diagnoses to materialize yet. She does, however, struggle with anxiety—a fact not unnoticed by her family members, human or otherwise. More on that soon.

Finally there's Nadja herself, a relative latecomer to her family's mental health melee. During Tilson's Covid-initiated doldrums, Nadja noticed a pattern while consulting with his doctors: while the symptoms psychiatrists were discussing pertained to Tilson's challenges, sometimes they also described hers.

"A lot of what the doctors said about Tilson also resonated with me," she recalls. While any loving mother would sympathize with her son, Nadja was *empathizing*—personally identifying with items on symptoms checklists.

Nadja shared her history with the doctors, including concentration problems in high school severe enough that she balked on college. They determined she suffered, in varying degrees, from ADHD, depression and anxiety. Nadja was, after all, her children's mom.

Yet the close-knit clan persisted, a loving, supportive household thriving despite mental health challenges. Speaking with Nadja, a confident thirtysomething with twentysomething looks and fortysomething poise, there is no hint of the stigmatizing shame that, for too long, has plagued those with mental health issues. No resentment at the universe

7. Mental Health: Rx Rescue

for not wiring their brains quite right. No inkling of victimhood—refreshing in an era when too many see oppression and self-pity first and progress-centric solutions second, if at all.

Against these stereotypes, Nadja speaks matter-of-factly, more "this is us" than "woe is us." She is endearingly candid—a proud Latina with a proud story. And when the rail-thin mother of three modestly referenced her "weight loss journey"—a transformative shedding of over 100 pounds—it became evident how scrappy and dedicated she is.

Like so many other sato parents I've met while developing this collection, Nadja Caban Lopez is a fighter. And now, for her family's sake, she was battling a policy she saw as unnecessary and unhelpful.

Like too many residential complexes, the building where the Guzman-Cabans live did not permit pets. While no doubt a rule meant to prevent a tenant from accumulating a small zoo in a contained community with shared walls and common areas, the notion that a family of five couldn't adopt a singular dog or cat is restrictive to the point of regression.

Nadja viewed the idea that a domicile can't contain a lone domestic animal as patently ridiculous. And now, she was asking for an exception to her building's pooch-averse policy, or else the powers that be could find themselves new tenants.

For Nadja, it was a hill worth dying on. But while she obviously believed getting a dog would benefit her children, she never could have foreseen the outsized impact a medium-sized mutt would have on their collective wellbeing.

The battle was short-lived. With pooch permission in hand, Nadja knew exactly where to turn for a dog: her homeland.

In early 2021, a dog that would come to have four wonderful names started her life just like Vector did: anonymous and hopeless. All of the rescued dogs in this collection began with very little chance for a happy, lengthy life. For the satos of Puerto Rico, though, the odds are even more daunting.

Over the long term, a stray dog's survival rate in Puerto Rico reaches zero. While no comprehensive survey can be conducted of the island's estimated half a million strays, it can safely be assumed that the older dogs roaming its beaches and cities and rural roads are recently dumped, not lifelong curs. The hot, humid, parasite-ridden facts are that Puerto Rico's conditions are too harsh to permit a full canine lifespan. By three, Vector had a year left, tops.

This is not a pathetic pooch pissing contest, an attempt to crown the unlikeliest and therefore grittiest canine survivor. It is only to reiterate how uniquely hellish life is for Puerto Rico's satos. And in early 2021, a dog that became an irreplaceable member of a stable middle-class family—a dog that would be infinitely loved and want for absolutely nothing—was existing in a trash receptacle in Puerto Rico. An actual dumpster in a doggie dumpster of an island. She was going to die, and soon.

And then she wasn't. Someone mentioned the miserable mutt to a volunteer for the Sato Project, which, since Vector's rescue, had grown by leaps and bounds into an established island entity. They fed, vetted, sheltered, and altogether loved the six-month-old puppy back to life. They named her Missy—an upscale name for a downtrodden dog.

Meanwhile, Nadja and her husband were actively searching online to make good on their hard-fought lease leniency. As discussed in Chapter 3, rescue dogs were harder to come by during the Covid-19 pandemic, so the couple agreed on just one prerequisite.

"It had to be black," Nadja said, "because we'd read that black dogs have the most trouble getting adopted." In short order, they'd clicked through pages of dark-haired doggies online, and each brought their top choice to the other.

"It was the same photo," Nadja smiles. "We picked Missy without the other knowing it."

That was that. On August 28, 2021, Missy, who came to be known as "Missy Foo" by Nadja's family, boarded a plane packed with more than 120 other strays. It was the second leg of the Sato Project's latest "Mission Possible"—the 14th such evacuation event featuring the organization's ambitious Freedom Flights from Puerto Rico to the U.S. mainland, typically the New York City and Boston metro areas.

Ironically enough, Nadja and her family were visiting relatives in Puerto Rico that week, so her mother fetched Missy from Newark Liberty International Airport. Still, Nadja wanted Missy to be a surprise for the kids. So she made matching "Guzman-Caban Pack" T-shirts, and invented a reason to wear them on the plane ride home.

It was only as they approached their building that Nadja broke out another Guzman-Caban-branded garment. Only this one had four leg holes. Her daughters gasped. Tilson welled up. Though the Guzman-Cabans hadn't formally met Missy yet, they were already in love.

Missy would need it. Despite being a stray for "only" six months, she was exhibiting anxiety above and beyond a "normal" dog getting accustomed to new surroundings. "She was very scared," Nadja recalled. She described Missy's curled-up, cowering, inconsolable tremors—a panic that paralleled Vector's early days with my wife and me. "She just wanted to be held."

But not by men. Missy didn't like men, hinting at some harm done at the hands of a Y-chromosomed culprit. It took treats and trust-building for Missy to warm up to Tilson and Nadja's husband, Stalin. Missy still

7. Mental Health: Rx Rescue

doesn't trust new men (who can blame her?), but today her dad and brother are exempted from her growling gender bias. So is her grandpaw: when Missy hears Nadja's dad's car coming up the street, she leaps and yips in joyful anticipation.

Missy's other major hang-up was far more straightforward.

"She hated trash cans," laughs Nadja. "Still does. Won't go near them—walks around them on the street." Missy's had enough garbage for one life, thank you very much.

In any event, the Guzman-Caban clan grew from five to six. As with most rescues, the transition from rogue mongrel to family member took time and effort from everyone. For a family beset with various mental maladies, this neediness was Missy's first gift.

"Before Missy everyone was kind of in their own rooms, doing their own thing," Nadja says. "But she was this great new thing and they were drawn to her. Missy got them out of that and into more interacting."

"She's been very good at keeping us…" she pauses, "…together."

By "together" Nadja isn't speaking existentially. Her family was not going to disintegrate and separate without Missy. Rather, she meant physically, as in Missy disrupted the rhythm of everyday family life by making it less self-segregated and more group-centric.

All mental maladies aside, there is value in Missy's collective allure in our 2020s civilization. Because when Nadja alludes to her children retreating to their rooms for individual activities, it doesn't take a digital decoder to understand she's talking about tech. Computers, smartphones, tablets, online gaming … the cyber-lives most modern-day kids lead is all but unrecognizable from childhood even 20 years ago.

In an August 2022 Pew Research Center survey of more than 1,300 teens ages 13–17, an alarming 46 percent reported being online "almost constantly." That figure is twice as high as the number reported just seven years earlier. Ninety-seven percent reported using the internet every day.[2]

Notably, these aren't for academic purposes—it's not an app that children are using to upload homework assignments. Per the survey, the vast majority of this use constitutes social platforms like TikTok, YouTube, Instagram and Twitter. In fact, teens outpace Americans overall in social media use, 97 percent to 72 percent.

And that brings us back to mental health. Inundated with optimized, filtered images and boastful posts depicting others as far happier, more attractive and more moral than they really are, social media platforms preach connection and community while offering alienation and inferiority complexes.

Multiple studies have indicated what any astute observer could easily surmise: social media use correlates to increased risks of depression, loneliness, and anxiety. Per the Social Media Victims Law Center, credible research notes an adverse effect on self-esteem, with the age group most susceptible defined as girls between 10 and 14—Alexandra's age group.[3] In May 2023, the U.S. surgeon general, Dr. Vivek Murthy, warned that social media may harm children and adolescents.[4]

So Nadja had three kids with diagnosed mental health issues using, like the rest of their generation, technology proven to be detrimental to mental health. What's more, many mental illnesses—not just bipolar disorder and cyclothymia but also depression and anxiety—thrive on isolation, as well as opportunities for "less than" messages that prey on disease-driven proclivities toward lower-than-normal self-image.

Against these worrisome digital trends, Missy presented a wonderfully analog solution. "Get off your phones," her tail-wagging energy demanded, "and get me a treat." She was boisterous, barking bait to lure the Guzman-Caban kids out of their own rooms and into shared ones. They don't call it the living room for nothing.

"She pulls people out of their funks," Nadja contends. "She drags them, goads them. When she comes to you and wants to play, it has a way of guilting you out of a down mood."

Simply by being a delightful distraction, then, Missy threw a wrench in the arguably unhealthy habits that many people—children and adults alike—tend to fall into with too much alone time. She became a conduit for the Guzman-Cabans to spend more time in the same room or, even better, out for an obligatory walk or park excursion. Missy gave them a cute, lovable reason to congregate—something they could all agree on and simultaneously enjoy.

But of course, any dog could have accomplished that. Missy didn't need to spend six months in a disease-ridden dumpster to give the Guzman-Cabans something to dote over—a pick-me-up for a family impacted by mental health challenges.

But a fraught past likely was necessary for Missy to perform her next role with such surgical precision. Paging Dr. Missy, resident rescue of the Guzman-Caban Center for Mental Health.

Incredibly, as Missy became acclimated, she shot past getting to know her new family members to knowing them better than they know themselves. She began gravitating toward whatever family member she sensed was having a poor mental health day—a doggie diagnostic tool giving Nadja a heads-up that someone needed some extra love, even if that someone was Nadja herself.

"She just knows when something's up," Nadja says. "She's right next to that person and doesn't want to leave their side."

7. Mental Health: Rx Rescue

Whether or not Missy's role as psychologic psychic is directly due to her inauspicious beginnings is debatable. However, there certainly seems to be a "you rescued me, so I'm rescuing you" element to the extra dedication Missy shows to whichever family member she thinks needs it.

Recently Nadja's youngest, Marie, required a surgery unrelated to her mental health. Surgeries are scary for anyone, let alone seven-year-olds, and Marie's anxiety was approaching panic-level. She was barely sleeping. And the longer it went on, the less Missy left her sister's side.

Eventually, the young girl paid less attention to her own worry and more attention to her doggie. Missy made it known that she wasn't going away until that positive result was reached—a smother-you-with-love approach that is counterproductively annoying when humans employ it, but endearingly effective when animals do. It's not a stretch to insist that Missy was the only Guzman-Caban capable of quieting her sister's insomnia-inducing nerves.

Alexandra is no stranger to Missy's proactive pestering either. Unsurprisingly for an adolescent, she tends to bottle up and hunker down when her mental health issues resurface.

Missy will have exactly none of it. Waiting and barking outside Alexandra's room. Scratching at the bathroom door. Bringing chew toys to her middle sister in an endless game of fetch. Missy does her part to break down the barriers of a preteen prone to moping. "I can't solve your mental maladies," her ceaseless attention says, "but I can help you forget about them and alleviate them. Now throw the damn toy already."

Meanwhile, at 17, Tilson has learned to preemptively employ Missy's mental health services.

"He's gotten to a point where he knows how he's feeling, and feels a funk coming," Nadja says, justifiably proud that her son is so self-aware and honest. When he and Missy are closer than usual, Nadja knows Tilson may have a bipolar high or low looming.

In protecting her family against themselves, Missy showcases levels of love and loyalty exceptional even for a species known for such qualities. She's like Lassie, only with five Timmies. It's as if she's seen enough hurt and anguish and hopelessness for one life—six months in the trash will do that to a soul—and has taken it upon herself that her family unit will suffer as little of it as possible.

Nadja clearly agrees with this sentiment—it says so right on her car. The family vehicle sports a bumper sticker that not only sums up their relationship with Missy, but could also double as an alternate title for this book. The rhetorical, chicken-or-the-egg quandary speaks to their mutual healing: "Who Rescued Whom?"

Dr. Missy Foo Guzman-Caban, off duty for a birthday celebration (courtesy Nadja Caban Lopez).

At least some of Missy's magic is likely attributable to another doggie differentiator: a prodigious sense of smell. While expert opinions vary regarding precisely how much more acute dogs' scent-detecting abilities are compared to humans, even modest estimates place them from 1,000 to 10,000 times better.[5] Some put the figure closer to 100,000 times keener.[6]

Whatever the exact figure—one likely dependent on breed, among other factors—that's exponentially more advanced than even the most sophisticated man-made instruments. Some dogs possess snouts powerful enough to detect substances at concentrations of one part per *trillion*—akin to a single drop of liquid in 20 Olympic-size swimming pools.[7] If your dog ever ripped open a delivery box with food inside ... well, that's why.

It's no wonder, then, that many service dogs have been trained to identify smells associated with human medical conditions—particularly those that relapse and remit unexpectedly and dramatically. Dogs have been trained to sense recurring tumors, as well as pending episodes tied to diabetes, hypoglycemia and other conditions where fair warning can be invaluable. For example, with a heads up from a four-legged companion, an epilepsy sufferer can be alerted that a seizure is imminent; she can then lie down on the ground to prevent a collapse-caused head injury or, if driving, pull over and park.[8] Here, a barking alarm bell can mean the difference between safety and serious injury.

One organization at the forefront of advancements in canine-assisted living is Indianapolis-based Medical Mutts. Partnering with researchers, the service dogs provider was among the first to demonstrate canines' ability to warn humans of both epileptic seizures and hypoglycemic episodes. Medical Mutts also has trained dogs to detect subtler conditions such as postural orthostatic tachycardia syndrome (POTS); defined by an inability to regulate blood pressure and heart rate, POTS can cause, among other symptoms, distracting dizziness or even dangerous fainting spells.

Returning to this chapter's theme, Medical Mutts also has trained dogs to sniff out early indications of a highly common mental illness: anxiety-related panic attacks. Officially termed panic disorder, the condition affects around six million adults in the United States, just shy of 3 percent of the 18 and over population.[9] Often downplayed or dismissed as mere nervousness or lack of fortitude, panic attacks are a mental-meets-physical condition that can cause heart palpitations, uncontrollable hyperventilation and even fainting. Think Tony Soprano passing out behind the wheel of his SUV.

Several studies have indicated that certain human emotions have associated scents. Recalling Missy and the Guzman-Caban family, while scientifically vetted studies are still lacking, anecdotal evidence suggests dogs also can smell certain chemicals associated with bipolar disorder, specifically those tied to pending manic episodes.[10] While these reports are largely limited to first-person testimony—such as those highlighted in a November 2018 article on *Bipolar Hope's* website—for lack of motive it seems unlikely people are lying about, or even imagining, their dogs' scent-centric diagnostic powers.[11] Again, we're talking about a species whose olfactory sensitivity is several thousand times more sophisticated than ours; the idea that they can sniff out a sudden chemical shift in someone they live with is far from far-fetched.

Of course, Medical Mutts trains dogs to be more than the mental health equivalent of smoke alarms. The organization also trains dogs to serve humans with a wide range of chronic and permanent mental disorders (meaning those that affect sufferers perpetually rather than episodically). In fact, one of Medical Mutts' specialties is a category called psychiatric service dogs, which entails a set of parameters distinct from therapy, emotional support or even conventional service dogs.

The purview of psychiatric service dogs surpasses mere helpfulness into mission-critical or harm-reducing tasks. For example, while therapy or emotional support dogs can, by their very presence, help calm down their agitated humans, psychiatric dogs can be trained to rouse PTSD sufferers from damaging nightmares or flashbacks, or to purposefully disrupt situations causing emotional overload. They also can remind their humans to take crucial medications, and even persistently nag them until they follow through. This last responsibility—medicine adherence monitoring—cannot be overstated, since mental illnesses often provoke in their sufferers a reluctance or refusal to follow vital prescription drug regimens.[12]

One of Medical Mutts' clients is Joe, who in adulthood developed schizoaffective disorder, a condition that combines schizophrenia symptoms such as hallucinations or delusions with mood disorder issues like depression or mania. In moderate to severe cases, schizoaffective disorder can lead to highly awkward or adverse social situations, trouble maintaining relationships, and difficulty holding down a job.

"I got to a point where traditional methods weren't doing enough," Joe shares on a video on Medical Mutts' website. "I was locked up in [my] apartment, too afraid to ever leave. Panic attacks would be overwhelming."

Joe was paired with a brown, medium-sized mix named Ray. Progress was both expedient and extraordinary.

"He's kept any paranoid thoughts out of my head when we're out," Joe says. "I'm completely focused on what he's doing."

Joe's condition is alienating, and his cognizance of that is both frustrating and intimidating. With Ray, he has a companion whom he knows isn't judging his every move or utterance—a connection that, as the pair stroll down the street or through the park, has proven literally liberating. And when he notices his adorable point of focus prompting smiles in passersby, he feels more connected not only to Ray but to humanity as well. If a medication exists that can produce a similar effect, I've yet to learn about it.

"When people see a service dog, they tend to be attracted to them, drawn to them," said Dr. Jennifer Cattet, co-founder and executive director for Medical Mutts, whose lengthy career in animal well-being began with a PhD in animal behavior studies. "They come up and ask about the dog in a way that is overwhelmingly positive. The dog is a catalyst of healthy human interactions for those who might otherwise struggle with that."

That's the medical aspect of Medical Mutts. But just as powerful is the mutts part. These aren't carefully cultivated canines bred and groomed to be lifesavers. The dogs Medical Mutts mentors are fellow spared souls trained to pay forward the unconditional love bestowed upon them. Each and every service dog the organization houses, trains and places is a rescue. It's salvation, squared.

Still, the organization is careful not to sacrifice service for sentimentality's sake. The selection progress is both extensive and expansive.

"It's not easy to find the right rescue dogs for these purposes," said Dr. Cattet. "We frequently travel across Indiana and well into neighboring states to find suitable program candidates." Among other variables, Medical Mutts prefers dogs in the one- to two-year age range—old enough to display a predictive temperament but young enough to have a lengthy life ahead of them.

Those selected from shelters have their work cut out for them. All dogs must pass rigorous, repeatable tests to ensure they can accomplish the numerous, often customized roles their humans will require of them. Further, some behavioral prerequisites comprise traits not always associated with once-desperate dogs. Medical Mutts service dogs mustn't startle easily, nor be overly motivated by food. And they must be reasonably tolerant of other dogs even while recognizing and mitigating potential threats. Vector, bless his heart, would have been the class dunce.

In the real world, these dogs must navigate complicated, often highly demanding situations and, for that reason, the selection process must be uncompromisingly discerning. In fact, only about one in four dogs successfully completes the training and gets placed with needs-based clients.

But whether dean's listers or dropouts, all Medical Mutts graduate to a happily ever after. Dogs who don't make the grade are placed with suitable, non-service-requiring forever families; in these instances, the Medical Mutts team is essentially a loving foster family.

And like Ray, the ones who pass with flying colors go on to become more than heartwarming stray-to-service sagas. There's sound psychiatry here, with the impact of these dogs' daily super-canine duties bolstered by their tears-inducing backstories.

These dogs once faced highly uncertain futures. They were abandoned, ailing, alone. They not only survived but thrived. They found their place in the world—found peace, purpose and connection. They found a forever home with a forever human whose life has been similarly marked by undeserved misfortune. They want to help these humans—and, of course, help themselves. Dr. Cattet notes a self-preservation aspect to many of the organization's service dog success stories.

"What's unique about rescued service dogs is that the trauma of being abandoned often triggers an understandable anxiety in the dogs about being abandoned again," Dr. Cattet explains. "So these dogs tend to be a little more clingy."

She drives the point home by using an often disparaging term that, for Medical Mutts' mission, suddenly becomes high praise.

"A lot of them are what you'd call 'Velcro dogs.'"

Medical Mutts, she explains, needs dogs that are highly in tune with their persons. By contrast, a dog fully comfortable and content being by itself—in another room napping, or sniffing around the backyard—is likelier to miss emotional or physical warning signs in their person, scent-related or otherwise.

"That little bit of overattachment brings tangible values," she adds. "The dog who wants to constantly be by your side is better suited to picking up on all those subtle signs, whether it's a smell, change in behavior or environmental shift."

It's not, of course, a perfect process. There can be difficult-to-foresee downsides when a dog affixes itself so firmly to its person—especially when that person has psychiatric issues.

"Some dogs, because they have a proclivity to attachment and are trained to be super-sensitive to their person's moods, become emotionally impacted themselves," Dr. Cattet says. "Unfortunately, some dogs become too sensitized and accrue their own set of anxieties or other issues that can make them less effective from a service perspective."

She discusses a client who suffered debilitating anxiety, and also had a free-flying bird in his home. While the initial training went well, the dog had difficulty handling that living situation, as well as the bustling streets of New York City, where his person resides. The dog had to be returned to Medical Mutts—something that, fortunately, happens very rarely.

Indeed, psychiatric service dog successes far outpace the well-intending misfires. And a substantial reason for this is rescue-related.

"From the patient's perspective, it makes the dog more relatable," Dr. Cattet contends. "They each have a difficult past, and a bond is facilitated and strengthened that way."

Medical Mutts once supplied a service dog for a boy, Kyle,* who'd been given up for adoption as an infant, then abandoned by his adopted family when he was six. By age 11, now with his third (and current) set of parents, Kyle had understandably developed considerable anxiety and abandonment issues that manifested in disruptive and even destructive behavior, both at school and at home. Kyle wasn't to blame—but he wasn't OK.

"He was too young to diagnose with PTSD, but his level of fear definitely pointed toward that," said his adopted mother, Stephanie. "And who could blame him for worrying about being deserted again?"

Medical Mutts trained and supplied Kyle and his family with Darcy, a Labradoodle whose initial owners had returned her to a shelter for not exhibiting her breed's trademark curly locks of hair. (Pardon the brief

---

* Name changed to protect anonymity of a minor with mental illness/medical conditions.

editorial, but that might be the least valid reason to abandon an animal imaginable.)

Stephanie knew her son loved animals. But the rapid, significant improvement Kyle displayed once Darcy joined their family was, she said, almost unbelievable. Kyle's boyhood expressiveness played a role in that.

"Kyle's psychiatric issues are so physical that Darcy is able to read him fairly easily," she said. "So Darcy intervenes. 'Don't run away, don't punch the wall. Pet me.'" Stephanie explains that Darcy, upon realizing Kyle is becoming upset, typically leans on his legs as a means of interrupting and therefore diffusing the situation.

Notably, Kyle cites Darcy's backstory as a major factor to his lifted spirits. There's empathy there—and an endearing symbiosis.

"More than once, Kyle has said something to the effect of 'People were

Darcy the medical mutt (courtesy Jennifer Cattet).

wrong about Darcy, but this is where she's supposed to be.' And he knows that this is where he's supposed to be as well."

That certainty has cemented over time. Kyle is now 17. That he and Darcy have a forever family is now evident to each of them.

"They rely on each other," Dr. Cattet says, speaking both specifically about Kyle and Darcy, and broadly about rescued service dogs and their humans. "Neither will ever be abandoned again."

Like Vector, these dogs are not panaceas. But to say they aren't uniquely positioned to significantly help people with mental illnesses is selling them well short. Their practical service capabilities help their humans live fuller, more independent lives; their hard-luck histories provide their people with leaping, licking proof that, despite their discouraging conditions, they indeed have worth—that they can do right by an innocent being by providing a permanent loving home, and gain a beastie bestie in the process.

8

Marriage and Relationships
V for Victory

Neither of us looked very good.

Let's start with the guilty party. My face is puffy, showing flashes of a double-chin. In the best of the photos, I'm leaning forward to diminish an overly fleshy chest; in the worst of them, man boobs are on full display. A sweater that once fit perfectly hugs my torso. My pants are too tight, their 36 inches of available waistline maxed out and then some. It was clear my descent from a booze-bloated 240 pounds was far from finished business.

Then there's the innocent victim. Simply put, this is not the young lady I fell in love with, or the middle-aged one I remain in love with today. In this snapshot in time, Patty is easily 15 pounds heavier than normal—noticeable given her 4'11" frame—and, past such skin-deep superficiality, just looks … off. Overweight and under-rested, she appears like a woman put through the wringer. And she appears that way because that's exactly what she is.

The photo roll continues. Us looking not-that-great in front of our fireplace. Us seeming older than our years sitting in the dining room. Us walking frumpily through a nearby park.

But more importantly, us looking relieved. Us looking honestly happy, boasting unrestrained smiles rather than the feigned for-the-camera smirks that, for too long, were the disingenuous norm. Us looking like a couple that intends to stay that way.

And we were. And this fact was on display every bit as vividly as my moobs. Interspersed with photos of a too-chubby twosome showering each other with hugs by the hearth and pecks in the park is a third subject—one decidedly lither and livelier. He is sleeker and browner than he is now, a being in the very prime of his once incredibly tenuous existence.

Vector sitting upright on the living room rug. Vector clutching a rope toy. Vector begging for a treat then, in the very next photo, outstretched as he begins a zeroed-in leap reminiscent of a zoo seal-feeding. Vector

Patty and me in late 2014: two people emerging from the wringer of my addiction (Mike Stella Photography).

leashed up, striding between his mom and dad in the peace and quiet of a park in wintertime. Vector back home, head down on the couch, eyes half closed in semi-slumber.

The two people in these photos have been to hell, and are still finding their way back. When Patty Li married Christopher Dale, on April 28, 2007, she knew he had his share of issues, clinical depression foremost among them. What she did not know is that, less than a year after the wedding, her husband would become a borderline alcoholic and, soon thereafter, a full-blown cocaine addict.

It was an exceptionally long, pothole-laden road to get to that photo shoot in late 2014. Even after the bottles and baggies ceased and my personal recovery commenced—a prerequisite to any mutual recovery together—we dodged dead-ends on numerous occasions. We were hostages of the horror-show our union became, the hurt and humiliation and lies and resentments imperiling our recovery as a couple even as my abstinence from drugs and alcohol trended toward permanence.

Those few dozen photos were not the first taken in our recovery. But they were the first formal, posterity-preserving pics we'd taken in years. They were, in essence, re-wedding pictures—an outward-facing representation of a couple's revived vows. And this time we weren't just a couple; we were a family. Because of Vector.

8. Marriage and Relationships: V for Victory

Still, shuffling through the pics nearly a decade hence, I can see the slightest taint of hesitance, a tepidness between two people striving to wholeheartedly embrace each other but not quite there yet. Patty and Chris version 2.0 still had some bugs to fix.

By contrast, Vector is fresh, pristine, unencumbered. In some photos, he is engrossed in the scents of the park; in others, he stares matter-of-factly ahead from a position of pride: his parents' feet. In a few, his head is cocked quizzically, no doubt wondering who this stranger with the strange contraption—the photographer with his camera—could possibly be. And of course, the most amusing photos involve his single-minded mission to pluck a treatsie from my too-high hands.

One thread permeates Vector's photos: they show a being certain of where he should be, and equally certain that he is there. He is with us, and that is right. Period, end of story, cue treatsie.

I regret a *lot* of what I did to Patty in active addiction. She regrets a few of the things she did to me in recovery—especially during that fraught period of our fledgling recommitment. But neither of us regret anything about our relationship with Vector.

We (ok, mostly me) have done so much wrong to each other. But when it comes to the being that transitioned us from a couple still wearing yesteryear's wounds to a fully forward-looking family, we've pitched about as close to a perfect game as possible. And to two far-from-perfect people, that shared success goes a long way toward wiping a messy slate as close to clean as possible.

There is beauty in capturing the imperfections of two people on an intricate, incomplete journey, however emotionally and physically compromised it has left them. The lion's share of these photos are haunting and hopeful and awkward and altogether real. A thousand words apiece wouldn't do them justice.

But there is one shot that stands out for its succinct simplicity. Patty on the left, me on the right, lips in full kiss formation. In between, a smushed sato receives simultaneous smooches to both sides of his scarred snout. Its message can be conveyed in just six wonderful words.

We were going to make it.

On October 11, 2011, Patty was waiting when, after a night in jail, I appeared before a judge for a DUI. I was finished driving for a year, and figured Patty and I were just plain finished.

She could have left. We'd been staying with my relatives as I tried to get clean, so our apartment was empty. The next day, Patty could have gotten up, packed her bags, and went home.

Instead, she got up, packed a lunch, and went to work. We didn't

Vector turned a still-struggling couple into a full-fledged family (Mike Stella Photography).

know it yet, but that was our bottom—my last inebriating substance, and our closest brush with divorce.

But it's not that simple.

In marriage, one partner's early sobriety is a deceptively dangerous time, one masked by its decisive preference over active addiction. Absent a round-the-clock five-alarm emergency, the pressure gauge dropped from a 10 to … say, a 7½. We could catch our breaths and catch up with a life suspended by addiction's insults, indignities and overall insufferableness.

We took that breather. And since we liked the fresh air … we stayed there.

This alluring, indefinite pause showcases the sneaky challenges of post-addiction marital recovery. Two road-weary travelers downshift from life in the emergency lane. But instead of continuing at a reasonable pace, the newfound peace is so compelling they pull over entirely.

Going nowhere feels much better than hurtling toward divorce. That's how a union once barreling at breakneck speeds toward disaster ends up in park. And that's how Patty and I ended up a few months into my recovery, going nowhere fast in our mission-critical *mutual* recovery.

We simply didn't know any better. Nobody told us what to expect when no longer expecting the worst. This issue is so confounding—and, I believe, so common—that my first book, *Better Halves: Rebuilding a Post-Addiction Marriage*, was an attempt to help mitigate such ignorance-driven missteps.

There was, for starters, an egregious discrepancy of resources. For me, Alcoholics Anonymous provided a well-trodden path. I just needed a catalyst; my DUI, with its inglorious hit and run and even less glorious pants-pissing, provided that. I only needed to give up and get in. I'm proud to say I did. It isn't enough to *need* recovery. I know plenty of dead people who needed recovery. It must be *wanted*.

Meanwhile Patty had ... what? Al-Anon? She found it a group of people griping about their mostly still-using loved ones. Psychiatry perhaps? But wasn't *I* the one with the problem?

Only one of us—me—had both an existential need and clear, consistent direction. As recovery commences, society does a far more admirable job meeting addicts where they are—the gutter—than meeting their spouses where *they* are: the curb.

Early sobriety demands expedited progress to parlay what brings addicts into recovery—existential fear—into something with a more durable foundation. In short order, I went from hopeless active addiction to exceedingly hopeful abstinence. Ignorantly, though, I left Patty out of it. I figured this was my fight, and that actions spoke louder than the words of a conniving addict. Besides, none of this was Patty's fault. Why should *she* have work to do?

It's a notion as reasonable as it is unhelpful. However unfairly, Patty was a worse person—angrier, more cynical, less trusting—than before my addiction. In hindsight, that Patty needed her own parallel recovery seems obvious; in real time—like so many other couples—we were oblivious.

So I made prodigious progress while my more mature partner didn't. Eventually the inevitable occurred: I ran right up Patty's ass. As I reclaimed ground on a lopsided landscape, landlord Patty wasn't having it.

Resentments are lethal. And when the person you resent most is your spouse, the marriage is unsustainable. Patty hadn't forgiven me, because doing so required processing and addressing the deep damage I'd caused her. Worse, neither of us *recognized* this—a prerequisite for any resolution. It took several near-separations to realize the problem, bewilderingly, was ... Patty. This time I couldn't fix what I'd broken: my wife. The choice was Patty's alone. Either be perpetually owed an unpayable debt, or work to transcend traumas and remain married.

This is all messy, confusing, convoluted. It's all very unfair and fucked up. And it exemplifies why so many marriages face deal-breaking challenges during one partner's early sobriety.[1] We had to reset, reacclimate and reaffirm our commitment to each other while accepting, airing and addressing the harms my addiction had inflicted upon us both. Remember, I had a tried-and-true program of recovery; Patty did not.

We got lucky. We stumbled into success before being dragged into divorce. We moved forward and, soon, moved out of my relatives' place, purchasing our first home. We were committed now. But we were also at each other's throats—this time, in a good way.

As we recovered together, working to diminish our character defects (regardless of their singular source—me) meant calling each other out. It meant helping each other recognize the detritus of my addiction *within* each other. It meant constructive conflict with the occasional cathartic shouting match. Our new doors got slammed, our new neighbors got an earful.

This wasn't regression, but rather progress. We were getting in each other's faces, getting loud about it ... then cooling off and *getting better*. Sometimes a couple emerging from years of trauma needs to unravel their stubbornly tangled knot spat by spat. That shit just needed to come out before we could do anything useful with it.

We weren't in danger, but could clearly benefit from a safe space. We could use something to agree upon entirely, that we'd both unquestionably and unceasingly see as 100 percent good. And if that something furthered our renewed commitment to each other, all the better.

Later, Patty would contend she was already thinking it. But I said it first. I uttered what remains as important to our union as any five-word phrase, up to and including "in sickness and in health" and "'til death do us part."

"We should get a dog."

That was, I acknowledge, a rather winding road. But marriage is complicated, and precisely how Vector fits into our personal puzzle requires context. Next chapter, we'll meet other couples with their own disparate circumstances—unique love stories made lovelier by their equally unique four-legged family members.

None, including Patty and I, would insist their rescue dogs made their marriages work. However, all would attest their rescue dogs made their marriages *better*.

For starters, Vector was just ... well, himself. A defenses-dropping, smile-inducing pet for a couple that needed to step back, lay off and just chill the hell out once in a while. From the moment he set paw in our home, Vector, who no doubt had experienced his share of violent Caribbean thunder, became the opposite of a lightning rod. He became a storm-stopper—a doggie diffusion device that quieted down the winds of any nuptial nor'easter.

8. Marriage and Relationships: V for Victory

We were still stumbling through our imperfect path forward—and that included learning how to fight for change rather than conquest. When things got hot-tempered, Vector was a cute, cuddly coolant. When impasses led to silence, Vector was an irresistible icebreaker.

Dogs do that. Their adorability and innocence is compelling and disarming. We are drawn to them, and drawn to be calmer and more accepting *by* them. Dogs are really good company that, merely by association, seem to make those in their vicinity better company, too. It's really hard to be an uncompromising asshole with a playful puppy in the room.

Vector allowed us to put our guards completely down, to abandon our pretenses, hangups and disagreements du jour and just dote upon something cute and pure and wonderful. He was an untainted soul in a marriage that, while improving, still had stains from years of neglect.

We ooh-ed, we ahh-ed, we aww-ed. We loved him effortlessly and effusively. And for now, we did that exclusively: Patty and I weren't ready to disarm so fully with each other. In providing an outlet for such naked, unreserved affection, Vector helped steer us toward the unmitigated trust, respect and love that marriage professes, aspires to, and hopefully espouses. Vector was a vessel—a vehicle that transported us to happiness and harmony, if only for the duration of a good boy belly rub.

But Vector was more than a distraction, or even a disruptor capable of cutting through tension. Vector was a change agent, a doggie Sherpa trudging us toward a distant yet reachable peak. The outpouring of ebullient baby-talk ("Who's a good boy! Who? WHO? *YOU'RE* a good boy!! Yaaaay!!"), playful rambunctiousness and overall good tidings Vector evoked in us were more than mood-altering diversions. Our interactions with him hinted at where we wanted to go as we continued to slowly repair our relationship. If Patty and I could be half as happy to see each other as we were Vector, we'd be in the Marriage Hall of Fame.

Granted, this is a magic trick any dog could have performed; or, at least, any dog with Veckie's caliber of cuddly cuteness. His status as an endearing, adorable love magnet for a couple still smarting from a bruising recent history did not require him to be a rescue animal. There are facets of his feat that do not need a sob story to be adequately effective. Vector would have brought value to our relationship even if he'd been purchased from a pet store rather than salvaged from the hot, humid doggie wasteland into which he was born.

But of course, Vector *was* a rescue. And like so many other dogs we're meeting in this collection, he had an origin story that was pitiful then plentiful, malignant then miraculous, heartbreaking then heartwarming.

Sound familiar? For Patty and I, this was more than a little on the nose—or rather the snout. Vector's stark before and after pictures drew parallels to ours. We didn't just love him; we *identified* with him. He fought to survive; we fought for our marriage's survival. And now, he was safe and fed and happy because we were scratching and clawing and ultimately growing, together. He was here, right where he belonged, because we were doing the honest but honestly exhausting hard work that healing a post-addiction marriage demands.

As a fellow reclamation project, Vector was our renewed commitment incarnate. His sound health and growing confidence in his new-and-improved environs not only gave reassurance *to* us, but also reflected *upon* us. His trauma, trials and newfound triumph didn't just resonate *with* us, they became part *of* us. Vector was validation that we were on the right road, however bumpy.

There was an affirming forward momentum to all of this. Part of Vector's wizardry wasn't what he was, but rather what he represented. Adopting Vector was an outward expression of our unrealized intentions—not just about where we wanted to go in life but *who we wanted to be*, both as individuals and as a couple.

For two people clumsily working through the wreckage of the past—knowing full well they were doing so imperfectly and incompletely—Vector was a walking welcome sign that read "damaged souls accepted here," or maybe "apply within for second chances." He was Vector the projector.

We found a battered dog with a tortured past and decided that the remainder of his life would be filled with hugs and kisses and park excursions and treatsies. In promising this to Vector, we were implicitly promising to provide that love together—not just to him or each other but, ideally, everyone in our inner circle.

On our wedding day, we promised to love and honor each other forever. In short order, I took those vows and snorted them up my nose. When I finally got my head out of my ass and my ass into group-centric recovery, we started the arduous process of reestablishing that indefinite, all-encompassing commitment.

But unlike our nuptials, that commitment required far more than words. They required Patty and Chris to undo the damage that came right up to the brink of dissolving our union. Revisiting our vows wasn't enough. For Patty and Chris to have a path to forever again, each of us needed to evolve.

My evolution was mandatory—it was necessary for my continued viability as a living, breathing, free-willed adult. Physical abstinence is rarely enough to defeat addiction over the long run. If I didn't work to diminish the personality flaws that had led me to drink and drug in the first place, I was doomed to go back there. And going back there meant any combination of death, unemployment, prison or divorce. I changed to survive—a foxhole prayer in action.

Patty's change was far less existential, but no less critical to the long-term viability of our marriage. Classic Chris wasn't coming back, because Classic Chris would inevitably descend into cocaine Chris and, from there, dead, divorced or incarcerated Chris. Not a very good Chris.

Rather, Patty had Chris 2.0 on her hands. And she was either going to recommit to this Chris under revised rules of engagement, or she wasn't. She was either coming along for the ride, or she wasn't. With her husband growing out of sheer necessity, Patty alone dictated whether we, as a couple, would grow together or grow apart.

We had to become re-compatible. I am convinced that the failure to do so—a failure overwhelmingly attributable to innocent ignorance—is responsible for far too many early recovery divorces. Today, our weller-than-well, better-than-ever marriage is proof positive that Patty passed this test with flying colors. That she did so is far, far, *far* more impressive than my gun-to-his-head transformation. I changed, or else. Patty changed with several other options on the table.

It took introspection and honesty and, in our case, a fair amount of arguing to redefine and reaccept each other not for who we married but for who we were becoming. We basically got re-married—it was an "I do-over."

Where's Vector in all this, you ask? Simple. He's part bellwether, part guiding light.

The bellwether part is straightforward: Vector was as real a commitment to staying together as our wedding rings. He exemplified where we were in September 2013—confident enough in our marriage's salvation that we could confidently save another, together. Satisfied enough with our progress thus far to turn our recovery into a three-covery.

With a big fat caveat, though. Less than two years since my not-so-fond farewell to drugs and alcohol, we weren't ready for the commitment of all commitments: the one that involved diapers and cribs and crying and 3 a.m. feedings. We weren't ready just yet for the pitter-patter of little feet. But we *were* ready for what so many call a first step toward it: the chit-chit-chit of paws prancing across floorboards.

And we were ready to honor our journey by making that special someone a special sato—a dog that looked oblivion square in the face and spat in it. We were ready to parlay our fledgling success into promising the same for another family member. We were ready for Vector.

What we weren't prepared for was that Vector's near-death and rapid rebirth would come to signify not just a snapshot in time—not just September 2013—but also a point on a more hopeful horizon.

If we were strong enough to nurse and love this tremoring, cowering, traumatized wreck of a cur back from the brink, we could become ready to extend that patience and hospitality and understanding to others in our lives. And when Vector rewarded our efforts by becoming, within mere months, a leaping, licking, loving companion, it pushed Patty and I closer to all in on all of it. Those first few months with Vector helped us discover, then double down upon, the type of couple we wanted to become, and the type of home we wanted to make.

Most married couples, I suppose, come to this organically. They tie the knot, store some money away, purchase a home … then intuitively know what to do with their blessings. Their souls largely unscarred, and their confidence in each other never seriously shaken, they go about extending the warmth, non-judgmentalism, and support they have for each other to those around them. To family, friends and, in due time, to sons and daughters.

Patty and I enjoyed no such normalcy. I obliterated any chance at so linear a life-building with three years and $100,000 of cocaine. I nearly killed our union in its cradle, and myself along with it. A couple can take one of myriad paths from there, but each has one thing in common: none of them are conventional. I had guaranteed that nothing would ever come naturally to us as a couple—at least for the foreseeable future.

We were left constructing those convictions—humility, generosity, gratitude—one brick at a time, and only rarely in perfect unison. In rallying around Vector, Patty and I came to learn what was important not just to each of us as individuals, but to us *both*. Vector helped Patty and I embrace these ideals together—extreme emphasis on the word "together." Our shared sato led to shared values.

Do we live up to those lofty ideals? Sometimes, I guess. Sort of, maybe. But Vector helped us sniff them out, and serves as a live-in reminder to strive for them.

Finally, Vector's tale—including his lack of, well, a tail—helped cement for us that our experiences, however humiliating and cringeworthy and altogether awful, can come to benefit others.

Let's be honest: the story of the first few years of our marriage isn't just tragic and sad. It's fucking embarrassing. And there are reasons galore to tuck it away in a closet and seldom speak of it again to the outside world—a world that, per last chapter's mini-rant, is increasingly full of disingenuous social media personas pretending to be far more moral and happy than they actually are. We live in a society that rewards not only reputation-guarding reticence but also posed, filtered phoniness.

Against this, I and especially Patty had to be dragged into openness about our history. To friends, families and most recently my employer, the

8. Marriage and Relationships: V for Victory

truth eked out in drips and drabs over months and years. But as my first book attests, we got there. And that candor has been repaid a hundredfold in the joy of having our friends actually know the real Patty and Chris rather than their public relations representatives.

Is this all Vector's doing? Of course not. But living with and loving a family member that lost a tail and a toe and chunks of his ear to exceptionally harsh circumstances made us realize how gritty and gutsy he must have been to survive all that. Vector isn't shamed; he is strong. If he can live freely in the light, so can we. And since Vector can't talk, we must.

As we became more open about our struggles—and proud of our successes—something amazing happened: close friends and family became even dearer. They appreciated our candor, and saw it as an invitation to be open and honest with us about their own, typically less existential problems. Fairweather friends faded away, and what remains is a close-knit circle of confidants that Patty and I feel truly privileged to truly know.

This all happened, we feel, on an expedited timeline. Having Vector in our lives put recovery on speed dial, fastening us together faster and more firmly. And it was a good thing, too, because we were approaching 40 and, so far as the next step was concerned, unyielding biology was becoming a factor.

We were making it happen, together—as a trio. And soon, we were ready for something else. We were ready to make Vector a big brother to a human sibling.

9

Marriage and Relationships

Yes We Canine

In the previous chapter we covered how, with a consistently love-affirming, endearingly adorable assist from our rescue dog, my wife and I battled back from the brink to rediscover each other and reclaim our union. Fortunately for both individual sanity and societal stability, most couples enjoy love affairs far more linear and less turbulent than ours.

Indeed, this collection has its share of outliers; we're diving into some pretty heavy stuff here. Alienating mental health disorders. Low-bottom addiction and scarring trauma. Grueling grief (see Chapters 12 and 13) and intricate, difficult-to-resolve relationship issues. Throughout, we've seen the inspiring ability of rescue dogs to meet us where we are—often, a deep ditch—and drag us someplace safer, kinder, happier.

But not every tale needs to teeter on death, devastation or divorce for the value of rescue dogs to resonate. Like cherries atop sundaes, our adopted four-legged family members also improve situations that are already inviting.

Compared with Patty and me, Cassidy and Marek Harabin are a wonderfully fresh-faced, uncomplicated love story. Cassidy was born and raised near Albany, New York, and met Marek, who is from Stamford, Connecticut, while the two attended nearby colleges. They started dating in 2016, their junior year. When I spoke with Cassidy, the mid-20s couple had just celebrated six months of marriage.

Their life together is young. And shortly before congregating on a beautiful altar to say "I do," Cassidy and Marek congregated on a cramped commercial airplane to say "I dog." Her name is Carmen (originally Valentina), and she was just days old when the Sato Project—Vector's benefactor—salvaged her from the unforgiving streets of Yabucoa, Puerto Rico. Either abandoned or orphaned, the helpless puppy was just a few hundred yards from Playa Lucia, more notoriously known as Dead Dog Beach.

Carmen was going to die—right there, and really soon. She was too

9. Marriage and Relationships: Yes We Canine

new and too tiny to fend for herself. While Vector somehow lasted three years before becoming a dead dog walking—courtesy of parasitic disease and lifelong malnourishment—Carmen would have succumbed to exposure or thirst in less than a week.

Her existence never would have gotten off the ground. She would have been even more of a nonentity than most of her hopeless fellow satos, if that's even possible.

And then she wasn't. Too young to mentally fear humans or physically flee from them, she was not hard to corral. In all of ten seconds, Carmen's expected remaining lifespan jumped from under a week to … well, about 12 years, a dog's average lifespan. The Sato Project didn't save Carmen's life; it *gave* her a life—one that was about to end before it even began.

Carmen didn't come to the U.S. mainland scarred and scared like Vector. She has no idea how close she came to never really existing. She was delivered from perhaps the world's worst environment for strays unharmed and unhaunted, with both her medical chart and her soul spotless. She is exceptionally fortunate—as close to a sato unicorn as can be.

So Carmen was a young, relatively unscathed rescue for a young, relatively unscathed couple. But we're not there yet.

In July 2021, Cassidy Arocho and her fiancé, Marek, did something they'd been anticipating for quite some time. In reality it was about 16 months. To them and to pretty much everyone else on the planet, it felt like forever.

They were about to take a vacation.

It was the duo's first true taste of freedom since the Covid-19 pandemic shut down first travel, then restaurants, the office, family gatherings and every other lifeline to normalcy. Freshly vaccinated, the healthy young couple were embarking on what could be described as sun and fun with a purpose.

"First of all, obviously we just needed to get away to someplace tropical," said Cassidy, whose hometown of Boston is anything but palm trees and piña coladas. "But I also wanted to trace some of my roots."

Cassidy is Latina—specifically, Puerto Rican. She and Marek planned a trip combining sun, sand and surf with exploring the area surrounding Aguadilla, on the island's northwest coast. It was where Cassidy's *abuelo* and *abuela*—her grandparents—were born and raised, and she'd never seen it in person.

She'd also never seen so many stray dogs. Like, ever.

"They were just … everywhere," she recalls. "Living in a major city like Boston, you see your share of stray animals, but this was just a whole different level of desperation. Far more dogs in far worse shape."

Cassidy and Marek came to Puerto Rico intending to escape the harsh realities of the Covid era. They needed, and had earned, a release valve—some good old-fashioned un-adulting. And they definitely enjoyed facets of that.

But unintentionally, Cassidy and Marek also matured on that trip—and in a fashion that bound them even closer together. They flew to Puerto Rico expecting a carefree romantic getaway. They flew back recognizing how their commitment to each other could expand into a dutybound engagement with the larger world. Two individuals still six months from formally exchanging their vows were realizing their responsibility—as a stable, reasonably affluent aspiring family unit—to do their small part toward righting a grievous wrong.

They flew to Puerto Rico as a couple. They flew back as a household. And that household was about to grow.

"Right on that plane, we promised each other we were adopting one of those dogs," said Cassidy. "Period. It almost didn't need to be spoken. We couldn't…" she pauses, "…we couldn't *not* adopt one after witnessing that."

For them, it was glaringly obvious—nothing more complex than a transitive property of decency. (A) Any decent people with means would see the tragedy of Puerto Rico's satos and want to do something—*anything*—about it. (B) Cassidy and Marek were two decent people. Therefore, (C) Cassidy and Marek were going to do whatever well-intending thing they could to alleviate this seemingly impossible crisis.

Their search did not take long. They Googled "rescue dogs + Puerto Rico," and up popped an organization celebrating its tenth year of sheltering, vetting and evacuating thousands of formerly doomed dogs from the island.

Cassidy and Marek initially thought they'd need to return to the island to adopt. A quick perusal of the Sato Project's website proved otherwise. Less than two months later, Valentina arrived in late August, during the same "Mission Possible" airlift that brought Missy to the Guzman-Caban family, profiled in Chapter 7. Cassidy and Marek made the four-hour drive down to New Jersey for the airport pickup. Cassidy plucked the three-month-old pooch into her arms. Valentina got a new name, new parents and a new home in one fell scoop.

Listening to Cassidy recall their journey to Carmen, it all seems so … normal. So normal that, for a cocaine-addicted, clinically depressed, partially blind miscreant like me, it seems decidedly abnormal. However, I and anyone with such issues must see this relatively unmarred couple's shared joy as no less beautiful for its comparative lack of struggle. Good for Cassidy, good for Marek and, especially, good for Carmen.

And good Samaritanism. And unbeknownst to the young couple,

9. Marriage and Relationships: Yes We Canine

Cassidy and Marek Harabin with their sato, Carmen (courtesy Cassidy Harabin).

so much more than that. In setting Carmen up with a nurturing forever home, they were setting themselves up with a better chance to keep that home intact, indefinitely. Relationships are hard—God knows Patty and I realize that—and anything that helps two people learn, care and persevere together is a blessing.

"We were never patient enough with each other," Cassidy said. "Maybe we thought that, since we each knew we loved and were committed to each other, everything else would sort of fall into place."

Carmen is describing what many otherwise happy couples experience:

the blurred lines between content comfort and conflict-causing complacency. It's what happens when two people think sharing their lives *with* each other will always mean sharing the same expectations *of* each other. To some extent, all long-term partners likely experience some degree of this confusing push-pull.

"Dealing with a puppy helped build more of a realistic mindset—first for Carmen and, maybe by extension, each other," Cassidy recalls. "Getting Carmen acclimated and housetrained took patience and, for us as a couple, developing a workable care routine that shared responsibilities took clear communication."

Cassidy also explains that working with Marek toward a common, undeniably noble goal—getting Carmen settled in as a full-fledged family member—made them more accepting of each other's shortcomings. It made two people reasonably new to cohabitating—and *very* new to dog parenthood—less likely to bicker over well-intending mistakes, and more happy to pick up any slack the other needed for lack of time. Carmen presented two people already moving toward something inherently good—marriage—with a mandated master class in patience, tolerance and communication, three things they'll need in spades to live happily ever after.

At first, it was Cassidy who needed to communicate, and Marek who needed to absorb and remain teachable. Cassidy grew up with dogs; Marek did not.

"I had to teach him to take care of a dog," she says. "And he had to be willing to learn, and be a little more flexible." The two owned a cat (with a hilariously human name: Rick), but soon learned that a dog required far more attention. As Marek grew into the role, of course, Cassidy had to be willing to step back and let him do things his own way, even if they didn't quite jive with her preferences or experiences. Compromise. Results over process. Not letting perfection be the enemy of progress … gee, marriage must-haves much?

Of course, such qualities can be learned and earned in a variety of ways. But for Cassidy and Marek and countless rescue dog parents, such humble pie is far more palatable when the beneficiaries include a blameless, pure-souled being such as Carmen. No rational person could resent so innocent an animal, leaving no viable excuses to not put in the work and grow as both individuals and a couple.

And of course, Carmen is … well, a dog. She expects her new home to be calm, and doesn't like it when it isn't.

"She barks when we fight," Cassidy shares. "She hates hearing us yell, especially when she senses we're yelling at each other. She's shut down arguments many times before either of us said something we'd probably regret." Carmen's referee role, Cassidy explains, is a tangible, real-time benefit to her joining the family. Cooler heads prevail and the couple continues forward.

Before Carmen, Cassidy and Marek were really, really good. With her they were even better. When the two tied the knot, Carmen stole the show at the newlywed's wedding brunch. Today, Cassidy sees parallels between rescuing a dog and starting a marriage.

"You start from the beginning coming just as you are, imperfections and all. You take little steps every day and, slowly, it starts to blossom into something beautiful. And the next thing you know, you have a family member of your choosing who's helped you become more open, trusting and selfless."

In May of 2023, Cassidy and Marek doubled-down on doggie. The couple adopted a second sato, Tito, from the Sato Project. Tito has parents who've already reaped the benefits of a rescue dog in their lives together. He has his big sister to thank, and his own happily ever after ahead of him.

For a young couple like Cassidy and Marek, a rescue dog represents a promise. Carmen embodies the couple's commitment to building a union whose affection is both eternal and *external*—a lifelong love available not only to each other, but to *all* others near and dear to them.

By comparison, Yun and Zoe showcase that potential realized over the longer term—a mature, middle-aged marriage rooted in rescue dogs just as surely as it is each other. So inseparable that friends have Bennifer-ed them into "Yoe," the couple exemplifies what can happen when two individuals find the right partner, then see their love expand exponentially outward.

Yoe is not only a combination but a culmination. Though still individually young—Yun is 43, Zoe 39—as a duo they have arrived. They have transitioned from fledgling couple to forever family, with or without offspring. And they have done so far more organically than Patty and me, whose reclamation project of a marriage is, to put it generously, a chaotic outlier.

Unlike Patty and I, Yun and Zoe were never a black hole. Their now-expansive universe formed linearly, amassing gradually greater gravity. Their wedding bands represent fixed orbits surrounded by concentric circles of close companions. And on the innermost rings reside a trio of now-senior rescue dogs, beginning with a medical miracle of a mutt named Roxy.

But before the advent of Yoe there was ... just Yun and Zoe. Two solo women searching for Ms. Right.

Yun was born in Shanghai. Her parents fled China, whose oppressive government executed Yun's grandfather for speaking out against the Communist Party. The family immigrated to Costa Rica but, deeming the education system inadequate, eventually landed in Los Angeles. Yun proceeded to graduate from UCLA, earn a PhD in cognitive psychology from the University of Hawaii, and become a tenured professor.

Yun's mother clearly did a lot right. But she had a blind spot: an affinity for animals, minus the follow-through to adequately care for them.

"My mom loved Poodles, so we got a Poodle," she says matter-of-factly. "But she didn't know how to take care of a Poodle." Its needs unmet, the dog barked loudly and exhaustively in their apartment. "We didn't want to get evicted, so she gave the Poodle to a rescue organization."

Yun had seen this show before. Years earlier, her mom brought home a Spaniel. The dog got fleas, got them everywhere, and got returned.

Yun's mom had no animal animus; if she had, she wouldn't have brought dogs home in the first place. Her issue was perseverance. This lack of stick-to-itiveness stuck in the young Yun's craw. Later, Yun's own circumstances exacerbated her uneasiness. She was accepted to graduate school, and the university's housing didn't permit pets. Yun had to leave her dog, Bear, behind. With her ex. Yuck.

"Then and there, I promised myself I wouldn't get another dog until I had real stability," she recalls.

For Yun, stability meant not just somewhere to stay, but a place to *belong*. To give a dog a deserving home she needed permanence, roots. She thrived in school, returned to Los Angeles, began teaching. She had a nice place and promising career. Still, the pitter-patter of little paws eluded her apartment—but not her heart.

"I would go run errands and inevitably wind up at the dog shelter," she says. "I'd just go see the dogs, knowing I wasn't ready to commit to adopting yet."

Yun's "yet" kept the canines' cages closed. It wasn't something missing, but some*one*. Yun was flailing to find her yang. And as she meandered through dead-end relationships, she only got pickier.

"I developed this set of conditions that I wanted in my ideal partner," she explains. "I called it API: appreciation, priority and inclusivity." Unfortunately, the only person who checked each box was left unchecked—buried under less suitable bachelorettes in Yun's long-ignored dating app inbox.

Zoe is a native New Yorker. Thoughtful, introverted and dog-averse from childhood, she retains two of those qualities today.

At eight, Zoe was bitten hard by a dog … right on the rear end. Combined with her father's untrained, rambunctious chocolate Labrador, she began watching her back (and butt) around all dogs—a youth-ingrained, disproportionately heightened fear reminiscent of Deanna Cheng's experiences in Chapter 3.

Zoe's doggie discomfort persisted through early adulthood. She earned a Bachelor of Fine Arts from New York University's renowned Tisch School of the Arts. She moved to Los Angeles, America's entertainment industry hub, and became first a camera assistant, then a camera operator. When Covid-19 halted most productions, Zoe pivoted, creating a camera log app now popular with TV crews and moviemakers. This admirable adaptability will become mission-critically relevant soon.

Seven years earlier, though, 30-year-old Zoe was having her own underwhelming dating experiences. Her natural reticence, she explained, can be mistaken for standoffishness. The flip side, though, is whoever penetrates that guarded exterior feels privileged. Yun's chance arrived in October 2013. But she almost blew it.

Earlier that year, Zoe sent Yun a message through OKCupid, a decidedly non–Tinder dating platform that asks detailed questions to suggest compatible candidates. Ever-hesitant, Zoe didn't message many folks, but the pretty Asian-American on her screen was a 97 percent match—a rarity. It was an A+, even for two ladies grading on a curve.

Unfortunately, Yun had deactivated her account without checking messages. For seven months.

When Yun reactivated her account, she noticed the promising 97 percent compatibility rate and reached out—without ever seeing Zoe's initial message. It was either a match made in heaven, or with a hell of a lot of luck.

Their first date was October 22, 2013. Zoe said Yun broke down her walls quickly and completely—an unprecedented anomaly. For Yun, Zoe was similarly unique.

"I called her a unicorn," Yun said. "We don't argue. We always want the same things. We share the same values. It's like winning the lottery."

By their third date, they hardly spent a night apart. By early 2014 they were living together. Three months later, Yun proposed. Yun and Zoe officially became Yoe in April 2015, two years after California established marriage equality, two months ahead of America at large.

Yun knew she was home—stability, roots, permanence—right away. And for Yun, more than anything else that meant one face-licking, four-legged next step.

Here, we find a quality that distinguishes dogs from almost anything else short of parenthood. Had Yun looked forward to becoming an avid marathon runner or painter or gardener upon settling down with her better half, it's doubtful whether Zoe would have acquired running shoes, paintbrushes or a green thumb along with her—especially if Zoe were predisposed to dislike those passions. Had Yun taken an intense interest in marine life, it's unlikely Zoe would have come to regard the resulting sea anemones and tropical fish as an integral part of their union.

Hell, even if Yun were a (sigh) cat person, Zoe's involvement could have been minimal. While the ever-raging "cats vs. dogs" debate is certainly subjective, one indisputable fact is that, on an everyday basis, the former are far easier to care for than the latter. Cats require less attention, less money, even less affection.

Dogs are different, and that difference is the distinction between support and immersion. And when a dog person finds a human soulmate—particularly one apathetic toward or even afraid of dogs—that difference becomes crystal clear. Zoe would have *supported* Yun's interest in any reasonable passion, up to and including cat ownership. But dogs—and especially rescue dogs—require all-in adaptation. Life partner, meet lifestyle change.

Mere weeks after her successful 2014 proposal to Zoe, Yun visited a No-Kill Los Angeles shelter to find the perfect pooch for her perfectly apprehensive fiancée. They had known each other all of eight months, but Zoe had already given Yun the go-ahead to adopt a dog she deemed a fit for them. Some couples have a starter home; Yun was seeking a starter dog.

"My goal was a dog as unintimidating as possible," she remembers. "Small, easygoing, preferably an older dog."

At the shelter, Yun came across a mild, seemingly serene 16-pound mutt. A subsequent test showed a jumble of breeds including Springer Spaniel, Pomeranian and Mi-Ki—which itself is a blend of Shih Tzu, Maltese and Yorkshire Terrier. The dog was six, and her name was Roxy. The attendant opened the enclosure. Instead of frolicking and leaping, Roxy slowly sauntered up to Yun. It would be difficult to imagine a less threatening dog.

Roxy never returned to the kennel.

On the one hand this is a scene that, thankfully, plays out in shelters nearly 5,500 times each day in the U.S. alone; per the American Society for the Prevention of Cruelty to Animals, approximately two million rescue dogs find forever homes each year.[1] So while Yun was doing something special, she was also doing nothing special—an encouraging nod to America's standing as both the overall and per capita leader in dog ownership.[2]

On the other hand are the circumstances of Roxy's salvation—a dog that, as it turned out, had been adopted and abandoned twice before and, in the interim, hit by a car. When she tepidly moved toward Yun that June day, an aging orphan facing the likelihood of life behind bars took the first bracing steps toward fulfilling a solemn vow for her soon-to-be mom—a layered commitment whose prerequisite involved … well, a commitment.

9. Marriage and Relationships: Yes We Canine

Namely, Yun's commitment to finding the stability she swore she'd secure before adopting another dog.

Again, that stability wasn't a house with a big backyard, or a tenured teaching position. It was Zoe. Yun was sure about Roxy because she was sure about Zoe—and sure that Zoe was sure about her. Future wife at her side, Yun was finally on terra firma. She'd built a foundation upon which she could begin righting what she saw as the canine-centric wrongs of her past.

And then there's Zoe, the bite victim turned dog dodger. For decades, she was uncomfortable around dogs. Now, she was permitting one to occupy the same home as her.

That's not a doggie-driven about face. That's a Yun-driven trust. Early in their rapid ascent into love, conversations about dogs had turned to shelter browsing tagalongs. Soon, Zoe had such ironclad faith in Yun that, in less than a year, she'd decided not only to spend the rest of her life with Yun, but to allow Yun to significantly shift the dynamic of their happily ever after.

But it wasn't *all* Yun. For Zoe, going from OKCupid to OK canine so quickly needed more than total trust in the love of her life. It needed a higher purpose.

Yun would never consider buying from a breeder—and Zoe knew this unequivocally. Zoe, then, understood that Yun's desire for dog ownership stemmed not just from fondness but also *fealty*. Yun wanted to do right by an innocent soul whose life would otherwise be scary, lonely, confined, and likely cut short.

People are more willing to make major accommodations for worthy causes. Zoe saw that Yun was attempting to do something irrefutably good; they weren't going to enrich a shady breeder or pet store, but rather save a life through rescue. Zoe loved that about Yun. And certainly, Zoe also loved that Yun saw her as the impetus—the stable, foundation-building catalyst—for undertaking so noble an endeavor.

Zoe loved not only Yun but Yun's intentions. And in short order, she also loved Roxy. In endearing herself to her other new mom, the mild-mannered diminutive dog left Zoe reconsidering her wariness of all canines.

On her first new morning with Yun and Zoe, Roxy popped her head up on the side of her moms' bed. She wanted up. She got up. She's slept there every night since. Or rather, she's slept in Yun and Zoe's bed—which soon underwent a Roxy-required upgrade. Yun calls it "hyphenating," and an award-winning novelist couldn't concoct a more symbolic scene.

"Roxy insists on sleeping perpendicular to us," Yun explains, "with her face on my side and her butt on Zoe's side." A bit unfair for Zoe, but adorable nonetheless. "We like to think it's her way of making sure she's close to us both," she continues.

Unfortunately, the full-sized wouldn't cut it. "We needed something bigger." Soon, the nightly hyphenations transpired on a spacious new king-sized bed.

We wouldn't know it from our sensationalist 24/7 news cycle, but most people are inherently good. And when we find something good, we are attracted to it. We take joy in the positive influence, and are compelled to seek out more of it.

But what we *can* take at face value is that animals are *all* inherently good. We know that none of them deserve to spend a long, listless life enclosed in a cage, or a brief, terrifying existence on the hopeless beaches and streets of Puerto Rico or similarly ruthless, cutthroat environments.

That's how Zoe's fear of dogs, like Deanna Cheng's in Chapter 3, leap-frogged the level ground of indifference into an open-ended embrace. Zoe loved Roxy. And that love was ready to expand.

By 2017, the couple was ready for their first standalone house—no small financial feat in the expensive Los Angeles housing market. It took

Roxy on her first morning with Yun and Zoe: hyphen, here we come (courtesy Yun and Zoe).

9. Marriage and Relationships: Yes We Canine

a while to find the perfect home, especially considering their requirements.

"It needed to be a single-story house," Yun recalls, "so senior dogs wouldn't have to worry about stairs. And it needed to have a yard for them."

Contrary to Yun's pluralizations, the couple hadn't adopted another dog in the three years since Roxy. Rather, they had designs on fostering—something they couldn't do in the townhouse they occupied. The first accoutrements their new home received were a doggie door and a fence to secure the backyard.

Their first heartwarming houseguest was a 10-year-old Rottweiler with the rhyme-time name of Gina Galina. While all fosters are intended to be temporary, Yun and Zoe expected Gina's time with them to be particularly limited.

"She came to us with large growths on her belly and leg," Yun remembers, "and had been given anywhere from two weeks to two months to live." Gina's owner had been unable to cover her onerous, ongoing medical expenses, and had to give her away.

It was clear Gina hadn't been cared for particularly well—the type of dog that was set up outside and left to her own devices. Yun and Zoe soon discovered her fondness for walks, which they began to take several times each day.

Gina Galina: saving her best life for last (courtesy Yun and Zoe).

Gina had been given two months maximum. She stayed with Yun and Zoe for over a year, likely the most enjoyable time of her life. "I think she wanted to stick around and get in as many walkies as she could," Yun suggests, using a doggie-talk word for their frequent strolls.

Their next fosters were a pair of Chihuahua mixes: Daisy, eight, and Queenie, seven. The tiny twosome each weigh about 13 pounds. Their elderly owner had passed away, and the rescue organization that took them in had scant room to care for them due, in part, to their advanced age.

It was a fabulous foster fail. And this time, it was mostly Zoe's doing. She quickly fell in love with Queenie—"her dog" to this day. They were both staying.

One might think three was enough—that Yun and Zoe's fledgling career as foster parents was, at the very least, indefinitely suspended. Quite the opposite occurred. Daisy and Queenie's age-related predicament—the difficulty older dogs have finding forever homes—inspired them to foster more seniors.

Let's recap. Two people, one dog averse, fell in love. That love brought trust, and that trust birthed a new chance at a happy life for one lucky little mutt. The dog started as a symbol of the couple's trust, love, and commitment to do good together.

"Roxy changed our marriage in unimaginable ways," Yun declares. "As only a dog can."

They loved their new family member—and loved that giving her a home was an unquestionably positive, life-affirming act. Soon, that love grew into more innocent beings to love—and with it, more love and trust and respect for each other, and for what they were building together.

Yun expressed all this with a pragmatic, chicken-or-the-egg paradox: "I have never sat down to think about how the dogs have affected our marriage," she shares, "because they have always been part of it."

Yun and Zoe are perfect for each other. Their love would have flourished without rescue dogs. When Yun contracted breast cancer and was left bedridden with chemotherapy side effects, Zoe handled the household affairs while caring for her wife, up to and including mopping up projectile vomiting. That's love. Fortunately, Yun is now cancer-free.

But in rooting their lives in rescue dogs, Yun and Zoe's bond is all the more unbreakable. It's the difference between *being right for* each other and *doing right with* each other, and in a fashion that pays daily dividends in the form of three now-senior playful pooches.

Fast forward to present day. The couple has tried unsuccessfully to conceive a human baby, their trio of tough mutts the ultimate consolation prize. Roxy, Daisy and Queenie are 15, 14 and 13, respectively. Now a decided dog person, Zoe, who dabbles in custom furniture, has

9. Marriage and Relationships: Yes We Canine

Queenie (left) and Daisy. Queenie quickly became "Zoe's dog" (courtesy Yun and Zoe).

constructed a low-to-the-ground bedframe so Roxy, the family's aging paw-triarch, can retain her hyphenating autonomy.

Roxy has been living with cancer for years. She nearly passed away on two occasions, only to reward them with a rebound. Still, Roxy is worse for wear; among other signs, she noticeably limps. Her parents absorb this fading note into life's background music, likening the now-erratic nail tapping of Roxy's compromised gait to arhythmic jazz. The family band plays on.

One day in the not-so-distant future, though, Roxy will not get back up.

The inevitable is approaching. Anticipatory grief sometimes saturates the household—a pre-emptiness that, as Vector's own age-related limitations mount, permeates my home as well. But as they brace for heartbreak, Yun and Zoe—and Daisy and Queenie—embrace in love. They hug, they hold hands, they hyphenate. They take turns crying.

But they also look to the future—one fewer in number but just as broad in scope.

"We plan to foster as many dogs as possible," Yun says. That will, however, involve another loss. "This means not replacing our dogs as they pass away, until we are down to one."

Yun and Zoe's plans might seem somewhat arbitrary; on the contrary, they are strategic. They are altruism mixed with realism.

"It's so hard when a foster dog goes to their forever home," Yun explains. "It's sad because they are leaving you, happy because they found their permanent home, and gratifying to see how much they blossomed with us."

However, Yun and Zoe know they couldn't handle the carousel of conflicting emotions inherent to fostering without a full-time dog of their own. Hence the planned two-foster, one-forever ratio. They still plan to skew toward senior dogs but—further testament to Zoe's transformation into a full-on dog person—also will welcome larger dogs, including oft-neglected breeds like pit bulls.

Sooner rather than later, their three senior dogs will become two. Eventually one elderly dog, likely with little time left herself, will remain, along with a revolving doggie door of fosters. That's a lot of logistical turnover and emotional baggage. Probably too much for one person.

But not for two seamless spouses—not for Yun and Zoe. Together, they are capable of physically accomplishing and emotionally absorbing exponentially more than either could alone. Their total is far greater than the sum of its parts; fittingly, both the cause and beneficiaries of this overflowing affection are one and the same.

One doted-upon dog at a time, the love circle continues to expand, with the duo known as Yoe at its center.

10

Parenthood
Doggie Bro-Bro

"Just make it to 11, buddy."

On a crisp March day in 2016, my wife Patty and I brought home our first and only child, Nicholas. As we pulled into the driveway, a moment that sparked both memory-making anticipation and paranoid new parent anxiety was upon us. It was time for Nicholas to meet his four-legged brother.

As Patty carried our fragile new cargo in a handheld bassinet, I entered the house first. Vector reserves his loudest yips and most rambunctious jumps for when I, his daddams, comes home, so the idea was to get those out of the way before Patty and Nicholas came inside. Basically, I was a 190-pound crash test dummy protecting a six-pound passenger.

Vector went berserk with joy, begged for and devoured the obligatory treatsie, then settled down into a nub-wagging contentedness. Patty walked in, a half-asleep newborn Nicholas in tow. She set the bassinet down near the front door, and we both kneeled over it. We beckoned Vector.

Vector approached, and paused quizzically. I doubt he noticed that his mummumsie's belly wasn't quite as round anymore, but he certainly knew something was … different. He stuck his neck out, and his head into Nicholas' bassinet. I held his harness, guarding against the 1-in-1,000 chance he flashed teeth.

But of course, he didn't. Veckie took several interested sniffs, sat down, seemed to process for a few seconds. Then he gave me one of his insanely cute, tilted head looks. Did he understand, from Nicholas' scent, what he was? Did he put together that one and one had suddenly made three, making us a family of four?

Probably not—but it was clear he knew, right from the get-go, that this was no ordinary visitor. This small, new-smelling thing wasn't going anywhere. Vector officially had a bro-bro.

So there Patty and I were, two first-time dog owners turned first-time parents. Understandably, we carefully monitored and refereed the interactions between Vector and Nicholas, wary of any signs of jealousy-driven aggression or, more likely, ignorance-inspired roughhousing. Three years ago, Vector had been surviving on the streets; now, we were asking him to understand that extreme gentleness was required of him when it came to this newest, tiniest member of his pack.

There was, simply, none of it. Not a trace of envy. Not the faintest growl when Nicholas' nails scraped across Vector's snout. No defensive nip when his baby brother saw his irresistible yet scarred sato ears and, unfortunately but inevitably, tugged them with glee.

Nicholas had mild jaundice, so Patty and I took to laying a blanket down in a sunny spot on the living room floor. Soon Vector, part sunbather part bodyguard, was lying alongside Nicholas. Their bond was quick and firm, and has proven permanent.

As March turned to April, the exhale of a settling scenario led to contemplation. I was taking stock of everything—my unlikely recovery from addiction, my just as unlikely recovered marriage, this recovered sato sitting beside me on the couch. Those first two things, I knew, would eventually be shared in their entirety with Nicholas. It's part of his family history and, besides, his dad wrote a book about them.

It was that third invaluable asset—Vector—that loomed unresolved. Nicholas remembering Vector—*really* remembering him, not just the wisps and blurry images I have of my mother, who died when I was three—depended on this sato seeing not only a happy life, but a reasonably lengthy one.

Vector was turning six in September—an educated estimate by a veteran veterinarian, but close enough. Nicholas was, of course, 0. I did the quick math in my head. Then I grabbed Vector by his sato cheeks, looked him in the eyes and pleadingly muttered the quote that opens this chapter. The magic number, I decided, was 11, making Nicholas five and a half and assuring that he'd remember his older brother for the rest of his life.

This was not a request. I *needed* Nicholas to remember Vector. And amid the whirlwind surreality of new routines, new concerns and a new family member, it might have been the first time I truly felt like a father. Because it was the first time I understood the importance of legacy.

Parents feel an instinctual need to pass various things—talents, traits, interests, behaviors—on to our children. I want Nicholas to have my love of reading and, especially, my obsession with baseball. Patty wants him to have her poise (and, by contrast, not my excitability) and an appreciation for her Chinese heritage. We both want him to enjoy travel, which we see as curiosity in action.

10. Parenthood: Doggie Bro-Bro

But the first thing I wanted—*needed*—Nicholas to embrace was a tailless mutt from a brutal background. I needed Nicholas to know Vector not only for who he is but what he represents. And I needed him to hug and love and learn from Vector firsthand rather than the way I experience my mother: through photo albums.

If you've read the preceding chapters, you already know that Vector did all this—all this plus one, actually. As I write this, Vector is 12½. He's slowed down some, but it's safe to say that Nicholas, now seven, will never, ever forget his doggie bro-bro.

So far as Nicholas is concerned, Vector has arrived at forever. He has seared his love into my son's soul, and has begun what Patty and I are

Vector's first Christmas with a baby brother, December 2016.

certain will be a lifelong love affair with rescue dogs. Eighty years from now, when the calendars begin with a "21-" rather than a "20-," Vector will live on in the memory of an octogenarian Nicholas. In the interim, a slew of rescue dogs in both our household and eventually Nicholas' will have Vector to thank for assuring our allegiance to their adoption.

But this is more than an interspecies sibling love story. Vector has done far more than serve as an adorable advocate for himself and his fellow satos. He has done more than secure a permanent home for himself, and a future home for his successors.

Through his harrowing history and unwitting wisdom, Vector not only has taught his younger brother a thing or two about life, but helped guide Patty and me along our imperfect parenting journey. Following are but a few examples.

In Chapter 6, which explored my struggles with depression, I referenced a March 2022 getaway that Patty and I took to the Caribbean. I discussed how Nicholas, then in kindergarten, stayed home with Patty's parents and didn't skip a beat, while Vector stayed at my dad's place and was utterly miserable in our absence.

The stark contrast in those daily check-in calls hammered home the value of Vector's permanent dependence upon me. Nicholas loves me; Vector *needs* me—an asset against a condition that thrives on worthlessness. For me, "needed people are valued people" espouses a straightforward, facts-over-feelings positivity that can pierce my depression's armor against all things uplifting.

Though just four days, that trip featured another memorable teaching moment. This one pertained to parenthood.

One evening, Patty and I were taking a stroll along the beach. As we meandered past the adjacent hotels and oceanfront restaurants, we came to a set of upscale, gated beach condominiums—the sort of place a couple with means might purchase in retirement. On one balcony, an older couple sat, a dog at their feet. The pooch began barking at us—not threateningly, just inquisitively, even playfully.

Suddenly, a shadow trotted across the beach a few hundred feet ahead of us. It was another dog. The thin, collarless, matted-haired animal clearly had no owner. It was forging for whatever it could find on the beach, and possibly sizing us up to beg for whatever morsels we might have.

It is one of those juxtapositions that people in cities and suburbs see regularly. One dog who wanted for nothing, another who wanted for everything. Perhaps it was the guard-down nature of a relaxing getaway that made this particular scene resonate so sharply.

In hindsight, I'm realizing how the owned versus stray anecdote exemplifies how animals—especially domesticated ones, who have no real place in the "wild"—can affect us more than people, even those in similar situations. A close human comparison to what I'd witnessed, for instance, would be a well-heeled businessman walking nonchalantly past a ragged homeless person. As a lifelong resident of the New York City area, I've seen that play out countless times.

But this human scene has limitations *simply for involving humans.* People can sabotage their lives in ways dogs cannot. Humans make choices. They make mistakes that are their own fault. Humans have agency. So as sorry as one might feel for a homeless person, there's always that nagging possibility that his lot in life is largely his own making—or, at least, that it could not be improved upon to any satisfactory extent.

Maybe he's a drug addict, the little voice says, or suffers from a severe mental illness that makes living a fulfilling life all but impossible. Maybe he's just a huge asshole who's alienated any and all persons who tried to help him. It's not *correct* of us to think these thoughts but, even if these doubts are mere subconscious notions, they influence us nevertheless. There's a defense mechanism element that allows us to deflect much of the guilt, shame or sorrow that witnessing such inexcusable inequity instigates.

But canines have no such extenuating circumstances. There are no "what ifs" to mitigate the emotional impact of seeing rich and poor so close in proximity but so far apart in fortune.

On an existential level—the lifesaving line separating the cur from the coddled, the forsaken from the rescued—dogs have no agency. Their fates are determined by fate itself and, failing that, by humans willing to alter it. Humans like Chrissy Beckles and her team at the Sato Project. And humans like us, who turn fosters into forever family members.

Patty and I continued walking. After 15 years of marriage, each knew the other was a bit shaken. I broke the saturated silence first.

"Their lives are completely dictated by the kindness of others," I said.

"Well," Patty responded, "that's why it's important to teach him to be kind." Him, of course, being Nicholas—the most important pronoun in either of our lives, the person we're responsible for raising into a competent, moral adult.

Patty and I got lucky with him. While it might ring hollow coming from a proud papa, we've really got a great kid on our hands: sweet, obedient (for a seven-year-old anyway) and, most noticeably, exceptionally intelligent. By four, he was reading on a first-grade level; by first grade, he's reading books meant for nine-and-ten-year-olds. Incredibly, at seven he can add and subtract double-digit numbers in his head, multiply, and recall conversations from weeks ago. His diction is crisp and clear, making him sound far older than he looks. OK, last gush (for now): He's also highly coordinated, shagging pop flies and smashing wiffleballs across our yard (and over our fence) like a kid several years his senior.

But there's one catch with Nicholas, and it's a biggie: his size—which, contrary to the protestations of many a male, certainly does matter. Nicholas is tiny. Like less-than-one-percentile, off-the-charts tiny. Like X-ray to check for proper bone maturation, endocrinologist assessment for growth hormone treatment tiny.

Hyperintelligent and undersized, Nicholas has already shown challenges making friends. Whether it's a natural introversion or a circumstantial one remains to be seen, but there's anecdotal evidence to suggest the latter. He's brighter and smaller than the overwhelming majority of his peers and, while being gifted is indeed a gift, in the short-term it brings a set of social challenges.

Generally, those challenges play out something like this. A fellow first grader is doing something innocently incorrect, and Nicholas feels the urge to intervene with his entirely accurate but entirely unsolicited wisdom. His frustration only grows if his friend listens but still doesn't fully grasp the task at hand. By his facial expression and tone of voice, it's easy to discern what Nicholas is thinking: something along the lines of "Is this kid stupid or something?" (Patty senses this too, adding a "he's definitely your son" barb.) This reaction is, I'm learning, simultaneously unavoidable and unacceptable.

My first concern, of course, is safety. Tiny kids that mouth off are apt to get their baby teeth removed prematurely. But equally important is his social maturation. A know-it-all can quickly turn into a pariah. I experienced semblances of this myself, though in all honesty Nicholas is likely more intelligent. And from what I've seen and heard about some of Nicholas' interactions with kids his age, there's been enough smoke that I've felt compelled to preempt some flames here and there.

"Buddy," I'll say, "remember what we said about being patient with kids your age. Give them time and be kind."

Those last two words—be kind—constitute an increasingly difficult ask. Our children are growing up in extraordinarily judgmental times. Not only must they deal with the inherent, naive cruelty of their peers—kids can be mean, we all know that—but our image-obsessed, hyper-partisan, cyber-trolling society often sets poor examples of tolerance and acceptance.

It's only getting worse, and the main driver is social media. Online, loudmouth cowards with pseudonyms are far crueler and crasser than they'd ever dare be in person. On the extreme right (which at this point has supplanted mainstream conservatism), insane conspiracy theories reign and "owning the libs" is everything, with neither facts nor tact a concern. Meanwhile, the extreme left (which at this point constitutes half of Twitter) is little more than sinners casting stones, with virtue signaling and cancel culture rooted in the same groupthink meanness that fuel the bigots and oppressors they claim to be calling out.

All of it is ridiculous—and none of it is kind. And as noted in Chapter 7, these days kids are growing up in near-constant cyber-connectivity, largely on social media platforms. Patty and I are left swimming upstream against a tech-tainted culture teaching our small kid with a big brain to weaponize his intelligence—to puff himself up by deflating others.

Luckily, Nicholas has a markedly inferior intellectual that he absolutely adores. His name is Vector.

"You wouldn't treat Veckie like that, would you?" I asked Nicholas after he dressed down a friend for one innocuous playtime infraction or another. "Be as kind to humans as you are to Vector—do that for daddy." Basically the Golden Rule, but with his dog in lieu of himself.

That Vector is a rescue only makes him more valuable as a "be kind" benchmark. Nicholas has the luxury of being born into a two-parent, upper-middle-class household where his every need is met. His tailless, scarred-snouted, diseased older sibling most definitely did not.

The lesson is clear: Are we going to punch down, or pull up? Are we going to judge people by their backgrounds … or acknowledge and accept the limitlessly disparate experiences people (and non-people) carry with them? Are we going to act better than someone simply for being born into more fortunate economic or familial or intellectual circumstances … or see our once-destitute and desperate doggie bro-bro as proof positive that kindness matters?

Not only is kindness necessary in and of itself—a foundation of tolerance and understanding—it is a prerequisite for another quality modern society sorely lacks: forgiveness.

A crucial consequence of this situation can be found in our eroding attitudes toward redemption. Political affiliations, social media silos and perceived microaggressions have all drawn lines in the sand beyond which "others" are deemed inexcusable and irredeemable.

And no, this isn't just a white, middle-aged, heterosexual cisgender male grumbling generically about Gen Z wokeness. In the September 26, 2022, edition of the liberal-leaning *Boston Globe*, psychologist Pamela Paresky and Sarah Lawrence College political professor Samuel Abrams reveal shocking trends showcasing what they call the "us versus them" mentality on today's university campuses:

> Students can become balkanized around identities and perceptions of power—an "us" vs. "them" mentality that turns potential friends into "allies" or enemies and contributes to both political self-censorship and an avoidance of

Nicholas petting his bro in the park.

personal self-disclosure. When it comes to sharing their views, 80 percent of students say they self-censor, according to a joint survey by the Foundation for Individual Rights and Expression and RealClearEducation [https://reports.collegepulse.com/college-free-speech-rankings-2021]. The primary reason students say they don't express their authentic views, according to a Heterodox Academy survey, is fear of peers taking offense [https://heterodoxacademy.org/wp-content/uploads/2022/02/CES-Report-2022-FINAL.pdf].[1]

Our children are growing up in a culture where the concepts of forgiveness and redemption are so foreign that they're afraid to make the slightest mistake, perceived or actual. Shame on educators for mistaking preprogrammed thinking with progress, and thought conformity with kindness.

It is clear Vector will teach Nicholas more about redemption than institutions of higher learning will—and several hundred thousand dollars less expensively to boot. In their journeys from shunned, seemingly doomed outcasts to beloved, full-fledged family members, rescue dogs show that no being is beyond redemption. If Vector can go from that loathsome beach to our lush backyard, anyone can make a comeback from anything. When our children understand this, they can not only forgive others, but also keep hope alive for their own progress and renewal no matter how difficult their situations or egregious their transgressions. If dogs can do it, so can we.

And then there's forgiveness, an outward projection of redemption. By wholeheartedly forgiving those who wrong us, we bolster their redemption and deepen our understanding that poor behavior and decisions can be amended. We may be punished for our sins, but never permanently excommunicated.

As a rescue dog, Vector has granted forgiveness on a level few humans do: he has forgiven the universe. In his redemption, he has forgiven fate itself for doing its best to kill him off before he found love and safety with his forever family. His canine amnesia holds inadvertent instruction for our children to emulate. Redemption is always possible, for ourselves as well as others. We strive to forgive and, in turn, deserve forgiveness ourselves.

Anyone who grew up with bruises in the shape of their parents' hands can appreciate the upside of the kinder, gentler parenting that permeates modern society. That the phrase "adverse childhood experiences" has even entered our childrearing lexicon is highly encouraging. And as someone who grew up awkward and anxious, I wholeheartedly endorse attempts to instill confidence and acceptance of others in today's children.

That said ... do all kids need to think they're great at *everything*—and *all the time*? If everybody is special all the time, doesn't the word "special" lose all meaning? Does everything need to be so ... soft?

Humans are great at overreacting and overreaching—at righting perceived wrongs by overcompensating. For millennia, it was common knowledge that men were smarter and more capable than women. To make up for this longstanding injustice, suddenly women are smarter and more capable than men. Neither, of course, is true. Men and women are equally smart and stupid, capable and incompetent.

But perhaps the most damaging overcompensation is the replacement of stifling conformity with individualism run amok. We tell everyone they're perfect just the way they are—a "you do you" mantra that is mere laziness masquerading as inclusivity. The problem, it seems, is never that we have hard work to do, never that we must embrace effort-driven progress to move toward a destination we haven't yet reached. You're great as-is—and here's another participation trophy to prove it. We blow past instilling confidence into instilling complacency.

It is understandable, then, that concerns have arisen about children not being raised with sufficient mental toughness—often termed "grit"—to thrive in the real world. These worries are expressed in an uptick in education-centric articles, such as an April 2020 *School Rubric* piece, discussing grit's importance, and even the incorporation of resilience lessons into many schools' curricula.[2]

One such class could easily be a parade of adopted rescue dogs. Rescues like Vector's presence—and very existence—commands respect for the determination and craftiness they must possess simply to have survived. They are battle-tested and street smart; they've seen worse and, through biography alone, seem to know better.

Vector is, simply, grit personified. His face-licking, fetch-playing joy belies the guile and guts he drew upon to make this enhanced existence, this life beyond his wildest dreams, possible. He hung in and pressed on as long and as hard as necessary and, albeit with some luck, his perseverance was infinitely rewarded.

Amidst a coddled childhood in which he is—understandably but perhaps overdramatically—encouraged to share, care and discuss his feelings, my son has come to know, love and forever remember a family member who made it by being just plain tough as nails. Both sides of this coin are valuable: Vector's vintage dogged determination complements rather than contradicts today's more sensitive, validating parenting. Feel your feelings, yes, but don't let them derail you. Never stop moving forward, and if life bites then bite it back.

That brings us to another lesson Nicholas isn't necessarily going to learn from the education system: that the world outside his small circle of family and friends will not be nearly as accommodating. That discouragement and discomfort and fear are inevitable consequences of the human condition.

Recently, several major U.S. colleges—including the University of Michigan[3] and Brandeis University in Massachusetts[4]—began discouraging both faculty and students from using a particular word: picnic. Apparently, it was once code for the disgusting lynchings of Black people that occurred throughout the South during the slavery and Jim Crow eras.

Whether one agrees that this word is offensive is irrelevant. For starters, regardless of its supposed use as code, it most certainly did not originate with lynching.[5] More importantly, however, is that it isn't realistic to remove a conventionally neutral word from our established vocabulary simply by claiming arcane ties to America's racist history. Picnic isn't an inherently racist word; it's people eating lunch outside in a park for God's sake. We're teaching adolescents to get offended by words they will innocently hear in the real world whether they like it or not. We're teaching them to get offended when absolutely no offense was intended.

Ditto for the greeting "hey guys" (misogynistic microaggression), the phrase "no can do" (which supposedly mocks the way Asian immigrants might speak English) and—the pinnacle of linguistic irony—"trigger warning" (reminds people of gun violence).[6] You know what else reminds my seven-year-old of gun violence? When his school conducts regular drills in which he hides in a closet to avoid getting slaughtered by a maniac with an assault rifle. Soft language, meet hard facts. I don't believe you've met.

As a parent, Vector is a constant reminder of my inability to shield Nicholas from discomfort, worry and even pain. I am reminded of this each time Patty, Nicholas and I prepare for a no-dogs-allowed family excursion. As we gather our coats and put on our shoes, Vector sits, stares, and prays I'm about to pull out his leash. Sometimes he even visibly shakes.

In these moments, I wish I could make Vector fully understand how deeply and unconditionally we love him. If he did, his separation anxiety and overall trepidation would substantially diminish. His life would be a lot smoother. But completely eliminating Vector's fear of abandonment, much of which is undoubtedly due to his tortured, fend-for-himself past, simply isn't going to happen. The point is clear: anxiety and fear are part of life, human or otherwise. Fighting that is futile.

Of course, I *can* make Nicholas understand the bottomless well of love his mother and I have for him. I can make him know that we'll love him no matter what, and that he can carry that love and support with him wherever it is life takes him.

What I *cannot* do is promise Nicholas that he'll never have to be confused, frustrated or fearful—that he'll never have to feel uncomfortable—ever again. Pointing to Vector's obvious abandonment issues, I've reinforced this message with Nicholas several times already. For example, when his first baby tooth began to wiggle, ache and bleed a little bit, Nicholas' concern was palpable. "Is this going to happen with all of them?" he asked.

"Yep," I said. "And there's absolutely nothing we can do about it. It's just part of growing up."

As much as his mom and I can quell unfounded fears and explain confusing new things, we can't stop Nicholas' teeth from falling out, one by one, in an awkward, painful process. Even with our son still in first grade, our roles as his protectors have limitations. Because nature.

And the more coddled he is at home, the less prepared for the real world he'll be. For Patty and me, being responsible parents means understanding that and preparing for it. Vector has needed to learn how to accept being uncomfortable—at least enough to, say, not rip the couch to shreds every time he's left alone. As he gets older, Nicholas will need to accept uncomfortableness in increasingly higher leverage situations. What's the alternative? Throwing a microaggression hissy fit when his boss invites him to the annual company picni … um, I mean "outside gathering"?

Patty and I refuse to raise a son that will cower into a safe space the moment he hears something with which he mildly disagrees. We want him

Nicholas and Vector in April 2019: looking out into the world beyond our living room.

to tolerate alternative ideas and tackle tough tasks and take advantage of opportunities for growth outside his comfort zone.

But of course, there's a fine line between being encouraged and enriched and challenged … and simply being overwhelmed. And today's children are walking that line like never before.

In addition to busy school days, after school programs and homework, my son's schedule is peppered with pianos lessons, tennis lessons, baseball practices and games, playdates, birthday parties, children's library events and more. Gung Gung and Paw Paw (Patty's parents—that's Chinese for "grandfather" and "grandmother," respectively) are Tuesday afternoons, Pop Pop (my dad) is Friday evening. Three times a week, his baseball-obsessed dad will pitch overhand batting practice and conduct fielding drills in a backyard that increasingly can't hold his moonshots. (And yes, that's me gushing again.)

This is Nicholas at age seven—a mere preview of the who-knows-what-else he'll be rushing off to along with his peers in a few short years.

The kids who are best prepared for this loaded landscape are those whose strides aren't easily broken. The fewer people, places and things capable of angering, cowering or otherwise derailing our children, the better they can move through their busy lives happily and effectively.

That's where rescues come in. By and large, our dogs are barking Buddhas. They are completely engrossed in the moment. In our "what's next?" culture, they are unburdened by the future; and in an increasingly coarse, cancel-happy society, altercations with the mail carrier conclude the very instant the USPS truck pulls away.

Here, it is a rescue's backstory that holds sway. The fact that so troubled a being can achieve such presentness—an ability to enjoy the moment unhaunted by the past and undaunted by the future—is simply incredible. As we age, our brains carry more memory of the past and, through experience, keener ability to anticipate the near future. We are either looking back or looking ahead, but are rarely locked into the here and now.

Rescues teach our kids to carry their carefree, unburdened mindset as far into adolescence, and ideally adulthood, as possible. Perhaps this gift, more than any other, exemplifies the value of rescue dogs in helping shape our children's formative years. In his pre-scarred prescience, Vector teaches my son that our pasts don't dictate our futures, and that the present should be experienced free of accrued grievances or guarded apprehension.

Vector isn't dwelling on his three years of hell and, even at a hobbled, largely deaf age 12, isn't fearful of his increasingly evident mortality. He's just sniffing that tree and deciding whether to piss on it—living his life to the fullest by living it one moment at a time.

Someday in the not-so-distant future, Vector will pass away. While Nicholas has lost a few relatives—two great-uncles, two great-grandparents—he has never experienced the loss of someone he lives with, someone he sees every day. As I discuss in Chapter 12, which is dedicated to grief, the loss will be profound and the mourning protracted.

Vector's passing and what comes next—another rescue dog, thanks in part to Vector's already-cemented legacy of love—also will mark a transition point in my most important role: Nicholas' father.

Of his three live-in family members, I am Vector's clear favorite. He loves his mummumsie and bro-bro, but he simply cannot do without his daddams.

This preference arose organically. When Vector first came to live with us, Patty was slightly less enthusiastic (as well as slightly allergic) about dog ownership than me. She was committed enough to adopt, yes—but I was simply overjoyed, having always wanted a dog.

Vector, then, bonded with me both first and irrevocably. And since his time with us predates Nicholas, our son never really had a shot at being Vector's alpha.

Patty's a big girl; she can deal (albeit sometimes a bit begrudgingly) with being Vector's second choice. But when the three of us come home to find Vector focusing 90 percent of his welcome wags and yips at me, I feel tinges of guilt for the message the situation sends to my highly perceptive son.

As Vector ages and Nicholas continues to mature, I'm realizing the importance of our next four-legged family member gravitating toward Nicholas at least as much as me, if not more. And I recognize this while knowing full well that I'll be hard-pressed to not kiss and hug and love and dote upon our next rescue so much that I once again become the undisputed, odds-on go-to human.

I am everything to Vector. I must be a little less than everything to our next rescue, for Nicholas' sake. After nearly a decade of having a sato shadow, I'm still not sure how I feel about that, or exactly what that intentionally shifted dynamic looks like. It will be a huge test of selflessness—likely the largest one of my fatherhood to that point.

Assuming I can't convince Patty to adopt two rescues following Vector's passing (I'm working on it, trust me), I will need to forfeit at least some degree of closeness and companionship—some amount of unadulterated and unconditional love—so that my offspring can experience these more comprehensively. That will be exceedingly difficult for me, and will make me miss Vector even more. While I'm not one to deify the dead, Vector is as pure a soul as I'll ever have lost, and grooming his successor to be more Nicholas' dog than my own will only reinforce how irreplaceable Veckie is.

But despite the heartache on the horizon, I am somehow assured that none of this will make me resent my son. Doing so would be beneath the sanctity of what Vector has given this family. And besides: nothing bad can come of a boy and his dog—and especially, a boy and his rescue dog. It is too beautiful a narrative to be blemished by petty jealousies or nostalgic longing for the way things were.

"Vector is yours," Patty said recently. "Our next one will be Nicholas'." Very succinct, very blunt. Very Patty.

And very accurate. And very bittersweet, inspiring, and altogether fitting. For both me and now my son, Vector has helped instill and instruct a variety of values and lessons. None is more important than this last one, which he will continue to teach posthumously: parents make sacrifices for their children so that they may thrive. I must cede ground so that Nicholas can experience a bond even greater than he has with Vector. I must do that with a broken heart, in hopes that the selfless act will refill it with pride and joy.

I will do this for my son, and because of Vector.

11

Parenthood
Foster/Mom

"We failed that dog."

When Jenny Franz was in elementary school, her parents brought a dog home. She was hoping for a Golden Retriever; her father opted for a Dalmatian. They named it Pepper.

"My dad was very thoughtful, very well-intending," Jenny said. "But Pepper was really the wrong breed for us."

"And of course," she continues, "it was far more than that."

She recalls a house "made of baby gates," an often futile effort to contain the large, high-energy dog. She described their too-small yard, typical of the family's densely populated Long Island suburb. But most of all, she remembers the biting. Here, she is careful not to dog-blame.

"It wasn't her fault, she was just…" she paused. I expected a more familiar doggie diagnosis. Traumatized. Anxious. Frightened. Instead, Jenny's assessment seemed shockingly mundane.

"She was just … bored."

The family didn't know what they didn't know. And what they didn't understand was that Pepper needed far more exercise than brief walks to relieve herself. She needed more interaction than a few minutes of fetch. And since Pepper couldn't talk, she needed her own way to convey that urgent message.

"What we misinterpreted as aggression was really just communication," Jenny contends. "Pepper was saying, 'Hey, I wasn't bred to sit in the house all day and not have exercise, and not have consistent stimulation.'" She noted Dalmatians' affinity for mastering tasks—a trait that has made them popular for jobs ranging from hunting partner to firehouse assistant.

Jenny is certain things would have been different had they been more educated about Pepper's breed-specific needs. Instead, they were an unprepared family with a dog that, likely, was rambunctious even for her boisterous breed. The result was a knowledge gap that, too often, came back to bite them. Literally.

"Pepper bit everyone in the family multiple times," Jenny said, wincing. These were more than nips; blood was often drawn. Jenny remembers her family being hesitant to have guests over, wondering aloud why they didn't simply crate Pepper. Again, what they didn't know was hurting them, this time forfeiting get-togethers for fear of another doggie disaster.

Finally, one too many of these incidents occurred. Pepper, now nine, bit one of Jenny's cousins at Thanksgiving with no discernible warning. Looking back, Jenny wonders why a dog with a history of biting was in the middle of the family living room around company.

A short while later, Pepper was put down.

"My mother still cries when we mention Pepper," Jenny said, regretfully.

This was a loving family. There was no premeditated malfeasance, no malice, no ill will. This was a tragedy rooted in naivete. It was a failure not of intention but rather imagination—one that also reflects the dearth of resources three decades ago, when the internet and its limitless library was in its infancy. Jenny's family couldn't YouTube "How to Care for a Dalmatian" for instant access to expert-driven videos. It was a different time and place.

Pepper's loss still haunts Jenny, now 42. But it helped instill a lesson that has become a mainstay of her adulthood, not only as a rescue dog adopter and advocate, but also as a (human) mother.

"We had this unrealistic, Hollywood glorified ideal of a dog in our minds and, when Pepper didn't fit squarely into that preconceived notion, we didn't properly adapt," she contends. "There was some denial going on there. Regardless of her breed, we didn't meet her where she was and treat her as an individual."

In early adulthood, Jenny and her new husband, Nate, would adopt their first dog, a 60-pound black mutt. At the shelter, the 10-week-old pup kept licking Nate's face. They named it Foster—ironic considering both Jenny's future and this book's overall narrative.

Jenny was in love; Foster was a nervous wreck. Foster was good off-leash, but only because he never wanted to be more than a few feet from Jenny. And he wasn't good with other dogs whatsoever—a trait Vector has showcased throughout his time with us. Foster growled and resource-guarded food when he sensed other dogs nearby.

Once again, Jenny found herself with a dog falling short of her expectations. Pepper's long shadow loomed.

Some time passed. Jenny and Nate had their first child, Jack, in 2010. Foster was good with immediate family, not so much with others. Jenny

The prophetically named Foster (courtesy Jenny Franz).

crated the anxious dog when company came over. When they traveled without Foster, the family hired a dog sitter, since they strongly suspected the anxious animal wouldn't handle kennels well.

They made efforts to understand what Foster was experiencing, and tailored their actions accordingly. They met Foster where he was, and he responded by living as happy and as lengthy a life with them as he could. Foster passed away in 2017, from cancer. Pepper's long shadow receded. A valuable lesson had given another dog a nurturing, understanding home.

It might seem natural, even obvious, to lead with empathy. But it isn't. Empathy is a learned reaction, a practice in attempting to see situations from the perspectives of others, human or otherwise.[1] Emotions aren't

11. Parenthood: Foster/Mom

enough; empathy requires emotional *intelligence*. And woefully, today the dogs returned to Jenny after a mere day or two in new "forever" homes showcase the often frightening lack of it in modern society.

"A dog acts even slightly different than someone thinks it would, and back it comes," Jenny says. "Very disappointing."

Last year, Jenny founded Better Together Dog Rescue, which transports strays from the U.S. South for fostering and adoption in western Massachusetts. She and Nate reside in the Amherst suburb of Belchertown. Jack is now 12, and the couple's second son, William, is nine.

Jenny is *in it*—smack dab in the middle of her children's formative years. And the experiences she's accrued adopting, fostering and now rescuing dogs has substantially shaped her motherhood. For one, as we've seen, Jenny has learned to always respect her children's individuality. She will meet them where they are, not where any romanticized perception of a typical family dynamic says they should be.

But the pitfalls and challenges—and failures and victories—through which Jenny has persevered have led to another takeaway, one not so easily digested but no less necessary to swallow. It's a lesson that requires far more than a singular sad anecdote reinforced with an 800-word introduction. It's a convoluted, imperfect nugget of wisdom with tangled tangents and variables. It's a parenthood-worthy mess.

"Life," Jenny said, matter-of-factly, "is really complicated."

Rescue dogs have been part and parcel to all of it, helping shape Jenny's maturation as a parent. In fact, Jenny's role as dog mom has made her role as human mom less complicated by turning hypothetical concepts into concrete examples. Let's explore.

Somewhere between leading the charge to build a proper animal shelter in her hometown and founding her own rescue organization, Jenny Franz began fostering dogs. This in addition to the family's permanent pooches, a roster that currently includes Wren, six; Callie, five; and three-year-old Marty Byrde, an homage to the protagonist played by Jason Bateman on the Netflix series *Ozark*.

Fostering dogs is an exercise in noble yet garbled gains and losses. It is an indisputably kind, decent act that usually ends in bittersweetness. It's simple: people who foster dogs tend to be (what else?) dog people—the same folks who become easily attached to dogs and are pained to see them leave, even when that separation means placement in a loving forever home.

This push-pull is exemplified by the reverse vocabulary connected with fostering animals. A "foster fail" occurs when someone simply cannot part with their foster, turning a temporary refuge into a forever home.

A foster fail is a fortunate fail—a beautiful bust leaving all parties in the best of spirits.

While wonderful as standalone stories, foster fails are unsustainable on a broader scale. If every foster family fell so head-over-paws in love that they kept most of the dogs they took in, they'd quickly run out of room—and rescue organizations would run out of foster families. Transitional caretakers are a critical link in the dog rescue chain.

But such sound logic doesn't always square with the facts on the ground—or on the couch, or in the backyard. Despite knowing that it's for the best, handing a foster over inevitably involves some degree of heartache.

A foster win is a sad success. Like Jenny's generalized-yet-exacting assessment of parenting, fostering is … well, complicated. Complicated enough that articles on popular pet sites like the aptly named *Rescue Dogs 101* are dedicated to navigating the emotional rollercoaster, as are threads on doggie discussion boards.[2]

Jenny had difficulty parting with her first foster, but soon became more adept at walking the balancing act between letting a needy dog into her home and, when the right forever home came along, letting that needy dog go.

And then came Glover.

Jenny had an immediate and deep connection with the 60-pound, three-year-old mix. Glover also got along famously with Jack and William, then 11 and eight, respectively. Glover felt like a dog the Franzes would have chosen outright among dozens of others—a stray standout for a clan already prone to seeing specialness in all rescued dogs.

Glover was with the Franz family for two months. For Jenny, the experience was akin to a time bomb with an erratic clock, one that could go off—or rather, go away—at any moment. Of course, the tragic irony of falling for a foster is that, in this metaphor, the detonator is a loving family. Glover gets a happy home; Jenny gets a hole blown in her heart.

When Glover's departure day came, Jenny the mother did something Jenny the fosterer didn't want to do. She let Glover go.

She cried that day, and the next one. She did not shield Jack and William from her sorrow. Instead, she took pains to communicate and reiterate to her sons that her tears betrayed the act rather than represented it. This was a happy ending—a bawling, sobbing success. All's well that ends welled up.

"That was the best decision *for Glover*," Jenny shares. "Sometimes the right decision doesn't feel good—at all—but the growth it leads to helps you make peace with it."

She continues: "For Jack and William to see me struggle but still be able to let him go … that was a really big moment for us."

Jenny Franz and Glover: Love at first lick (courtesy Jenny Franz).

Intentionally or not, in letting Glover go Jenny dispelled a misconception many experts feel is adversely affecting her sons' generation. She had shown Jack and William that feelings, while valid and honest and real, *are not facts*. Sometimes the right decision feels wrong, at least at first. Sometimes a strong game plan must be honored more than a strong gut reaction. Empathy takes even-keeled emotional intelligence, not heated, hysterical reactionism.

This ill-advised conflation of feelings with facts is no minor matter. It isn't just one of a lengthy list of warning signs concerning Generation Z, generally defined as children born from 1997 on. It's been argued that it's *one of the three most crucial* issues.

In September 2015, Jonathan Haidt, a social psychologist and professor of ethics at New York University, and Greg Lukianoff, a journalist and free speech activist, cowrote a piece for *The Atlantic* magazine, a bastion of well-reported longform commentary that, according to AllSides Media Bias, leans decidedly liberal.[3] The piece, "The Coddling of the American Mind," discussed on-campus trends the duo saw as alarming, including the disinviting of speakers with alternative viewpoints and the sheltering of students from well-rounded debates in the name of "safety."[4] This feelings-first narrative assumes that people should be able to avoid or eliminate any discourse they personally find troubling.

The piece drew enough attention that then–President Barack Obama weighed in. "Anybody who comes to speak to you whom you disagree with, you should have an argument with them," said the president. "But you shouldn't silence them by saying, 'You can't come because, you know, I'm too sensitive to hear what you have to say.' That's not the way we learn."[5]

Obama went on: "I don't agree that you, when you become students at colleges, have to be coddled and protected from different points of view."

In 2018, Haidt and Lukianoff expanded upon their views with a book of the same title.[6] Too many Gen Z kids, they contended, were entering college having somehow learned what they call the three Great Untruths— so named because they directly conflict both with modern psychology and ancient wisdom spanning myriad cultures. Those misconceptions are:

1. ***What doesn't kill you makes you weaker.*** This idea prompts people to avoid narratives that challenge their preconceived notions or personal experiences.
2. ***Always trust your feelings.*** Among other problems, unquestionably trusting our feelings leads to taking offense when none is intended.
3. ***Life is a battle between good and evil people.*** This leads to a blame-first mentality that assumes the worst about others rather than giving them the benefit of the doubt. This unforgiving mindset is often exacerbated on social media, where extremism is rewarded with likes and shares.

Haidt and Lukianoff didn't concoct these misconceptions randomly, no less daringly deem them "Great Untruths"; they leaned on research-driven data. In 2017, one Middle Tennessee State University survey of over 1,200 college students found that more than half (56 percent) favored disinviting at least some speakers. Perhaps more alarmingly, slightly more students (58 percent) agreed that "it's important to be part of a campus community where they are not exposed to intolerant or offensive ideas." Showcasing the ever-expanding definition of "offensive," 30 percent reported self-censoring because they thought their words would be offensive to others.[7]

That's not progress; it's Orwellian—and it leads to confusing contradictions. A 2022 Knight Foundation survey found more students than ever say the climate on their campus stifles free expression ... even while an unprecedented number of students—nearly one in five—report feeling "unsafe because of comments" made on campus.[8] Per President Obama's commentary, it's reasonable to assume most of these "safety-threatening" comments were not overt bigotry, but rather perceived triggers, microaggressions or other speech or literature found personally disagreeable. In other words, it's taking offense when none is intended.

Just as importantly, Haidt and Lukianoff selected these misconceptions because, they believe, they are preventing college students from accomplishing the overarching goal of adolescence: readiness for life in the real world.

Post-college life won't be muted by safe spaces and trigger warnings. It won't be padded in bubble wrap. Progress toward inclusivity and respect for others' experiences is wonderful, but we mustn't create children too fragile to function in the world outside our doors. As parents, our top priority should be raising competent, confident individuals capable of standing firm on their own two feet.

When she said a grueling goodbye to Glover, it's safe to assume Jenny Franz wasn't actively confuting the Great Untruths and their impact on her young sons' generation. Nevertheless, in one rescue dog-driven anecdote, she took the first two of these three fallacies—ones so widespread and worrisome that two insightful professionals dedicated an entire book to them—and completely dispelled them for Jack and William. Gee, Jenny, Supermom much?

That leaves the third misconception, the notion that life is a battle between good and evil. Recalling Jenny's comment about life requiring adjustments to both actions and expectations, if "life is really complicated" isn't a solid start to rebutting such nonsense, I don't know what is. Buttressing this, Jenny's double-booked life as a full-time mom and full-time dog rescuer have, at times, placed life's sacrifices and tradeoffs at the forefront of her relationship with Jack and William.

Life, Jenny shows William and Jack, isn't a battle between good and evil. It's a well-intentioned balancing act between priorities that all seem worthy of all our time, all at once. The only thing we have to battle is the clock. When we fill our existence with good deeds and good motives, we prove ourselves worthy of the benefit of the doubt.

Not only was this intentional, but it was also part of Jenny and Nate's overall family planning. Here, we see kids influencing dog rescue, which in turn influences kids—a life-affirming, almost symbiotic cycle of love and learning. Unlike Vector, this wasn't about one rescue exemplifying emulation-worthy traits, or instilling unintentionally profound lessons. Jenny's career as a dog rescuer doesn't just *inform* her role as a mother; it *completely permeates* it.

What's more, Jenny was fully cognizant that rescuing dogs would be entirely intertwined with her parenting. We know this because, when she decided to start her own rescue organization, Jenny did something that made her very uncomfortable.

She waited.

"I knew this was going to be a complicated time for me, that I was going to be extremely busy, very stressed and not as present," she said. "It was important for me that the children be at an age where they were not only a little more independent, but also could look back and say 'look at what my mom did.'"

Jenny's pre-paws pause wasn't just to let her kids grow out of a time-monopolizing stage—though, of course, that was a logistical perk. She delayed Better Together's launch because she wanted William and Jack to be old enough to recognize and appreciate what she was doing. She wanted them to know the rescue-driven reason why mommy wasn't instantly available all the time.

Jenny needed Better Together not just to rescue dogs, but also to serve as a role model experience for her sons. She wanted them to associate mommy's time impoverishment with a richness of spirit. She wanted them to see that *her absences* were *their sacrifices*—ones endured for a pure purpose: the salvation of defenseless, innocent beings. For Jack and William, their mother's often sporadic schedule is a lesson in selflessness for a greater good. Some parents make excuses; Jenny Franz has *reasons*.

"I think they'll look back and see that the effort and struggle is worth it—that the ends justify the means—and give me the benefit of the doubt for a noble effort," Jenny said.

The benefit of the doubt is, of course, a key ingredient toward *not* seeing the world in black and white terms—as a battle between good and evil, victims and oppressors. Jenny's sons may be a little disappointed when her schedule at Better Together gets unpredictably inundated, but they've seen and lived and experienced too much love to let their mother's good intentions bring bad tidings. And Jenny doesn't just suspect this; she knows it.

Recently, Jack and his sixth-grade class made cutouts of themselves so their parents could identify their desks during a parent-teacher conference night. On the shirt of Jack's doppelganger wasn't his favorite sports team, superhero or other personal effect. It was Better Together's logo.

Jack wasn't thinking about himself; there's no "I" in Better Together.

11. Parenthood: Foster/Mom

Here was a boy at a notoriously moody, self-seeking age emblazoning empathy on a self-portrait for an audience of two: mom and dad. Without saying a word, he told his mother he was strong and compassionate enough to understand why she isn't always around. It may seem at odds to simultaneously teach children grit and kindness. Jenny has proven otherwise—with an invaluable assist from each and every dog she saves.

Many of my most poignant papa points have been made with Vector as a guidepost—an example for my seven-year-old of resilience and perseverance, forgiveness and redemption, hope and kindness. By contrast, Jenny's major mama moments come not alongside an individual dog, but through an entire life built around rescuing them.

Chris the dad and Chris the rescue owner are intricately linked but invariably separable. By contrast, Jenny the mom and Jenny the dog rescuer present as one big, beautiful jumble. Her parenting lessons are funneled through her canine calling, because ... well, because basically everything in her existence is.

And in fact, Jenny's lifestyle itself is a lesson—one that balances examples of selflessness with the equally important need for healthy individualism.

"Even if it ends up having nothing to do with rescue dogs," Jenny exclaims, "I want them to follow their passions. Find something worthwhile and run with it—listen to your instincts and learn what makes you tick."

As we've already demonstrated, this isn't Jenny telling Jack and William to treat their feelings as facts. It's instructing them to honor inherent interests, proclivities and talents when they come across them—because those are the defining differentiators that make each of us who we are. A passion prompts proactive exploration rather than reactive resistance. While passions can help expand one's mind, feelings—and especially overemotional, kneejerk responses—can help close it.

Stifling passions would be akin to the countless college students currently self-censoring for fear of breaking some new or nebulous micro-rule they never knew existed. Counteracting this concerning trend, a child who grows up with a healthy understanding of free expression is more likely to see this principle through in college and beyond. And in the fall of 2021, Jenny Franz found a terrific way to show Jack and William how important it is to unabashedly pursue one's passions.

"I left them for six weeks," she grins. "Not alone, of course—with Nate."

For over a year, Jenny had been building toward becoming an accredited animal rescuer through a master's program offered by Southern Utah University. As a mandatory curriculum component, students must choose between a thesis-level paper exploring a rescue-related topic, or an intensive six-week training internship at a rescue organization spanning everything from intake and day-to-day operations to resource management and facilitation.

Which would it be, Jenny: the pen or the pound?

"I hate writing," Jenny confesses. "And it's not my strong suit."

Later dudes. Mama needs a masters and it's about 3,000 miles away.

It was like studying on steroids. Jenny spent the next month and a half absorbing the broad strokes and finer points of managing a rescue organization. And this wasn't a handful of dogs with a few volunteers giving pointers. This was a full-fledged sanctuary—and a prominent one at that.

Jenny found herself immersed in the everyday caring chaos of Best Friends Animal Society, which is based in Kanab, Utah, and has shelters across the country. Notably, the organization once made headlines for taking in nearly two dozen traumatized canines from the property of former National Football League quarterback Michael Vick, who was arrested and convicted for his part in a dogfighting ring. (A 2015 documentary, *The Champions*, follows several of the dogs on their recovery journey. Great for a feel-good tear or 200.) To editorialize briefly, the fact that Vick served only 21 months behind bars for his brutality is completely disgusting; the fact that the NFL ever allowed him to set foot on a field again—the Philadelphia Eagles signed him shortly after he left prison—is completely unforgivable. Meanwhile, another talented quarterback kneels during the national anthem to protest police brutality and is blackballed from the league indefinitely. Hypocritical and gross.

In any event, Jenny thrived in Utah, returned home to her loving sons and husband, and got down to the business of ramping up the fledgling Better Together. The time apart, Jenny shares, was another milestone for the Franz family.

"The fact that I was able not only to leave for six weeks, but leave *without guilt*, that was everything," she said. Her three favorite men weren't resentful of her; they were rooting *for* her. She didn't need to hesitate or half-step, second-guess or slow roll. She could press forward with this life-affirming passion knowing everyone was on board.

And soon, Jenny would be showing her boys the results of her efforts and their sacrifice. Filling out and filing legal paperwork. Developing and strengthening ties in the local foster community. Liaising with on-the-ground rescuers from Texas, Tennessee, and elsewhere. Arranging for initial animal vetting and transportation up north. And of course, beginning the construction process toward Better Together's very own facility.

11. Parenthood: Foster/Mom

Jenny transports rescue dogs from Tennessee to New England in autumn 2022 (courtesy Jenny Franz).

All this, though, is more than a noble pain in the neck in service of stray dogs in need. Long hard day after long hard day, Jenny is showing Jack and William that pursuing a passion means hard work and, if necessary, acquiring extra education and skills. She finds herself doing the work of two or three people, all the while leaning on knowledge and experience she never would have gained without her solo six weeks in Utah.

The message is clear: Passions are motivation to study up and work hard, not something that necessarily come easier just because they bring you joy or fulfillment. Here, Better Together is a symbol—one bolstered by years of fostering scores of dogs leading up to its founding. Jack and William have seen mommy's work up close and personal, have experienced its love, have blessed it with their hugs and kisses. They've played an *active role* in their mother's passion, and have had ample opportunity to recognize it for the utterly upstanding endeavor that it is. It would be easy for a child to begrudge a parent's passion projects given the time and energy expended upon it. But if any child could begrudge a dog rescue, it certainly isn't either of Jenny's kids.

And besides, if you indulge mom in her passions, she'll indulge you in yours, right?

Right.

"Ok," Jenny says, "so let me tell you about Tiny Elvis."

It's a good thing Jenny kept talking, because you can't promise details on something called "Tiny Elvis" and not deliver. This is The King we're talking about. Or at least a miniature version of him.

Anyway, Tiny Elvis was a really traumatized rescue. As Jenny shares his story, it becomes clear the little guy was a really special do…

… no wait, he was a mouse. A baby mouse. Hence the "Tiny."

Tiny Elvis was a newborn mouse that Jack found near the family home in autumn 2022. So young its eyes were still closed, the rodent was unable to care for itself. Jack wanted to bring him inside. At first, Jenny refused.

"I told Jack that we needed to leave him, to see if his mother comes back to him," Jenny remembers. It was a no, but a highly sensible no.

But mama mouse never showed. The next day, the helpless rodent pup was in the same place. And when Jack noticed this, its next stop was the Franz family home. Jenny started to protest again. And then…

"Once I accepted it, I went to the pet store and bought an entire kingdom," Jenny recalls, pun likely unintended. The King was getting a new castle.

But while mom was footing the bill, Jenny made sure Jack realized this was a responsibility rather than a reaction. Passion projects require more than a moment of Good Samaritanism. It's what comes next that matters.

Together, Jenny and Jack researched how to feed and care for a newborn mouse, discovering that it was a painstaking process whose near-round-the-clock care required, among other musts, delicately administering food and water every two hours. They brought William into the mix, and took turns feeding their now-named newcomer using cotton swabs and fine-tip paintbrushes. Nate pitched in overnight.

What started with Jack's passionate plea—one driven by empathy and kindness—had turned into the entire family's sleep-deprived support, steep learning curve be damned. And this despite one overwhelming likelihood.

"Tiny Elvis had a very slim chance of surviving," Jenny knew. "We could do everything right and it was highly likely that it wouldn't be enough to save him."

It wasn't. The mouse passed away after six days. He died in Jenny's hands. She cried. The boys cried. But while Tiny Elvis' brief life was over, Jack's need to do right by him was not. It was time for Jenny—who, less than a year prior, followed her own passion thousands of miles to a dog sanctuary—to abide by her own example.

"Jack wanted to bury him," she shares, "so I followed his lead."

They bought a little wooden box and a river rock, adorning it with Tiny Elvis' name. They held a short but sweet service and laid him to rest under a shady tree in the front yard. It was a burial fit for The King.

With the purest of intentions, the Franzes had done their utmost to save Tiny Elvis' life. That their fervent efforts fell short only drove the point home further: a passion is worth pursuing regardless the result. Success is neither guaranteed nor necessarily the point.

Every time Jack passes Tiny Elvis' tiny gravestone, he is reminded that his passions are respected in this family—that what drives him to positive-minded action will be valued and encouraged. William was undoubtedly left with the same confidence-instilling impression.

Jenny's sons know that if they find something worth fighting for, their parents will fight for them. Some kids grow up never knowing that; Jack and William learned it before either is even a teenager.

There are points in this book where a passage unrelated to rescue dogs requires an explanation, if not an apology, for digressing at length. This is not one of those instances. Because Tiny Elvis doesn't get the mouse version of the ICU without Jenny's role as rescuer in chief.

In fact, an attempt to portray Jenny's parenting prowess through individual dog-driven anecdotes does not do her and her boys justice; it is missing the forest for a few peed-upon trees. This is because the similarities between Jenny the mom and Jenny the rescuer are more than mere parallels. At some point, the lines merge and meld.

"My kids are very different," Jenny observes. "Meeting them where they are, seeing them as individuals, letting go of what you thought it might be like rather than grieving for who they aren't. We try to adjust and meet those needs rather than prematurely give up."

Somewhere, Pepper just smiled. So did Foster and every other down-on-its-luck dog that ever passed through Jenny's doors.

What about rescue dogs makes them ideal foundations for life lessons so important that they shape not only us, but our sons and daughters as well? What about salvaged strays makes the impact of these messages simultaneously less preachy and more profound? Can the scale be fully balanced by the combined clout of adorable, undeniably innocent beings and admirable, undeniably virtuous acts? Maybe. But seeing this impact extend across generations suggests something less quantifiable.

Recently Jenny noticed Jack and William playing an online simulation, a "you're the mayor"-type game where participants construct their own towns from scratch. As their cyberworlds sprouted, Jack and William outfitted their humble towns with the basics of municipal life. Schools and supermarkets. Playgrounds and police stations. And of course…

"They both built dog kennels," Jenny gushes. "Maybe they figured mama needed a place to work."

And work she will. Better Together Dog Rescue recently passed its first full year of transporting strays from the U.S. South. Jenny and her team have rescued and fostered more than 250 dogs, with an eye toward doubling that figure in their second full year of operations. They also are working toward a spay and neutering program in Cleveland, Texas—an attempt to lower the area's unsustainable stray dog population.

For now, dogs transported north are cared for by volunteer foster families. Soon, this will be supplemented by a dedicated facility. The fosters will continue to flow in and out of the Franz family home. The mom these destitute dogs have forged for Jack and William could exist no other way. Both boys are better for it.

12

Grief

Good Grief

It was my first full day without him.

I remember very little. It must have been a Friday, since he died on a Thursday. It's odd how death days of the week seem to stick in our minds. My mother died on a Monday more than four decades ago. I couldn't tell you the exact date.

I'd gone to the office that fretful Friday, anticipating a staggered-at-best work schedule for the following week amid all the miserable details death brings—agonizing arrangements, crying en route to cremation.

I walked in the front door. My two-year-old ran to his dada, arms outstretched. "Hold you! Hold you!" he blurted, his inverted, baby-talk way of demanding I pick him up. I comply, dropping my emotional baggage for 20 pounds of adorable purity. The relief is short-lived, and carries the added weight of guilt at forgetting, even for the briefest of moments, the deceased—as if the space between my ears is his only place left on Earth.

I wander out to the backyard. My dad is there, head sunk, hands on hips. Likely he'd attempted, as I had, to extract some measure of alleviation from his alluringly oblivious young grandson; and likely, he'd found the same bittersweet split-second amnesia I'd just experienced. For us both, the culpability of utilizing the toddler for a doting yet fleeting hit of dopamine had another woeful layer: the knowledge that this same bundle of joy would never get to know his dearly departed family member. Guilt shot, meet gut punch.

Thus is the flailing of early-stage, benumbed grief. Neither of us had cried in the 24-plus hours since tragedy had transpired. And certainly, neither of us had smiled.

I walked over and sat on the bench near the garden. I looked down, to where my best friend would typically lie. On the grass. At my feet.

And there he was. On the grass. At my feet.

"I figured it would have been you," I said. I wasn't wishing for a role reversal, merely stating a logical fact. I really did think he'd be next, be the first close-knit family member I'd lose since age three, all those Mondays ago.

But it wasn't—and he was indeed there. This wasn't a fever dream. Vector was still very much alive. My father's older brother, whom we both loved effusively, was not.

We humans employ various tools for coping with the inevitability of death. One of those is math. We calculate current age and expected lifespan, and when those two numbers begin to align it removes some level of shock, albeit seldom sadness, from what we all know is a natural part of life: its conclusion.

In this equation, Vector was "on deck" among my innermost orbit—those people (OK, those beings) I truly and intimately knew and loved. Let's get real: for most of us, myself included, that number can be counted on two hands if we're lucky, one if we're not. And among those most favored few, Vector's lifespan made him the likeliest to leave first. "I figured it would have been you" was an acknowledgment that I, though probably only subconsciously, had been steeling myself against his eventual passing.

Instead, Uncle Steve dropped first. It hit me, and us all, like a ton of bricks. This was not the inevitable conclusion of a lengthy terminal illness. This was sudden—kiss your wife goodnight, wake up suffering a massive heart attack, never regain consciousness sudden.

Unsurprisingly, Vector became the second being who dared showcase a sunny disposition on this incredibly dark day. And along with his biped bro-bro, he was one of only two I would have allowed to display such situationally inappropriate mirth.

But again, with my son Nicholas there is a deep sadness—the tragedy of a robbed relationship. Fast forward to today, on my desk at work sits a framed photo my aunt took. Uncle Steve and Nicholas, backs turned, pace away from the camera amid a row of library books, my uncle's lanky arms reaching down to hold the hand of his grand-nephew at his knees.

It is the best worst photograph I've ever seen. My son will only know this remarkable man the way I know my mother: from this and hundreds of other pictures and recordings. Nicholas deserved to know him and, as he sprouts toward adolescence, vice versa. In the immediate aftermath of Uncle Steve's death, my son became a reminder of what would never be rather than a bright spot in bleak times. It's terrible to type that, but true nonetheless.

However, the equally naïve being in my backyard brought none of these tortured tidings. His joy had no strings attached, no "what coulda beens" to consider. He had known and loved Uncle Steve for nearly five years—almost half a doggie lifetime. Now, Vector was reinforcing a message delivered by Nicholas just moments ago, and by Uncle Steve countless times before that: Happiness will return. Maybe not today or tomorrow, but it will—and it should be enjoyed without constraints.

That Vector was a rescue added a hardened street cred to the soft, easy love he was now showing me—that he always showed me, his daddams. A fellow human, however hardscrabble his history, would be spitting in the face of a freshly grieving man for displaying a fraction of Vector's ebullience. Vector alone could show me, in all his bounding, yipping, licking joy, that light and life and love will eventually resurface and, once they did, I should embrace them both gratefully and guiltlessly.

From wherever his newly body-free soul was, I was certain my uncle approved of Vector's hopeful message.

One mid–August Thursday in 2018, my phone rang. It was Uncle Steve.

Only it wasn't. It was his friend. In tears. "Steve had a heart attack," he blurted. "We're at the hospital. Get here quick."

I wasn't quick enough. Stephen Robert Dale died moments later. He was 69.

We were exceptionally close. In Chapter 6, I mentioned our parallels battling clinical depression, which is known to run in families.[1] My experience takes a logical yet presumptuous additional step: should "strains" of depression exist, I believe we shared one. We were depression doppelgangers, our mental maladies so synced it bordered on condition-specific telekinesis.

When Uncle Steve was depressed, I could immediately tell and emphatically empathize. His shoulders slumped. Responses were delayed, the same "astronaut to mission control" stupefaction I've displayed. Smiles went from frequent to forced, more grimace than grin. Ouch, squared and shared. "I feel your pain" sounds like a bullshit platitude, until it's not.

Uncle Steve was a mentor, safety net, and inspiration, fighting depression's darkness with the light of generosity. From his career in child welfare to harboring his drug-addicted nephew (me), he was always helping someone. He lived the depression-quelling concept of self-esteem through estimable acts.

Uncle Steve provided not only consolation but identification, freeing my depression from the isolation of my brain into the warmth of his living room. He was just always … there. And there appropriately.

During my eyesight scare, solace from others was lacking. Patty was too young, my father too panicky. From friends, it was mostly "It'll work out, hang in there." Gee, thanks.

Not that I blame them. What can you say to a 24-year-old losing his eyesight? "At least you won't need to drive in NYC traffic?" "You've always wanted a dog?" "Look on the bright side, no pun intended?"

Uncle Steve was the only person who offered something truly useful. "OK," he said, "so it's probably bad. But maybe it's not *that* bad." His background in depression, and in *me*, produced the most optimistic assessment I could stomach: partly-cloudy with low visibility. He validated my dread—a sanity-verifying island in a sea of intelligence-insulting "it'll be OK" dithering—while dissuading our mutual, disease-driven inclination to assume the worst.

Uncle Steve knew I'd rather be dead than blind; he was trying to prevent the former despite possessing zero control over the latter. He was the thin thread tying me to reality during that protracted, panic-stricken period.

He intervened again a few years later, following my rooftop flirtation with suicide and subsequent depression-related hospitalization. "People don't think about us as much as we think they do. They're too busy thinking about themselves."

No one just pulls such fortune cookie fodder out of nowhere. No one says that unless they've been there. On that rooftop. Or tying that noose, or loading that pistol. Uncle Steve had seen familiar, troubling signs emerge in me. Persistent pessimism. Unbudgeable unhappiness. Paranoia. I was convinced everyone hated me, that I was irredeemable.

Uncle Steve knew my code-red-level depression wouldn't listen to brightside-ism so he pitted my cynicism against it: "People are selfish assholes," he continued, "so don't kill yourself over them."

My head jerked up. He knew I was suicidal. He knew my mind could be a dangerous cage because his could be too. I wasn't alone—and because of that, I wasn't revisiting the apartment building's roof anytime soon. "Nobody understands" no longer worked as an excuse.

When he came across a crisis he couldn't dent directly—namely, my addiction—he and his wife did the next best thing: took me into their home while I gave it my best go. And when it finally stuck, knowing he noticed my progress meant everything.

"You used to be the angriest person I knew, and now ... you're probably third," he joked. "I'm proud of you. Keep going."

In the ensuing years, he would be my chief consoler when my wife miscarried ("Allow yourself to be in pain. This is appropriate sadness, not depression"); my balance beam upon suffering a small stroke shortly before finally becoming a father ("Leave your fears with the doctors for now. When the baby comes, your aunt and I are here—lean on us"); and my primary point of reference when fatherhood began to sink in ("You're going to worry about him for the rest of your life, so just accept that without being overwhelmed by it").

Then the wisest voice I've ever known fell silent, forever. Uncle Steve's passing left me not only deeply sad, but also severed from a seemingly indispensable source of identification. Grieving, yes, but also feeling abandoned—and ashamed for feeling selfish before his corpse was cold. He is irreplaceable. His death remains the most challenging event of my post-addiction life.

Uncle Steve was a rescue dog owner himself. Well, sort of.

All of 10 pounds soaking wet, Xena (a.k.a. "Z," a.k.a. "Z Girl") came to live with my aunt and uncle when a close friend was hospitalized with an extended illness. Unfortunately, she never recovered. She died too young.

If there's any blessing in this, it's that this lovely woman knew her precious little pooch would be well taken care of. And perhaps she foresaw that Xena would, in turn, help care for Uncle Steve. Not that my aunt didn't love Z. Of course she did. But my aunt doesn't have Uncle Steve's demons. My aunt loved Xena, yes ... but Uncle Steve *needed* Xena, especially in the wake of his friend's untimely death.

Xena was always on his stomach. My aunt would let me in, I'd step into the living room, and Uncle Steve would be stretched out on the couch, back on the cushions. There contentedly lay a 6'5", 200-plus-pound man with a fluffy, white Bichon Frisé treating his tummy like a pillow. In short order this diminutive dog, tiny even for her petite breed, went from a literal consolation prize to an irreplaceable family member.

Uncle Steve had always been surrounded by love—his wife, his son, the extended family and friends that someone so warm and welcoming attracts. But per this book's theme, Xena was something else. She was, simultaneously, an endearing reminder of his fallen friend, a pact to move forward despite a heavy heart, and a tail-wagging, face-licking example of his success in doing exactly that. Xena's happiness helped mitigate Uncle Steve's sadness.

Let me qualify that. Of course Uncle Steve, my aunt and everyone who knew and loved Xena's original mom were sad—and appropriately so. But Uncle Steve had, as I have, that extra, clinically recognized tendency to shoot past measured melancholy into debilitating, even dangerous depression. There's a difference, and it's a big one.

For depressives like Uncle Steve and I, tragic events come with their own inward-facing, triggering twists. They are compounded by the lurking potential for a diseased response. We have a tough time identifying the blurred line between proportionate sadness and abnormal depression.

Can a dog cure depression? Of course not. But as we've seen in

My uncle, Stephen Dale, with his beautiful, bequeathed Bichon Frisé, Xena.

previous chapters, they can certainly help alleviate it. In Xena, Uncle Steve had a joined-at-the-hip (OK, the ankle) companion to do right by, just as he'd done right by his friend. And in walking, feeding, and snoozing on the couch with Z, he also had a front row seat to a soul healing from the same loss he'd sustained.

"It's OK," Xena's eyes, ears and tail said. "It's OK to feel some happiness again."

Watching this Bichon Frisé shepherd her adopted dad back toward the light was the first time I'd ever witnessed, up close and personal, a dog provide a grieving person such comfort. The second time I experienced this distinctly animal ability was when Vector consoled me that terrible August day in 2018. The tragic irony is not lost on me that Uncle Steve was the mourner in the first instance, the mourned in the second.

Dogs have a way of pulling us out of ourselves, even if it's to wonder what the hell they're thinking. Did Xena know she was helping every bit as much as she was being helped? Was she knowingly uplifting someone she sensed was down, or simply angling for a treat? How much of this was cognizance and emotional sensitivity … and how much was just inherent doggie goodness?

And of course: considering the undeniably positive impacts dogs can make while we grieve, how much, if at all, does all that really matter? After all, results are more important than intent.

12. Grief: Good Grief

Ricky Gervais' *After Life*, which ran for three seasons on Netflix, might be the greatest grief-centric series in television history. Despite confounding Emmy Award snubs and short-sighted middling reviews, including *The Guardian*'s reaction to its first season, the comedian has called it the best project of his career.[2] That's saying a lot from the creator of *The Office*.

Like life, the series was brief. Each season was six half-hour episodes, essentially one long movie apiece. Gervais plays Tony, a local journalist in small-town England who loses his fortysomething wife, Lisa, to a protracted battle with cancer. As it became clear her situation was terminal, Lisa recorded a long-goodbye series of videos. Each episode, we find Tony wistfully watching these sentimental snippets, along with clips of their happy pre-diagnosis lives together.

The takeaway from these living love letters is clear: this was no ordinary marriage, if such a thing exists. Tony and Lisa's union was the striven-for yet often unrealized portrait of an idyllic partnership, one where man and wife are truly best friends. All marriages are special; theirs seemed especially so.

We find Tony barely functioning. Angry, withdrawn and inching toward alcoholism, he alternates between half-assing it at work and projecting his misery on those around him to camping out for hours at Lisa's gravesite. His grief is deep, debilitating, and non-linear, alleviating slightly before backsliding in a fashion that is romantic, raw and altogether real.

Any attempt at moving on seems like an insult to Lisa's memory. Even if he wanted to reengage with life, he couldn't—despite her deathbed pleas for him to find happiness once she's gone. The couple was childless, so we frequently find Tony alone with his demons.

But he is not really alone. Brandy, the couple's German Shepherd, is a living, live-in link between wife and widower.

Brandy is no mere context canine, no cutesy tack-on to showcase the happy home Tony and Lisa kept. In fact, next to Gervais, Brandy might be the show's most crucial character.

If that sounds like a stretch, those aren't my words—they're Gervais'. In the run-up to *After Life*'s third and final season, Gervais tweeted, "One of the main themes of *After Life* is that a dog can save your life. This is ramped up in season 3 & she becomes as important as any other character."[3] (He also took pains to reassure concerned fans that no, Brandy does not die in the last season, an acknowledgment of the dog's importance to the program and impact on its viewers.)

In fact, entertainment media have dedicated entire articles to Brandy's "more than just a dog" role in *After Life*'s success. Notably, this was recognized right from the get-go. Following the first season—and again, we're only talking about six half-hour episodes here—*Screen Rant* published a piece titled "After Life: 10 Moments Tony's Dog Stole the Show in Season 1."[4]

What at first glance could easily be dismissed as a vacuous clickbait listicle is a surprisingly poignant compilation of the myriad ways Brandy helps steer Tony through the worst of his grief. First and foremost, Brandy's contribution to Tony's stalled healing process is existential. No one gets to slowly deal with the death of a loved one if they also perish, and Brandy goes a long way toward saving Tony's life on more than one occasion.

Often, these mission-critical moments are layered in Gervais' signature, wittingly insulting comedy. In one scene, Brandy is eagerly awaiting her breakfast. Tony, unmotivated in his grief to perform even the simplest of tasks, begrudgingly opens a can of dog food and remarks: "If you could open a tin, I'd be dead now. But you can't, can you? Because you're useless." The acerbic comment belies the affectionate way Tony strokes Brandy's back as she eats. Brandy is anything but useless, and he damn well knows it.

Tony's fake insult is rooted in real, life-threatening pain. Another scene finds him in the bathtub, where he reaches for a razor blade and moves it slowly toward his wrist. The grief has overwhelmed him, and he is contemplating the ultimate escape from it.

Knowingly or not, Brandy comes running in. She senses something is off and begins barking. Tony's head turns and the tension snaps, rendering whether he would have gone through with it temporarily irrelevant.

But only temporarily. In the next episode, Tony is walking Brandy along a beach he once frequented with Lisa. He flashes back to fond times, Lisa in a lounge chair and Brandy by her side. Almost catatonically, Tony begins walking, fully clothed, toward the ocean. This is not the thoughtful contemplation of the bathtub. Tony is not thinking clearly; he is resigned, and therefore committed. Expressionless, he wades in to his hips, his neck, his head…

… and then the most urgent bark in dog acting history pierces the shoreline breeze. Brandy bounds into the water, a literal lifeguard. Tony begins to swim back. When they reach the shore, there is no affection between the two. His senses dulled by deep grief, Gervais is still expressionless. His soul has not been saved—but his life has. Brandy has delivered another stay of execution, allowing him to fight another day. He picks up the leash and the two continue walking.

Here, Brandy was more than a canine substitute for a would-be human rescuer. There's a reason Gervais casts Brandy in a role that, to others, might have best been given a son, daughter or other loved one.

At its suicidal worst, grief and depression intermingle, practically to the point where a Venn diagram becomes two stacked circles. If only for a few moments, Tony's grief stripped him of his sanity, of his ability to make clear decisions. While one could argue that, in this situation, suicide could be construed as rational, the show goes to great lengths to portray Lisa all but begging Tony to go on with his life—his *After Life*—once she passes. Suicide, then, would directly defy the orders of the only person that mattered to Tony.

Where he was, though, a human could not reach him. He was done with the whole endeavor of grief, including the people around him who, while indeed caring, offered trite advice that seemed only to worsen matters. As he walked into the waves, Tony had no good will toward mankind left. He could justify their disappointment and sadness. But he certainly had good will toward Brandy, and he could not justify doing this to her.

Not even Tony's befogged mind could concoct a viable reason to hurt a creature—*his* creature—who is 100 percent good. That's what Brandy was because that's what all dogs are.

Whether Brandy's desperate beach barking translated to "Don't do it, I love you" or merely "How the hell am I supposed to survive without you?" matters little. Tony would go on, providing Brandy with additional opportunities to work her wordless wonder. And work it she does.

As the season progresses, we see Brandy as both a barking bond between Tony and Lisa—similar to Xena's role in Uncle Steve's grief—and a guide dog in Tony's slow climb out of abject misery. Per the former, we see videos of Lisa cuddling with Brandy interspersed with Brandy lying atop her grave, as Tony watches each scenario with a mix of love and longing. Brandy is both a piece of Lisa and a fellow mourning soul. Abandoning her is unthinkable.

But of course, there's a distinct difference between *having* to live and *wanting* to live. On cue, we soon see Brandy, having saved Tony's physical existence, help make that existence bearable. This is conveyed by nothing more complicated than a stroll through the park on a sunny day, with Brandy nudging Tony until he plays fetch with her. She is happy and, for the briefest of moments, a faint smile cracks his forlorn face.

It is no small thing that this happiness is guilt-free. Brandy is not a relative or close friend, or even a son or daughter. Her relationship with Lisa was not complicated, but rather 100 percent love. There is no hurt to unpack, no contentiousness to set aside en route to a brief glimmer of contentedness on a sunny day in the park. Brandy can deliver this because Lisa's love for her is pure and unencumbered by the messiness inherent to us humans. She is uniquely qualified to chip away at Tony's seemingly immovable mountain of grief—a German Shepherd sherpa capable of leading where two-legged travelers simply cannot tread.

In our grief, this is what dogs do for us. Not only can they shield us from our darkest demons, but point us toward the light.

I see shades of Brandy in the role Vector played in my life following Uncle Steve's sudden death. While I never contemplated suicide, the deep connection my uncle and I shared—in depression and otherwise—left me feeling like no one truly understood the extent of my loss. And perhaps I was right.

But it was Vector's irrepressible, completely uncomplicated love of life that began to penetrate weeks of sheer gloom. He helped make it OK—allowable, even advisable—to be happy again, if only for a few distracted moments. Ironically, per the opening anecdote, my son was two years old and displayed a similarly irrepressible, completely uncomplicated love of life. However, as noted, that same sanguine naivete in Nicholas brought a double-edged sword: the sad truth that he'd never get to know his incredible, infinitely kind great-uncle.

And of course, toddlers have another built-in disadvantage: they grow up. Only Vector will remain so endearingly oblivious and infectiously happy. Humans embody these qualities for a brief moment. Dogs do so forever.

Until, of course, they don't. The final scene of *After Life* shows Tony and Brandy walking away from the camera, having just attended a town fair. Given the entire series' tone, for a moment viewers are left wondering if Tony survives his prolonged grief.

Then Brandy fades away and disappears. Tony is walking alone. The message is clear: Tony and Brandy move on with life together, Brandy having accomplished her mission until she succumbs to the reality of a canine's comparatively short lifespan.

And someday, in the not-too-distant future, Vector will follow in Brandy's paw-steps.

Books take a long time to write. Particularly when the book is (a) nonfiction and (b) includes in-depth interviews of third parties, as this effort does, the project itself can take up to two years to draft and, from there, another 12–18 months to reach store shelves and online retailers.

This book has taken … actually, I don't really know. Because despite appearing toward the end of this collection of stories, it's only the third chapter I've penned.

I just broke writing's "fourth wall" by carbon-dating a saga designed to be evergreen. But I did this for good reason: I'd prefer Vector alive for it. I'm not ready to write *that* chapter, the post mortem chapter. Not yet. Epilogues are typically authored last; if Vector passes while this book is being developed, I'll save his sendoff for this collection's farewell address.

12. Grief: Good Grief

With that, I'll reveal that it is March 2022 as I draft this chapter. We've had Vector for eight and a half years. Shortly after his "gotcha day" in September 2013, our vet placed Vector's age at "about three." So according to the most educated of guesses, a dog whose tough history includes physical injuries, dangerous medical conditions (especially chronic ehrlichia, sometimes called canine Lyme Disease) and at least some measure of PTSD, is now 11½.

It shows. Both my wife and I have "early Vector" pictures in the most prominent of places: our cell phones' home screens. (Placing our son there, we figure, could invite kidnappers.) Vector is at his physical peak: light brown hair, perky high-set ears, tongue-out smile, eyes aglow. In my pic, a tennis ball sits in the grass beside him, a reminder of his once-favorite game, half-fetch—so named because Vector loved chasing the ball far more than giving it back.

We now have a decidedly senior sato. Vector's coat, along with the vast majority of his whiskers, have faded to gray. His ears have lowered as his skin stretches.

His eyes have lost their luster, too, as the beginnings of cataracts form. Last summer we were kayaking at our summer home. I was in a tandem with my son and Vector, my wife in a single. As she paddled up to us and called him from about ten feet away, it was evident Vector recognized his mummumsie's voice ... but didn't really know where she was. The vet confirmed his condition, which may eventually require surgery.

Vector is also increasingly arthritic, stemming from both his age and his ehrlichia, which is so severe that the best our vet can do is manage the condition rather than eradicate it. As the arthritis slowly worsens, his paws twist and point outwards, and become more plantigrade. Where before he trod lightly, Vector now lumbers.

Vector is not done, though. Not yet. He still loves walks, albeit shorter and slower ones. He still scream-yips excitedly when his daddams, mummums or bro-bro come home. And if anything edible enters his line of scent, glimpses of his rambunctious, daredevil nature reemerge. Pizza 1, pain 0.

Vector's life still has more than enough value that the end isn't just around the corner. But nor is it beyond the horizon.

There are, I realize, blessings in all of this. Were he to die tomorrow, Vector would have had a reasonably long life—an incredibly long one considering the near-impossible circumstances into which he was born. He has lived with two people who love him unconditionally for eight and a half years, and a third, his little brother Nicholas, for six. Each evening, I ask Nicholas the same question, and he responds with a rhyming refrain.

Me: "Nicholas, how much do we love Vector?"

Nicholas: "All the way and every day, and that's the way it's gonna stay."

Recently, I added another line, "Even though he's old and gray."

We are grateful Vector has lived this long. Grateful a life that historically should have been cut down at its dawn can experience an extended sunset. Too many satos suffer a quick and violent death; Vector gets to enjoy a slow, peaceful passing.

He has earned his retirement, and then some. He has helped me through crises big and small, a silent, steady and salient life partner. He has turned a reticent non-dog person, my wife, into someone who couldn't imagine not having one—and not having him in particular. And as discussed in Chapter 10, he has instilled in my son what I'm sure will be a lifelong affinity for rescue animals. Every dog any of us rescue in the future has Vector to thank.

Vector preparing to half-fetch: "You throw it, I keep it."

He has become a four-legged, full-fledged member of this family. None of us are truly prepared for the time when his doggie bed will be eerily empty. When there's no chit-chit-chit of his nails on the hardwood floor. When there's no always-warm couch cuddler on a chilly night. When there's no one trying to sneakily steal our food.

We are headed into the great unknown. I was just a toddler the last time I lost a live-in family member. Neither my wife nor Nicholas has ever experienced such a loss—such a profound hole in the place they call home.

I will admit it freely: with the exception of my wife and son, I love Vector as much, if not more, than any human in this world. And despite any understandable but unfortunate notions of him being "just a pet," my emotions upon losing him will not be species-specific. Ditto for my wife and Nicholas.

Vector's passing, then, will be the death of a family member unrecognized outside our inner sanctum. It will be an indignity both to our feelings and his legacy. There will be a depth and length of mourning many will deem excessive, but we will know is necessary and altogether fitting.

I am projecting, I realize, for lack of foresight. I honestly have no clue how any of this will play out. I cannot fully envision it. Or maybe I just refuse to.

Somewhere, Uncle Steve is on a big couch in the sky. Xena is on his stomach. Soon, they'll both be making room for Veckie.

My future is less certain. I have not grappled with the totality of what Vector's death will mean. This is partly born of a commitment to enjoying his remaining time with us. But it is also because I fear the full impact of his looming absence. My brain knows it is coming; my heart has not accepted it. And I doubt it will until life without Vector goes from pending to permanent.

Let's meet someone who, unfortunately, has experienced what I have yet to endure—the loss of her closest canine companion.

13

Grief

Ophelia (You're Breaking My Heart)

On her website, Katya Lidsky describes herself as a "writer, podcaster and animal person." Getting to know her is realizing those roles are not ranked in order. If anything they are inverted, because everything she creates seems to flow from her unconditional love of animals—and dogs in particular.

She wears many hats. In addition to being a wife, mother and foster mom to a rotating roster of rescue dogs, Katya is a former dog trainer and current certified Family Paws Parent Educator, providing tutorial programs that increase safety and decrease stress for dog families. She is a sometimes actress and an all-the-time activist.

Much of her writing is tips-based, practical and sprinkled with levity. Highlights include "10 Mindset Shifts When Bringing Home a Rescue Dog," "Top Reasons to Get a Lick Mat for Your Dog," and in the grand tradition of "write what you know," "Why Oh Why Does My Dog Pee on My Bed?" and "How I Dog-Trained My Husband."[1]

This playful writing style belies a much deeper, purposeful persona. Among other not-so-side projects, Katya runs a support group for people with aging pets. The forums are often joined by experts, who impart knowledge on both senior animal health (for example, as I'm finding with Vector, their heightened need for dental care) and the emotional wellbeing of their owners. Its stated goal is to help make senior pets happier and more comfortable for whatever time they have left, while acknowledging the strain their end-of-life journeys are placing on us, their human family members.

"We get it," its webpage reads. "We get all of it, and we are here to help process any and all emotions, to have a chuckle, to share what has worked or what has not. Because none of us have to go through this alone."[2]

The kicker: "It's not a small thing. It's not silly. It's a sacred love we're talking about."

In the context of this book Katya could check a lot of boxes. Person in

13. Grief: Ophelia (You're Breaking My Heart)

recovery. Mental disorder. Trauma. Her story is engaging and ultimately uplifting enough to have fit into any of those categories. She is the focus of a chapter on grief for the same reason she founded a senior dog support group. Her name is Ophelia and, by Katya's own admission, she saved Katya from herself.

The 17 years Ophelia walked the Earth started with Katya's mid–20s, and ended in her early 40s. During that time, Ophelia was a constant who played pivotal roles in Katya's maturation from a troubled post-adolescent to the sincere, loving adult she so obviously is today.

But since January 26, 2022—two months before our series of interviews for this collection began—that sincere, loving person has been gutted. And lost. And more than a little angry at the universe. As much as anything, what her experience shows is that all this is unavoidable, fitting and altogether beautiful. It shows that Katya loved Ophelia with a fearless, even reckless abandon that knew a hurt this deep was inevitable, but nonetheless sprinted head-over-heels forward, cliff be damned.

Ophelia: A 17-year constant in Katya Lidsky's journey from a troubled past to content adulthood (courtesy Katya Lidsky).

Ophelia's life was as circular as her name's first letter. Ophelia helped build a person capable of overcoming the loss of a partner as endearing and enriching as … herself. That Katya may not fully realize this (yet) is testament to the power of the amazing and unique bond dogs and humans can share.

The daughter of Jewish immigrants from Cuba, Katya was raised in Laredo, a Texas border city. Like many future addiction sufferers, including me, she was an uncomfortable child.

"I come from a family of eating disorders who don't know they have eating disorders," Katya says, half-jokingly. "I'm a Cuban Jew. We spend breakfast talking about lunch and dinner."

Katya describes her older sister as exceptionally attractive. "She would light up a room," she remarks. Katya felt overshadowed. A pattern prevalent in addictive behavior emerged: To garner attention, Katya became a perpetual performer, a people-pleasing chameleon playing various roles at the expense of developing her own identity.

She developed an eating disorder. "I couldn't change my face, or make myself taller," she recalls, "but I could make myself thinner."

By 11, she was limiting herself to 600 calories daily. If this self-imposed ceiling was exceeded, she subtracted from the following day's intake. Seven hundred today? Bad girl, Katya. Five hundred tomorrow.

"I'm a restrictor," she explains. Rigid self-discipline helped quiet her inferiority and insignificance—a sort of "it saved my life before it ruined my life" familiar to addiction settings.

"Eating disorders are wildly misunderstood—even by people experiencing them," she said. "For me, it felt very embarrassing—a privileged problem. Kids are starving in Africa, but I won't eat the food readily available to me. There's a guilt factor that makes both the suffering person and society at large uncomfortable addressing it."

A school employee reported that Katya regularly trashed her lunch. Exposed, the 68-pound sixth grader was reduced to eating in front of her family like, she recalls, "a monkey in a cage." The already sensitive child withdrew further.

Perhaps sparked by her analogy, Katya pivots to rare moments that brought relief from her display-case dining and overactive emotions. "The only time I felt it wasn't wrong to be sensitive," she remembers, "was around animals."

Katya could be herself around animals without fearing the judgments, real or perceived, human relationships comprise. Guard down, she could feel the range of emotions, from cold to compassionate, without potential penalty. And free from the complexities of people, she no longer

13. Grief: Ophelia (You're Breaking My Heart)

needed to be a people pleaser. "I don't think I knew that back then," she admits, "but I *felt* it. That's why animals are so magical."

Unfortunately, Katya soon found herself in what, for her condition, became a detrimental environment: boarding school. "Not a good place for someone with an eating disorder," she recalls. "Too much freedom, too many girls comparing bodies."

Compelled to "eat normal" with schoolmates but fearful of the caloric consequences, Katya transitioned from an imperfectly recovering anorexic to a full-blown bulimic. Often, meals began at the table and ended in the toilet. It got bad quickly, and stayed bad for a full decade.

Her depravities exemplify addiction's desperation. While I stole from my wife's purse to buy cocaine, Katya robbed supermarkets to binge and purge in the parking lot. While I scrounged for one last line from a baggie's dusty dregs, Katya discarded then desperately retrieved food from garbage bins—a rancid, rented meal that, with the help of a finger and a gag reflex, ended up right where it started.

It was ugly and dirty and dangerous. Katya's body and psyche were deteriorating. The girl who always wanted attention risked becoming a nonentity.

Her intelligence also worked against her. The book smart bulimic graduated high school with honors and excelled at New York University. (Disclosure: I also attended NYU; Katya and I share a mutual friend.) She moved to Los Angeles and began acting and writing.

Of all things, opulence finally interceded. At a cousin's wedding, Katya found herself at a decadent castle—a celebratory day on a lush green estate. An upscale upchucking provided desperately needed dichotomy.

"It's easy to justify lowly behavior when you're puking in a dumpster," she said. "Not at a lavish reception in a castle." Recovery commenced with six simple words.

"Mom, I have a big problem."

Thus began, however halting, her escape from bulimia's chokehold. She moved to Texas' picturesque capital, Austin, just a few hours' drive from her parents in Laredo. It was not a clean sweep. Like my own struggle with cocaine, Katya's bulimia bent before it broke—promising periods of abstinence interrupted by disheartening relapse.

Then, suddenly and forever, her path got immeasurably easier.

One day Katya came across a man selling puppies, of all places, behind a local taco joint. It was a backyard breeder, minus the backyard.

While Katya wasn't about to reward illegal breeding with money, there was one mutt too sick to sell. She offered to take the pup off his hands, and he agreed.

She took the beleaguered Beagle mix to the vet, where it was determined to have parvovirus. Commonly called parvo, the contagious disease is spread by dog-to-dog contact with contaminated feces or environments—such as the cramped, negligent conditions typical of puppy mills. Parvo wreaks havoc on dogs' gastrointestinal tracts, and is fatal in up to 80 percent of cases.[3]

This puppy survived but, as Katya recalls in tongue-in-cheek fashion, wasn't particularly thrilled about it.

"She was constantly hysterical. She was jumpy, morose, even morbid. It looked like she wanted to commit suicide."

Ever the gallows humorist, the aspiring actress with a love for Shakespeare named her seemingly life-ambivalent little dog Ophelia, after a Hamlet character who intentionally drowns herself.

Ophelia was stubborn, scarred, unyielding despite her obvious neediness … and it was exactly what Katya needed. She spent weeks just trying to get Ophelia to eat and drink, with water often administered via the squirt gun approach of an oral syringe.

As she became consumed with keeping this fledgling life from fading away, Katya slowly realized what was no longer consuming her: herself, and everything that came with it, including her obsessive urges to binge eat and purge. The selflessness of tending to a dog's urgent emergency had begun to chip away at her own protracted one. When this reprieve became evident, she instinctively doubled down on this simple effectiveness.

"All I knew," she recalls, "is that I needed to be OK for *her* to be OK." Encouragingly, as her bulimia waned, her emotional state also improved. She was building self-esteem in the most reliable of ways: through estimable acts. And all of this stemmed from Ophelia.

"I stopped pleasing people to please Ophelia," she says. "I started saying no to people because Ophelia mattered more."

Katya was always in her head. But Ophelia was *out there*. In *front* of her. You can't be in your head and consciously cuddling on the couch with a loved one at the same time.

It's never this simple, of course, but that's how a sickly puppy saved a sickly person. They would both grow up, together. It was the beginning of a beautiful, inseparable relationship that ranks among the most important of Katya's life.

With Ophelia as a foundation, Katya laid the cornerstones for a productive, content life. She met and married her husband, and settled down in Austin. They had two beautiful children. Career highlights began to accrue, including her aptly titled one-woman show, *I'm Sorry: How an Apologist Becomes an Activist*, running for two years in New York and Los Angeles. She sold a TV pilot for a show set in (where else?) an animal

13. Grief: Ophelia (You're Breaking My Heart)

shelter and, along with her husband, started a writer-centric production company called Pesky Moon Entertainment.

A life propelled from chaos because of Ophelia now included her in it, milestone by milestone.

Katya also found a calling. Her creative work started skewing heavily in the direction of animals. Protecting them, understanding them, helping their human family members do right by them. She wanted everyone to share in her life-altering love, one sparked and spurred by her darling doggie. Ophelia was the angel, Katya the evangelical.

Katya practiced what she preached. Among other life-affirming actions, this meant a steady stream of foster dogs that, at last count, surpassed 60. It also meant becoming a licensed animal trainer—a means of complementing passion with education. She was now a full-fledged animal person, one whose head followed her heart. And under everything was her underfoot life companion.

"Ophelia didn't open my heart—she blew it up," Katya insists. "I feel her love and a higher power in every connection I have—especially to other animals."

All the while, of course, Ophelia did what all of us do. She got older.

That Ophelia's aging tracks with a flurry of Katya's creativity is no coincidence. For starters, there was the launch of her podcast, *The Animal That Changed You*. The program bills itself as "a touching and funny

Katya with her bulimia-busting Beagle mix, Ophelia (courtesy Katya Lidsky).

podcast that explores how extraordinary people have been changed by an extraordinary animal." (Among those "extraordinary" people was me, and one of the extraordinarily animals—sarcastic quotation marks intentionally omitted—was Vector.)

Again, we find Katya identifying the special love she shares with Ophelia, understanding that there's no way such a bond is unique to them, and spreading this message example by hourlong example. It was a salve for Katya, for whom coping and caring seem symbiotic.

The show became an ever more important channel come the summer of 2021. That's when Ophelia, by then 16, was diagnosed with kidney failure. The blow to her dog's kidneys was a blow to Katya's soul.

"Her mortality was becoming clearer and clearer … and my self-talk was getting more and more ugly," she recalls. Her recovering addict brain wisely threw up a red flag. She was backsliding.

"I started feeling like my abstinence from bulimia was in jeopardy. I was worried about emotional regression leading to physical relapse."

Into action she went. A few episodes became 30, 40, 50. Like many recovery tools, it's now a mainstay she couldn't imagine abandoning; to borrow 12 Step parlance, it works, so she works it. Successfully recovered addicts replace bad habits with good ones.

"I love animal welfare people. Maybe it's because I find them a little bit addict-y. They just found a terrific, life-affirming way to channel away from their inner demons."

Next came the senior dog support group, a means for the families of aging dogs to swap advice, learn from experts and, most of all, identify with the pre-grief each member is experiencing.

That pre-grief, Katya finds, is unique to pets. A common thread weaving through the support group is a longing for the way a dog "used to be." This is because, unlike (for example) children, dogs typically remain consistent (in size, personality, etc.) throughout their lives … until the very end approaches. As their beloved dogs gray, slow down and undergo temperament changes (Vector, for instance, gets more spooked by sounds than he used to), we are constantly faced with the mortality of a family member who'd been a reassuring constant for a decade or more. We want more of the same—but Father Time is unyielding.

"Our pets aren't stagnant," Katya explains. "They age and they change. For example, a dog that was once cuddly might develop arthritis and not want to snuggle as much. It's important to let people know to let pets grow into what they are. Pets have a right to grow old just like we do."

But of course, helping our dogs deal with their deteriorating bodies is a kindness we'd extend to any elderly family member.

"Dementia. Vision loss. Tiring more easily. People want concrete

13. Grief: Ophelia (You're Breaking My Heart)

examples of what's going on with their dogs' bodies and, relatedly, in their minds."

Katya found that, as their dogs age, the family members she regularly met with became more engaged with their pets, not less. There is a distinct difference, it seems, between letting our dogs age and letting our dogs go.

Helping prepare folks for the present with their pooches was far simpler than addressing the inevitable near-term future without them. This, despite a canine's concentrated lifespan clearly indicating death's relatively rapid approach.

Katya saw beauty in this. And she realized that the difficulty in even beginning to let go of an aging dog isn't an act of fear-based denial, but rather fearless selflessness. Always reliant on their human family members to meet their basic needs—food, shelter, healthcare—dogs become ever more dependent as their days dwindle. Given the circumstances, bracing oneself for this looming loss through some degree of emotional detachment is understandable.

But it isn't necessarily right, either. Especially not for Katya.

In an early 2022 article for *The Fix*, a longstanding but unfortunately now-defunct recovery website, Katya leans into this sentiment by proudly declaring how desperately she needed Ophelia. Amid a recovery landscape where codependency has become an increasingly dirty word, the thoughtfulness and elegance of the piece, titled "The Case for Codependency … with a Rescue Dog," proves it no mere kneejerk reaction to Ophelia's terminal, deteriorating condition.[4]

She begins by recognizing the pitfalls of classic codependency.

> It's a dangerous game when we can't speak our needs or share a truth, and I don't want to gloss over those agonizing elements of this unhealthy dynamic or make the dysfunction sound fun. But it's humans I've experienced this [negative feedback] with—it's people who have disappointed me when it comes to a codependent paradigm.

She then contrasts this with the selflessness and responsibility she feels toward Ophelia.

> [Ophelia] has never, not once, pushed me to forget myself, has never shoved her guilt onto me or held on tighter when I walked out the door. My dog waits patiently, she dances when I come home, she accepts what I want, and she lets me know what she wants, as if it's all okay just the way we are, as if we can be together or apart, but the love isn't dependent on either, and it won't ever be affected by imperfections or mistakes or feelings.

Society's labels, Katya writes in not so many words, can go to hell.

> I adore Ophelia, I am devoted to her, and because of her I have grown to love myself. Because of her, I've also adopted many other dogs and fostered many

other dogs, each time proving to myself again that being codependent on dogs is safe.

These were not empty words. As Ophelia started to age, Katya pivoted to prioritize senior dogs, including a geriatric dog with cancer who spent the last seven months of her life with Katya's family. Codependent or not, that's love.

Katya then embarks on an eminently convincing point-by-point list of why dog codependency is not only acceptable but exceptional. She gets as far as five, but in my opinion could have dropped the pen in victory after #1:

> #1. You never have to sell yourself out for a dog's affection and companionship. You never have to perform to earn their approval. You just have to be halfway decent. For me, going into an animal shelter, bearing that world of hurt and taking in the ugly smells and earsplitting barks and eager eyes from behind kennel bars ... was all I had to do to be rewarded with unconditional friendship from someone who needed just one friend in the world. *It makes me feel proud to be that friend, and I can admit that a part of me still needs to be needed* [emphasis added by me].

Finally, Katya realizes that, as it becomes clear Ophelia will pass away in days or weeks rather than months or years, her heart is slowly adapting to what her eyes are witnessing.

> As I engage in a sacred love with Ophelia, my codependency is morphing because I am in the practice of letting go. Because my precious pets will not live as long as I do, and thus I will have no choice but to grow the resilience and self-care needed in order to go on. In this most generous last act, dogs help heal us of codependency's grip, showing us what we're made of, how strong we really are, and that we can live beyond heartache.
>
> I look at Ophelia with utter gratitude even though I know what's coming. She will leave me standing on my own two feet, less codependent than I was before her. Proud of what we were together, forever.

This is not a woman in denial, or in an unhealthy relationship. It's a woman in love—and all the heartbreak, turmoil and unpredictability that comes with it.

"Don't hesitate and hedge and protect yourself," she relates. "Death isn't over the horizon—it's right around the corner. And you still love with reckless abandon and rigorous honesty, and you feel the feelings and you move forward."

"Unfortunately, I'm much more angry than sad," Katya remarked.

Both the content and forcefulness of her words surprised me. After all, on the topic of death, this was arguably the most emotionally prepared person in the history of dog ownership.

Article writing, animal-centric podcasting, support group starting,

13. Grief: Ophelia (You're Breaking My Heart)

Katya and Ophelia, contentedly codependent (courtesy Katya Lidsky).

terminally ill dog adopting. Katya had approached Ophelia's pending passing from as many angles as one could imagine and—spoiler alert—we haven't even gotten to the most moving one yet.

"I'm actually surprised that my greatest emotion at Ophelia's death is anger," she continues, validating my own confusion. "I feel angry that she left me with all these people. I'm mad that it has to be that way."

It's not Ophelia, she explains. It's … well, *everything else*. Herself. Her demons. Other humans. Life itself. God, maybe.

"I'm more mad at the universe than I am with her," she says, before pivoting inward. "I'm an addict and I want more," she exclaims—an honest nod to both bulimia and bullheadedness. "I want more Ophelia."

"I want to feel her all day and every day, and I don't," she says. "I have really amazing moments when I miss her so much, and that's when I feel her presence. But it doesn't happen as often as I want. I just want more."

"And in this way," she adds, "Ophelia is still teaching me." Ophelia's painful absence is forcing Katya to direct elsewhere her need to fawn and dote and love, something Katya's track record strongly suggests will occur in due time. But perhaps not yet—not a mere two months following so heavy a loss.

"I feel like my grief with Ophelia is just beginning," she surmises. "I'm very uncomfortable with it, and if I'm trying to get away from it, it's just going to linger."

She touches upon the grief paradox I professed in the previous chapter—the guilt of a loved one in mourning who dares disregard the recently departed, if only for a few fleeting moments. It's the same way I felt in the wake of Uncle Steve's passing—that I was somehow disrespecting his memory unless he was on my mind 24/7.

And it's the same way I know I'll feel upon Vector's passing. Well—that, coupled with the defensiveness of a dog owner justifying his deep, protracted grief against the "it's just a pet" judgments of non-dog people. Katya claims she feels sorry for these folks—that she and I are lucky to understand the profundity of a dog's life, and fortunate to mourn our pets for what they truly are: family members. If to mourn is to love, dog people love an expanded set of beings—and that can't be a bad thing, ever.

It's an amazingly tolerant outlook considering where she is. Two months into her grief journey, Katya is a voice-cracking, tear-welling, altogether appropriate mess. Her pain is as raw, real, and reactionary as someone who hadn't been building, block by block, toward this inevitability for quite some time.

And that brings us to the most remarkable of these building blocks. That brings us to "Ophelia, I Feel Ya."[5]

On October 1, 2021, Katya promised her dog (and really, herself) that she'd write Ophelia a letter each day until she passed away. Posted on her website, www.katyalidsky.com, the collection includes 118 missives, concluding with Ophelia's passing in late January.

The letters read like an endearing exercise in aspirational empathy. Without stating it in so many words, it is unabashed in its insistence that Ophelia means as much to Katya as most humans—and that this fact is not only perfectly acceptable (society be damned) but perfectly beautiful. It's a gut-wrenching yet heartwarming paradigm push, and she invites those with senior pets to pick up a pen and creatively commiserate.

"Got a senior pet?" the introduction page reads. "I highly recommend you write them a letter too…. Process the grief, the feelings, the loss, and the love. That last one stays forever."

The daily entries find Katya coping, hoping and groping for the precise words to properly honor her relationship with Ophelia—and to convince both her dog and herself that death is part of life. That she is both nakedly vulnerable and wholly unconvinced is part of the letters' beauty

13. Grief: Ophelia (You're Breaking My Heart)

and effectiveness. Post after post, her pre-grieving is all the more touching given the knowledge that the "pre-" has since been erased.

On Day 26, Katya gets a fleeting moment of vintage Ophelia.

> OMG Ophelia, you had a frisky moment today and played with me! You actually initiated play! It's been so long since you've done that, since you put your mouth on my arm, since you wiggled just so, since you panted joyfully, since you did that little growl like a gremlin.

Three weeks later, Day 46 finds Katya and Ophelia in a different, more diagnosis-defined place. In a post titled "You Are Not Dying Yet," Katya is defiant, even demanding.

> Today sucked. Watching you drag your feet and fall over, flop on the ground, become an overcooked noodle, it all took me down in a way even I didn't expect.... You were soaked from laying on my chest while you slept during another fit of my endless tears.

A few days later, Day 54, a calmer Katya has a hound-dog haiku showcasing the Zen of a dog following its nose.

> For you, Ophelia, Beagle of my heart, the one who broke me in for all hound dogs forever, and taught me about the stubborn powerlessness of following what you smell.
>
> > "An old funny dog,
> > Nose reaching up, out, beyond—
> > To catch the big life."

And on they go. Memories, musings and mundanities celebrating the life Katya and Ophelia made together. On January 5 (Day 97), Katya celebrates what she knows will be her final birthday with Ophelia at her side. As Katya reels off the blessings Ophelia helped her accrue, the narrative morphs from a love letter to a thank you note.

> The husband of my dreams who is more than what I dreamed. The children I would do literally everything the same over again if I had a magic wand, just to end up with them in the crook of my elbows at night. You, 17, you, who's seen me through all of it, you who took down the brick wall of my restraint and my resistance so that every animal after you could have easy access to where you'd been.
>
> It is scary AF to be content like this, to receive with my whole heart. I can. I will. I do. But only because you have shown me how.

Two days before Ophelia's passing—Letter 116—Katya is overwhelmed. Ophelia's condition has deteriorated to the point of frequent seizures and near-total immobility. The date has been set for Ophelia's euthanasia—the day after tomorrow.

We find Katya profane and, per the assessment that surprised both me and herself, pissed. Far from poised, but still poignant.

Fuckshitdamnitdickballs. It's at my throat, the top, under the chin. No, it's not The Return of Bulimia, there are no more movies in that series....

I am going to hate the world. I'm going to be bitchy, in a bad mood ... hostile and looking to pick fights because I will not be able to stand life for a little while, the unfairness of it, the prickly spikes that are part of living and loving.

The postmortem predictions begin to fly from Katya's fingertips.

I am going to come home and have to hold onto a wall, catch my breath as I remember again—as if I could forget—that you are not home.

I am going to dwell, bite my lip, as the guilt takes little tiny bites out of my flesh. Were you in pain? Did I wait too long?

I am going to cry when I'm sautéing spinach and you're not at my feet hoping a piece of something good will fall, only to be bummed ... when you realize it's spinach.

I'm going to go quiet. I'm going to take walks and look for you, searching every ladybug who wants a moment of peace but has to deal with my ogling eyeballs, staring at it, asking, Are you Ophelia?

And if all this wasn't brutally honest enough, the *coup de grâce*.

I am going to feel relieved from the constant cleaning and the constant worrying. I have to get that off my chest, it's not nice, forgive me, but there I said it. I'm going to breathe easier, no longer wringing my hands wondering if you had another seizure, if you were able to drag your body to the water ... or if you're just lying there thirsty. It's the idea of you needing and wanting and suffering that is so very hard for me to stomach.

Two days later, in the final entry, Katya channels Ophelia from the great beyond, turning the tearjerking tables. It is a reminder for Katya to love the way Ophelia taught her to love: completely, fearlessly, unconditionally, painfully. It deserves to be printed in full, and to conclude a chapter and topic—grief—where conclusions are elusive, even non-existent.

Dear Katya,

I am writing to you. Me, your Ophelia, taking over to tell you that our last walk together was exactly what I needed it to be. Just us. A lot of birds. Maybe too many lawnmowers and builders, but I'm a lady of compromise. It was cold. You wrapped me in a blanket. At first I was tired, lying down in the stroller, but then—did you see?—I sat up tall so I could sniff everything and take the world in once more. Then it was time to come home.

You had that joke in I'm Sorry, your one-woman show (which I also inspired you to write, by the way) about how you loved me so much it'd felt like you'd given birth to me out of your vagina. Well, today I went back into your body, but not your vag, luckily for me. I went directly through your ribcage and into your heart like a worm into an apple. I went as we stared into each other's eyes this morning, laying on the couch for hours. I went as you played "Simply the Best" by Tina Turner and stole that song right out from under Schitt's Creek's fame. I went as you gave me Ben & Jerry's Caramel Chocolate Cookie Dough ice cream while they administered the first shot. I went as Sassy said goodbye. I went as Eric cried and I did too because I'd never seen

13. Grief: Ophelia (You're Breaking My Heart)

Dad's face fall. I know you felt me slipping away because I'd completed my final task, which was to set up the Ophelia Channel in your brain. I could feel when you were on it these past few days so as I went, as we sat outside in the sunlight, I felt you there, right there, with me, as it happened, as I burrowed my me'ness into the center of your chest. I went, and you felt it, not in words, not in pictures, but as a feeling that burned warm. It tickled, almost made you laugh. It twisted, definitely made you cry. And now I am not another, I'm not outside of you, but I am part of you, part of the inside stuff that makes you you. If you're sore tomorrow, that's just the side effect of me tunneling in. You'll get used to it.

Us dogs, we are not mind readers. But we are communicating and seeking communication constantly. You did good, Mama, you did good tuning into me during my life, but I wanted these last days to make sure you understood that animals are ignored all the time, that the messages we're sending are often not received. So many dogs are just waiting for someone to hear them and see them, and I don't mean coming at a dog with human words and things to do and needs and the busy thoughts that run rampant in most minds so that we can't get through even if we're sitting close. I am talking about the hard easy work of letting everything fall away so you can truly connect with another. That loving attention. That here and now. I know you will wish you'd learned this from me sooner, not at the end, but this is how it had to be because with us it happened organically, because you would never have let something take you over by surprise like I did, if you'd known going in. You would have tried too hard. You would have made a whole thing out of the Ophelia Channel. We had to live it, Mama, we had to be it, so that before I died I could guide you gently into knowing that all creatures are waiting to be interlaced with, offering their presence up at every moment. I don't mean to lecture you, but I am saying this: You gave it to me. Thank you. And now you know what it is. Now you can tell others. Now you can give it to others.

18 is chai in Judaism, the number stands for good luck. Dying on day 118 of this blog felt like poetic justice to me. But the way you live now can be a daily letter to me, not only sitting down and typing on the keyboard, but in learning how to let things go so you can dial in. When you're with other dogs, other beings, your kids, your partner, your family, your friends, set down everything else, from the screens to the mental chatter to the multi-tasking, and sync up with the one you're with. And my channel, our channel, is still there, will always exist, I swear—all you have to do is get still, get quiet, and you'll find me because I'll be everywhere.

It is not just at the end of a life. It is not just about me, your Ophelia. It reminds me of that movie you love, Scrooged, in the final scene, where Bill Murray says, "It can happen every day, you've just got to want that feeling. And if you like it and you want it, you'll get greedy for it! You'll want it every day of your life and it can happen to you! I believe in it now! I believe it's going to happen to me now! I'm ready for it! And it's great. It's a good feeling, it's really better than I've felt in a long time. I, I, I'm ready."

I was ready, Mama, and now so are you to be without me. I loved you the most a being could love, which I know without a shadow of a doubt despite our real, raw relationships and the many ways we bugged the shit out of each other, that's exactly how you loved me. We got the thing life is about. We got it, together.

Miss me. Don't stop missing me. Because you gotta want the feeling, believe in it, want it every day of your life. Stay ready to love like this, and give it to everyone, to everything, do it for me. Do it forever.

Ophelia

Epilogue
Vectorious

We call them our sniff ba-tiff walks.

It's the latest in a long line of doggie-isms we've coined over Vector's lengthy life with us, the type of corny vernacular born of love and familiar to any dog owner. His rawhide chew is a "bone ja-brone." Dog biscuits are "tra-ta-tots." Vector himself is a "cute pa-toot" and "Tosh Ba-gosh"—a nod to a nickname, Tashi, his then-baby brother bestowed upon him, likely due to an inability to pronounce his dog's actual name.

So now we have sniff ba-tiff. A soft, playful moniker belying a hard, compromised reality. Vector is old, enfeebled, hobbled. The gulf between him and dogs in their prime grew so wide that it became necessary to limit the overall landscape. So we did that, and slapped a silly name on it.

My town has a weird, creek-side path about half a mile in length, branching off from the main street. It's part of an old canal system that dwindled and died at the hands of more efficient rail travel. The results are patchwork, makeshift miniature parks dotted across much of northern New Jersey. Most have no playgrounds, no scenery, and no real purpose. And because of that, little to no people.

Which is perfect for a walk that isn't really a walk. For an outing that makes a leisurely stroll seem like an all-out sprint. For a sniff ba-tiff.

A typical sniff ba-tiff excursion unfolds as follows. Vector and I file into my car and drive all of a quarter-mile to the pathway. We get out of the car ... and then Vector does absolutely anything he wants at whatever pace he pleases.

He ambles toward a bush, and a scent catches him. He is immediately consumed, absorbing whatever wonderful information he can process in his still-astute snout. He plods forward, limply, toward a tree. He tries to lift his leg and fails, pinched by arthritic pain. A second, more modest marking attempt succeeds, and my self-satisfied sato slowly moves on.

The walk lasts a solid half-hour. We journey all of a tenth of a mile roundtrip, passed by an octogenarian or two along the way. Sometimes, one looks at me, looks at Vector, then looks back at me with a knowing nod, as if to say "yep, getting old sucks."

This secluded slice of greenery, this not-quite-a-park, is exactly what Vector needs. The vibrancy of a proper park—running children, rambunctious dogs—is too boisterous for him. Its shrieks and barks are alarming to his largely deaf ears, penetrating his muted world to startle him; its distances, however reasonable to able-bodied beings, are too vast for his quickly depleted stamina.

But here, alone in a condensed yet still-verdant setting with just his daddams by his side, Vector's total relaxation is showcased by his complete engrossment in whatever scent tickles his fancy. Removed from the hubbub of more popular settings, Vector is closer to being one with this toned-down, scaled-back environment.

Vector at nearly 13 years: an old dog, a slow stroll, and the long shadow of a life well lived.

Or maybe I'm just imagining things—projecting my feelings to quiet my own fears concerning my beloved companion's mortality. Maybe I just like the narrative of a newfound place of peace, an old dog with a new routine. Maybe it's the satisfaction gained from side-stepping Vector's deterioration for whatever window Father Time permits. Maybe it's what *I* need—a waystation on the potholed road to a bittersweet goodbye.

But of course, life isn't linear, even as it approaches its inevitable conclusion. Even as his ears fail, his eyes cloud with cataracts, and his hips and haunches continue to wither and wilt with painful arthritis, Vector has flashes when the joyful excitement of the moment—the return of a family member, the anticipation of a treatsie (sorry, I meant "tra-ta-tot")—erases any cognizance of these intractable indignities from his mind.

Yipping with glee, he does his turn-in-circles thing then leaps up, back legs be damned. What happens from there is a coin flip: sometimes he lands upright, sometimes his rickety legs give out, no longer capable of serving as landing gear. Regardless, watching Vector forget he is dying inspires both admiration and, admittedly, a certain amount of envy.

Tellingly, those once-reliable doggie greetings have grown less frequent. Often his eyes glimmer and his nub wags, but his balky body won't permit its former exuberance. Sometimes, if Vector is in a different room when I open the front door, he simply doesn't hear me, and whatever low-key cycle of welcome-home happiness doesn't commence until he lays eyes on his unadulterated alpha. It is these instances—ones when Vector greets me from the TV room couch rather than the living room entrance—that the dichotomy between past and present cuts deepest.

Despite this not-so-slow sink toward our irrevocable severance, though, Vector and I are closer now than we've ever been. Taking a nod from Katya Lidsky's relationship with her terminally ill dog, as profiled in Chapter 13, I find myself leaning in with urgency rather than pulling back with a bracing self-preservation.

This says nothing about me, and everything about the beautiful being who survived the very worst of circumstances to bring out the very best in me. Vector has disarmed me throughout his life; his death will find me similarly defenseless. My Katya moment is coming—and Vector's legacy deserves that depth of unguarded grief. As much as I fear it, I cannot cower. My good boy has earned better.

But there's also a far more mundane reason I feel closer to Vector than ever: because I'm literally closer to him more frequently than I've ever been—and because for me, physical proximity carries extra clout.

As we explored in Chapter 2, my eyesight is exponentially worse than the average person's. If we're calling my vision 20/60 corrected (which is generous), I need to be three times as close as a normally-sighted person to see as crisply. If we're calling my vision 20/80 (which, begrudgingly, is probably more precise), I must be four times as close. And though I'm still able to accomplish midrange things like driving and playing baseball with my son, the finer details are lost to me.

How much detail? Who knows. Tragicomically, knowing exactly how much I'm missing would require a functioning set of eyes. I try not to think about all the memory bank photos made less memorable by the foggy lens that captured them.

For me, then, the term "nearest and dearest" takes on a whole new meaning. My most fully enriching encounters—my wife's younger-than-her years features, my son's subtle facial expressions—occur at close range. Like *very* close range. As in across the couch rather than across the room.

For me to get the full picture, I need the level of closeness required for something Vector will never lose the ability to do: cuddle, kiss, and curl up next to his daddams. And as my once-spritely sato gets more lethargic and less mobile, I find myself face-to-face and snout-to-chest with him with unprecedented regularity. By an otherwise cruel twist of medical fate, he is far more complete to me this way. Vector can barely move; I can barely see. And because of that, now more than ever, we are barely separable.

Our routines have adapted to his new normal. Boisterous homecomings have been supplanted by a more subdued but no less special ritual of Vector jumping onto our bed (he typically still has one decent leap in him). There, we enjoy a few minutes of scratches and smooches we've aptly named "reaffirming our love." With jumping back down a far more daunting task—the gravity and weight are too much on Vector's front legs—the cuddlefest concludes with my outstretched arms under his chest and groin, respectively. As I lower him down, my high-pitched forklift beeps complete the obvious analogy to my wife and son's delight.

Often, my next destination is the basement for an evening workout. I carry Vector down the stairs to prevent him from a halting, wincing descent—recognition that he will, now as a decade ago, endure great pain just to be with his daddams.

Sometimes, of course, reality rears its ugly head. Sometimes Vector is too hobbled even for brief walks, and ends up carried back from the shortest of sojourns. Sometimes his legs give out going *up* the stairs—usually an easier endeavor than going down—and he slides down several before regaining his footing. Sometimes he won't even get off the couch to beg for pizza or chicken or Cheerios—a scenario unimaginable even a year ago.

But the most jarring evidence of Vector's decline comes not from my own eyes but through those of others—from the people who've known and loved Vector nearly as long as Patty, Nicholas and I have.

Epilogue

When friends and relatives come to visit, I see their looks of pity. Their facial expressions change for just an instant, from the smiles of hello to the sobering surprise of seeing our diminished dog. The "awws" that once meant "he's so cute" now translate to "he's so old."

They notice, and I notice that they notice. They mean well, of course—a tacit acknowledgment that my family soon will suffer a painful loss. They feel bad, and I feel bad that they feel bad.

As these moments mount, I am tempted to cut through the sad, saturated air—through the tenseness of greetings that quickly become farewells in the making. But what I am compelled to convey isn't comforting or even kind, so I don't say it.

But I will say it here.

My long-simmering rant has little to do with loss. It has everything to do with victory.

Yes, I will be devastated when I wake up one morning and Vector does not, or when we take that final, one-way trip to the vet. And yes, I am certainly pre-mourning the pending passing of an already-elderly companion aging at six or seven times the rate of my human loved ones. The end of the runway is near, and anyone in my position would be bracing for impact.

But that's not about Vector. That's about *me*. That's about *my* feelings, and my wife's, and my son's. And while valid, they aren't the top of the marquee here. They matter, yes, but they don't matter the most.

No, the main attraction is a being relegated to history's trash heap, who survived against mountainous odds to do something very few humans do: realize his full potential. To live a life whose accomplishments would be nearly impossible to surpass given its circumstances. And to pitch damn near a perfect game while doing so.

Vector will leave behind a long, wide, straight trail of love, with several mundane miracles performed along the way. He helped a compromised couple become a content family. He taught his new dad that life need not be defined by traumas, however harsh or haunting, and that recovery against steep odds is all the more satisfying for its unlikelihood. He taught a new brother about emotional toughness, and new (human) parents about both the importance of living in the moment and the value of lasting legacy. And soon, he will teach us that grief means honoring a loved one's memory through action; in this case, by adopting our next four-legged family member from the universe's garbage dump.

And miraculously, he has achieved all this without being cognizant of any of it.

Per the Prologue, I set out to write this book in search of empathy, in search of people whose rescue dogs have performed similar magic against some of life's most vexing problems. I needed to know that I was not crazy—that I was not a lone nut heaping far too much praise upon a 22-pound stray dog. That my experiences with Vector were not entirely unique, and therefore not entirely suspect. I needed to make sure I was a credible witness—a must-have for a nonfiction writer.

My subsequent discussions with folks from all walks of life shot past exoneration and validation into education and fascination. Not only did I find kindred spirits rescued by their rescues, I discovered stories of mutual salvation I never could have imagined. I heard things that, like my connection with Vector, were almost too good to be true. But they are true, with whatever gap of seeming incredulity exemplifying the incredible, often intangible value rescue dogs bring to our lives.

I learned that my special relationship with Vector was far from … well, special. It was not limited to just us. When it comes to rescue dogs, the special Vector and I share is more the norm than the exception.

Our rescue dogs are gritty and cuddly, goofy and knowing, carefree and responsible. They make everything and everyone around them healthier and happier and altogether better. Researching and writing this book has cemented this into my being, turning feelings into facts.

If this book sells just one copy, and that lone copy brings a single stray dog to a loving forever family, that union will have repaid this well-intentioned effort a hundredfold—just as adopting Vector has.

Chapter Notes

Chapter 1

1. Hilary Hanson, "Group Devoted to Puerto Rico's Stray Dogs Is Flying Dozens to Safety," *The Huffington Post*, September 30, 2017 (accessed May 5, 2023), https://www.huffpost.com/entry/dead-dog-beach-hurricane-maria-puerto-rico_n_59cfbadde4b05f005d3482c6.

2. Joe Wallen, "India Has a Brutal Plan to Deal with Its Stray Dogs Problem," *The Telegraph Online*, March 9, 2023 (accessed May 5, 2023), https://www.telegraph.co.uk/global-health/climate-and-people/indias-stray-dog-days-finally/.

3. Javier Balmaceda, "Tax Credit Expansions Expected to Significantly Reduce Poverty in Puerto Rico," *Center on Budget & Policy Priorities*, March 14, 2022 (accessed May 5, 2023), https://www.cbpp.org/blog/tax-credit-expansions-expected-to-significantly-reduce-poverty-in-puerto-rico.

4. Jeffrey Acevedo, "Puerto Ricans Leaving Island for U.S. in Record Numbers," *CNN.com*, May 2, 2016 (accessed May 5, 2023), https://www.cnn.com/2016/05/02/americas/puerto-rico-exodus/index.html.

5. Marielle Segarra, "More Residents are Expected to Flee Puerto Rico, Contributing to the Brain Drain," *Marketplace.org*, September 27, 2017 (accessed May 5, 2023), https://www.marketplace.org/2017/09/27/more-residents-are-expected-flee-puerto-rico-contributing-brain-drain/.

6. Robin Finn, "Operation Paws," *The New York Times Online*, March 24, 2012 (accessed May 5, 2023), https://www.nytimes.com/2012/03/25/nyregion/christina-beckles-boxer-and-dog-rescuer.html.

Chapter 2

1. Irene Keliher, "These Mixed Breed Dogs Each Took a DNA Test. Can You Guess the Results?" *Rover.com* (accessed May 8, 2023), https://www.rover.com/blog/mixed-breed-dogs-took-dna-test-can-guess-results/.

Chapter 3

1. Dana Hedgpeth, "So Many Pets Have Been Adopted During the Pandemic That Shelters Are Running Out," *The Washington Post Online*, January 6, 2021 (accessed May 11, 2023), https://www.washingtonpost.com/dc-md-va/2021/01/06/animal-shelters-coronavirus-pandemic/.

2. "New ASPCA Survey Shows Overwhelming Majority of Dogs and Cats Adopted During the Pandemic Are Still in Their Homes," American Society for the Prevention of Cruelty to Animals—Organization press release, *ASPCA.org*, May 26, 2021 (accessed May 11, 2023), https://www.aspca.org/about-us/press-releases/new-aspca-survey-shows-overwhelming-majority-dogs-and-cats-acquired-during.

3. "Pandemic Pets Are Being Returned to Shelters at Alarming Rates—Or are They?" Animal Humane Society, *AnimalHumaneSociety.org*, August 19, 2021 (accessed May 11, 2023), https://www.animalhumanesociety.org/news/pandemic-pets-are-being-returned-shelters-alarming-rates-or-are-they.

4. Jacob Bogage, "Americans Adopted Millions of Dogs During the Pandemic. Now What Do We Do with Them?" *The Washington Post Online*, January 7, 2022

(accessed May 11, 2023), https://www.washingtonpost.com/business/2022/01/07/covid-dogs-return-to-work/.

5. "Income and Outcome Data Comparison for Q1 of 2021 and 2022," Shelter Animals Count, *ShelterAnimals Count.org*, May 3, 2022 (accessed May 11, 2023), https://www.shelteranimals count.org/intake-andoutcome-data-com parison-for-q1-of-2021-and-2022/.

6. Kelli Bender, "100,000 More Pets in Shelters Now Compared to January 2021 Due to Pandemic, Animal Group Finds," *People Magazine Online*, January 28, 2022 (accessed May 11, 2023), https://people.com/pets/100000-more-pets-waiting-shelters-due-to-pandemic/.

7. Carol Mithers, "Most Americans Have Pets. Almost One Third Can't Afford Their Vet Care," *TalkPoverty.org*, November 12, 2021 (accessed May 11, 2023), https://talkpoverty.org/2021/11/12/low-income-veterinary-care-affordability/.

8. Anthony Johnson, "How Inflation is Causing a Crisis at Some Local Animal Shelters," *ABC7ny.com*, July 28, 2022 (accessed May 11, 2023), https://abc7ny.com/nj-animal-shelters-inflation-pets-pet-food-costs/12080158/.

9. Michelle Megna, "Pet Ownership Statistics 2023," *Forbes.com*, April 10, 2023 (accessed May 11, 2023), https://www.forbes.com/advisor/pet-insurance/pet-ownership-statistics/.

10. Jillian McKoy, "Depression Rates in U.S. Tripled When the Pandemic First Hit—Now, They're Even Worse," *bu.edu* (Boston University), October 7, 2021 (accessed May 11, 2023), https://www.bu.edu/articles/2021/depression-rates-tripled-when-pandemic-first-hit/.

11. "Dr. Sims on Parvo: Everything You Need to Know About Canine Parvovirus," Pembroke Animal Hospital, *pemah.com* (accessed May 11, 2023), https://pemah.com/dr-sims-on-parvo-everything-you-need-to-know-about-canine-parvovirus/.

12. "Which Animals Are Used," American Anti-Vivisection Society, *AAVS.org* (accessed May 11, 2023), https://aavs.org/animals-science/animals-used/dogs/.

13. "Undercover Investigation Reveals Animal Suffering in Toxicology Laboratory," Humane Society—Organization Report, *HumaneSociety.org*, April 2022 (accessed May 11, 2023), https://www.humanesociety.org/sites/default/files/docs/HSUS_Inotiv-Investigation-Report.pdf.

14. Chuck Johnson, "4,000 Beagles Will Be Rescued from a Virginia Breeding Facility," *CNN.com*, July 18, 2022 (accessed May 11, 2023), https://amp.cnn.com/cnn/2022/07/12/us/beagles-virginia-facility-rescue/index.html.

15. "Beagle Freedom Project Rescued 34 Dogs and 7 Cats from a Testing Facility in Oklahoma," Beagle Freedom Project, YouTube [Video], September 29, 2022 (accessed May 11, 2023), https://www.youtube.com/watch?app=desktop&v=xf6TBm3a4qE.

16. Michael Ray, "Sandy Hook Elementary School Shooting," *Encyclopedia Britannica Online*, updated April 24, 2023 (accessed May 11, 2023), https://www.britannica.com/event/Sandy-Hook-Elementary-School-shooting.

17. Thomas Black, "Americans Have More Guns Than Anywhere Else in the World and They Keep Buying More," *Bloomberg.com*, May 25, 2022 (accessed May 11, 2023), https://www.bloomberg.com/news/articles/2022-05-25/how-many-guns-in-the-us-buying-spree-bolsters-lead-as-most-armed-country#xj4y7vzkg.

18. "In Your Own Words: Mental Health on Campus," *The New York Times Online*, February 21, 2019 (accessed May 11, 2023), https://www.nytimes.com/2019/02/21/education/learning/student-responses-mental-health-on-campus.html.

Chapter 4

1. "Who, What, How, and Why" [Pamphlet], Narcotics Anonymous, 1976 (accessed May 14, 2023), https://na.org/admin/include/spaw2/uploads/pdf/litfiles/us_english/IP/EN3101.pdf.

2. Cesar Millan, "Saving the Satos—Stray Dogs," *The Huffington Post*, May 2, 2012 (accessed May 14, 2023), https://www.huffpost.com/entry/saving-the-satos-stray-do_b_1470597?ref=travel.

3. "The Twelve Steps," Alcoholics Anonymous, accessed May 14, 2023, https://www.aa.org/the-twelve-steps.

Chapter 5

1. "COVID Data Tracker," Centers for Disease Control and Prevention, *CDC.gov*, accessed May 19, 2023, https://covid.cdc.gov/COVID-data-tracker/#datatracker-home.
2. Zachary Rogers, "Fentanyl Becomes Leading Cause of Death in Americans Aged 18–45," *KATV.com*, December 17, 2021 (accessed May 19, 2023), https://katv.com/news/nation-world/fentanyl-overdoses-surge-become-leading-cause-of-death-in-americans-aged-18-45-families-against-james-rauh-drug.
3. "Fentanyl," United States Drug Enforcement Administration, *DEA.gov*, accessed May 19, 2023, https://www.dea.gov/factsheets/fentanyl.
4. "Opioid Manufacturer Purdue Pharma Pleads Guilty to Fraud and Kickback Conspiracies," U.S. Department of Justice—Organization press release, *Justice.gov*, November 24, 2020 (accessed May 19, 2023), https://www.justice.gov/opa/pr/opioid-manufacturer-purdue-pharma-pleads-guilty-fraud-and-kickback-conspiracies.
5. "Murphy: 'Fentanyl Is Killing More Young Americans Than COVID-19,'" Office of U.S Congressman Gregory F. Murphy, M.D., *Murphy.House.gov*, February 15, 2022 (accessed May 19, 2023), https://murphy.house.gov/media/press-releases/murphy-fentanyl-killing-more-young-americans-covid-19.
6. "Drug Overdose Death Rates," National Institute on Drug Abuse, *NIDA. NIH.gov*, accessed May 19, 2023, https://nida.nih.gov/research-topics/trends-statistics/overdose-death-rates.
7. "Synthetic Opioid Overdose Data," Centers for Disease Control and Prevention, *CDC.gov*, updated June 6, 2022 (accessed May 19, 2023), https://www.cdc.gov/drugoverdose/deaths/synthetic/index.html.
8. Rhitu Chatterjee, "Overdose Deaths Continued to Rise in 2021, Reaching Historic Highs," *NPR.org*, May 11, 2022 (accessed May 19, 2023), https://www.npr.org/sections/health-shots/2022/05/11/1098314220/overdose-deaths-continued-to-rise-in-2021-reaching-historic-highs.
9. Quinn Owen, "DEA Seized Enough Fentanyl to Kill Every American in 2022," *ABCnews.go.com*, December 20, 2022 (accessed May 19, 2023), https://abcnews.go.com/Politics/dea-seized-fentanyl-kill-american-2022/story?id=95625574.
10. "How Much Do Drugs Cost: The Steep Price of Addiction," Addiction Center, *AddictionCenter.com*, accessed May 19, 2023, https://www.addictioncenter.com/drugs/how-much-do-drugs-cost/.
11. "Music Therapy and Addiction Treatment," American Music Therapy Association, *MusicTherapy.org*, accessed May 19, 2023, https://www.musictherapy.org/assets/1/7/FactSheet_Music_Therapy_and_Addiction_Treatment_2021.pdf.
12. Hayley Cutt, BSc, Billie Giles-Corti, Ph.D., Matthew Knuiman, Ph.D., Anna Timperio, Ph.D., and Fiona Bull, Ph.D., "Understanding Dog Owners' Increased Levels of Physical Activity: Results from RESIDE," National Institutes of Health, January 2008 (accessed May 19, 2023), https://pubmed.ncbi.nlm.nih.gov/18048786/.
13. "Best Pets for Your First Year Sober," *IAmSober.com*, updated December 10, 2021 (accessed May 19, 2023), https://iamsober.com/blog/pets-for-first-year-sober/.
14. Brian Marschhauser, "Mahopac Resident Pleads Guilty to Animal Cruelty," *TapInto.net*, January 8, 2017 (accessed May 19, 2023), https://www.tapinto.net/towns/mahopac/sections/law-and-justice/articles/mahopac-resident-pleads-guilty-to-animal-cruelty.

Chapter 6

1. Erica Cirino, "Understanding Situational Depression," *Healthline.com*, October 3, 2018 (accessed May 23, 2023), https://www.healthline.com/health/depression/situational-depression.
2. "Depression—Overview," World Health Organization, *WHO.int*, accessed May 23, 2023, https://www.who.int/health-topics/depression#tab=tab_1.
3. Maria A. Villarroel, Ph.D., and Emily P. Terlizzi, M.P.H., "Symptoms of Depression Among Adults, United States, 2019," Centers for Disease Control and

Prevention, *CDC.gov*, September 2020 (accessed May 23, 2023), https://www.cdc.gov/nchs/products/databriefs/db379.htm.

4. "Major Depression," National Institute of Mental Health, *NIMH.NIH.gov*, updated January 2022 (accessed May 23, 2023), https://www.nimh.nih.gov/health/statistics/major-depression.

5. "Exercise for Depression," National Health Service, *NHS.uk*, last reviewed September 7, 2022 (accessed May 23, 2023), https://www.nhs.uk/mental-health/self-help/guides-tools-and-activities/exercise-for-depression/.

6. Kara Mayer Robinson; medically reviewed by Brunilda Nazario, M.D., "How Pets Help Manage Depression," *WebMD.com*, December 4, 2017 (accessed May 23, 2023), https://www.webmd.com/depression/features/pets-depression.

7. Ann Robinson, "'Dogs Have a Magic Effect': How Pets Can Improve Our Mental Health," *TheGuardian.com*, March 17, 2020 (accessed May 23, 2023), https://www.theguardian.com/society/2020/mar/17/dogs-have-a-magic-effect-the-power-of-pets-on-our-mental-health.

8. Luke E. Stoeckel, Lori S. Palley, Randy L. Gollub, Steven M. Niemi, and Anne Eden Evins, "Patterns of Brain Activation When Mothers View Their Own Child and Dog: An fMRI Study," *Journals.PLOS.org*, October 3, 2014 (accessed May 23, 2023), https://journals.plos.org/plosone/article?id=10.1371/journal.pone.0107205.

9. Julie Hecht, "Is the Gaze from Those Big Puppy Eyes the Look of Your Doggie's Love?" *ScientificAmerican.com*, April 16, 2015 (accessed May 23, 2023), https://www.scientificamerican.com/article/is-the-gaze-from-those-big-puppy-eyes-the-look-of-your-doggie-s-love/.

10. Brandon Keim, "Antidepressants May Thwart Quest for True Love," *Wired.com*, February 25, 2009 (accessed May 23, 2023), https://www.wired.com/2009/02/antidepressants/.

Chapter 7

1. "Cyclothymia (cyclothymic disorder)," Mayo Clinic, *MayoClinic.org*, updated December 13, 2022 (accessed May 28, 2023), https://www.mayoclinic.org/diseases-conditions/cyclothymia/symptoms-causes/syc-20371275.

2. Stefan Ellerbeck, "Half of U.S. Teens Use the Internet 'Almost Constantly.' But Where Are They Spending Their Time Online?" World Economic Forum, *WEForum.org*, August 30, 2022 (accessed May 28, 2023), https://www.weforum.org/agenda/2022/08/social-media-internet-online-teenagers-screens-us/.

3. "Social Media's Effects on Self-Esteem," Social Media Victims Law Center, *SocialMediaLawVictims.org*, updated May 17, 2023 (accessed May 28, 2023), https://socialmediavictims.org/mental-health/self-esteem/.

4. Matt Richtel, Catherine Pearson, and Michael Levenson, "Surgeon General Warns That Social Media May Harm Children and Adolescents," *The New York Times Online*, May 24, 2023 (accessed May 28, 2023), https://www.nytimes.com/2023/05/23/health/surgeon-general-social-media-mental-health.html?smid=nytcore-ios-share&referringSource=articleShare.

5. Ryan Llera, BSc DVM, and Lynn Buzhardt, DVM, "How Dogs Use Smell to Perceive the World," VCA Animal Hospitals, *VCAHospitals.com*, accessed May 28, 2023, https://vcahospitals.com/know-your-pet/how-dogs-use-smell-to-perceive-the-world.

6. Jan Reisen, "The Nose Knows: Is There Anything Like a Dog's Nose?" American Kennel Club, *AKC.org*, July 21, 2020 (accessed May 28, 2023), https://www.akc.org/expert-advice/news/the-nose-knows/.

7. Mia Rozenbaum, "The Science of Sniffs: Disease Smelling Dogs," *UnderstandingAnimalResearch.org.uk*, June 19, 2020 (accessed May 28, 2023), https://www.understandinganimalresearch.org.uk/news/the-science-of-sniffs-disease-smelling-dogs.

8. Emily Willingham, "Dogs Detect the Scent of Seizures," *Scientific American.com*, March 28, 2019 (accessed May 28, 2023), https://www.scientificamerican.com/article/dogs-detect-the-scent-of-seizures/.

9. "Anxiety Disorders: Facts & Statistics," Anxiety & Depression Association of America, *ADAA.org*, accessed May 28, 2023, https://adaa.org/understanding-anxiety/facts-statistics.

10. Linda Cole, "Can Dogs Sense Bipolar Disorder?" *WagWalking.com*, April 10, 2018 (accessed May 28, 2023), https://wagwalking.com/sense/can-dogs-sense-bipolar-disorder.

11. Carin Meyer, "My Dog Alerts Me to My Bipolar 'Cycling,'" *BPHope.com*, November 8, 2018 (accessed May 28, 2023), https://www.bphope.com/pets/how-my-dog-senses-my-mental-health-struggles-before-i-do-and-provides-invaluable-comfort/.

12. Mengjie Deng, Shuyi Zhai, Xuan Ouyang, Zhening Liu, and Brendan Ross, "Factors Influencing Medication Adherence Among Patients with Severe Mental Disorders from the Perspective of Mental Health Professionals," BMC Psychiatry, *BMCPsychiatry.Biomed Central.com*, January 7, 2022 (accessed May 28, 2023), https://bmcpsychiatry.biomedcentral.com/articles/10.1186/s12888-021-03681-6.

Chapter 8

1. Saya Des Marais, MSW, "Marriage After Sobriety: What to Expect," *PsychCentral.com*, updated January 23, 2023 (accessed June 6, 2023), https://psychcentral.com/relationships/marriage-after-sobriety.

Chapter 9

1. "Pet Statistics," American Society for the Prevention of Cruelty to Animals, *ASPCA.org*, accessed June 14, 2023, https://www.aspca.org/helping-people-pets/shelter-intake-and-surrender/pet-statistics.

2. "Countries with the Most Dogs Worldwide," *WorldAtlas.com*, accessed June 14, 2023, https://www.worldatlas.com/articles/countries-with-the-most-dogs-worldwide.html.

Chapter 10

1. Pamela Paresky and Samuel Abrams, "An 'Us' vs. 'Them' Mentality on Campuses Turns Potential Friends into Allies—or Enemies," *The Boston Globe Online*, September 26, 2022 (accessed June 19, 2023), https://www.bostonglobe.com/2022/09/26/opinion/an-us-vs-them-mentality-campuses-turns-potential-friends-into-allies-or-enemies/.

2. Tim Shirk, "What Is Grit, Why Is It Important & How Can We Develop It?" *SchoolRubric.com*, April 5, 2020 (accessed June 19, 2023), https://schoolrubric.com/what-is-grit-why-is-it-important-how-can-we-develop-it/.

3. Holden Walter-Warner, "University of Michigan Is Blasted as 'Parochial and Moronic' After 'Woke' IT Task Force Bans Words Like 'Picnic,'" *The Daily Mail Online*, December 24, 2020 (accessed June 19, 2023), https://www.dailymail.co.uk/news/article-9085007/University-Michigan-task-force-claims-words-picnic-brown-bag-blacklist-offensive.html.

4. Bernadette Hogan, Carl Campanile, and Bruce Golding, "Brandeis Warns Students Not to Say 'Picnic,' 'Rule of Thumb,' Calling Words 'Oppressive,'" *New York Post Online*, June 24, 2021 (accessed June 19, 2023), https://nypost.com/2021/06/24/brandeis-warns-students-not-to-say-picnic-rule-of-thumb/.

5. "Fact Check: The Word 'Picnic' Does Not Originate from Racist Lynchings," *Reuters*, July 13, 2020 (accessed June 19, 2023), https://www.reuters.com/article/uk-factcheck-picnic-origin-lynchings/fact-check-the-word-picnic-does-not-originate-from-racist-lynchings-idUSKCN24E21V.

6. John McWhorter, "Even 'Trigger Warning' Is Now Off-limits," *The Atlantic Online*, July 4, 2021 (accessed June 19, 2023), https://www.theatlantic.com/ideas/archive/2021/07/brandeis-language-police-have-suggestions-you/619347/.

Chapter 11

1. Peg Streep, "6 Things You Need to Know About Empathy," *PsychologyToday.com*, January 23, 2017 (accessed June 25, 2023), https://www.psychologytoday.com/us/blog/tech-support/201701/6-things-you-need-know-about-empathy.

2. "Fostering a Dog—Foster Fail?" *RescueDogs101.com*, accessed June 25, 2023, https://www.rescuedogs101.com/fostering-a-dog-foster-fail/.

3. "The Atlantic," All Sides Media Bias, *AllSides.com*, accessed June 25, 2023, https://www.allsides.com/news-source/atlantic.

4. Jonathan Haidt and Greg Lukianoff, "The Coddling of the American Mind," *The Atlantic Magazine Online*, September 2015 (accessed June 25, 2023), https://www.theatlantic.com/magazine/archive/2015/09/the-coddling-of-the-american-mind/399356/.

5. "President Obama: College Students Shouldn't Be 'Coddled and Protected from Different Points of View,'" Foundation for Individual Rights and Expression, *TheFIRE.org*, September 15, 2015 (accessed June 25, 2023), https://www.thefire.org/news/president-obama-college-students-shouldnt-be-coddled-and-protected-different-points-view.

6. Jonathan Haidt and Greg Lukianoff, *The Coddling of the American Mind: How Good Intentions and Bad Ideas Are Setting Up a Generation for Failure* (New York: Penguin, 2018), https://www.penguinrandomhouse.com/books/557315/the-coddling-of-the-american-mind-by-greg-lukianoff-and-jonathan-haidt/.

7. Ronald K.L. Collins, "New Report: What Students Think About Expression at American Colleges," Middle Tennessee State University, *MTSU.edu*, October 11, 2017 (accessed June 25, 2023), https://www.mtsu.edu/first-amendment/post/63/new-report-what-students-think-about-expression-at-american-colleges.

8. "College Student Views on Free Expression and Campus Speech 2022," Knight Foundation, *KnightFoundation.org*, January 25, 2022 (accessed June 25, 2023), https://knightfoundation.org/reports/college-student-views-on-free-expression-and-campus-speech-2022/.

Chapter 12

1. Douglas F. Levinson, M.D., and Walter E. Nicholas, M.D., "Major Depression and Genetics," Stanford Medicine, *Stanford.edu*, accessed June 30, 2023, https://med.stanford.edu/depressiongenetics/mddandgenes.html.

2. Stuart Heritage, "Ricky Gervais Calls After Life the Best Thing He's Done. This Is Patently False." *TheGuardian.com*, March 11, 2019 (accessed June 30, 2023), https://www.theguardian.com/tv-and-radio/2019/mar/11/ricky-gervais-calls-after-life-the-best-thing-hes-done-this-is-patently-false.

3. Ricky Gervais [@rickygervais], "One of the main themes of AfterLife is that a dog can save your life. This is ramped up in season 3 & she becomes as important as any other character," Twitter post, August 13, 2021, 5:55 a.m., https://twitter.com/rickygervais/status/1426120172096606210?lang=en.

4. Lynn Gibbs, "After Life: 10 Moments Tony's Dog Stole the Show in Season 1," *ScreenRant.com*, January 23, 2020 (accessed June 30, 2023), https://screenrant.com/after-life-brandy-dog-season-1-best-scenes/.

Chapter 13

1. Katya Lidsky, "Recent Publications," *KatyaLidsky.com*, accessed July 3, 2023, https://www.katyalidsky.com/writing.

2. Katya Lidsky, "Join Our Senior Pet Support Group," *KatyaLidsky.com*, accessed July 3, 2023, https://www.katyalidsky.com/senior-support.

3. "Dr. Sims on Parvo: Everything You Need to Know About Canine Parvovirus," Pembroke Animal Hospital, *pemah.com*, accessed May 11, 2023, https://pemah.com/dr-sims-on-parvo-everything-you-need-to-know-about-canine-parvovirus/.

4. Katya Lidsky, "The Case for Codependency … with a Rescue Dog," *TheFix.com* (defunct), March 8, 2022, link unavailable.

5. Katya Lidsky, "Ophelia, I Feel Ya" [blog series], *KatyaLidsky.com*, updated January 26, 2022 (accessed July 3, 2023), https://www.katyalidsky.com/letters-to-my-dog.

Bibliography

Abrams, Samuel, and Pamela Paresky. "An 'Us' vs. 'Them' Mentality on Campuses Turns Potential Friends into Allies—or Enemies." *The Boston Globe Online*. September 26, 2022 (accessed June 19, 2023). https://www.bostonglobe.com/2022/09/26/opinion/an-us-vs-them-mentality-campuses-turns-potential-friends-into-allies-or-enemies/.

Acevedo, Jeffrey. "Puerto Ricans Leaving Island for U.S. in Record Numbers." *CNN.com*. May 2, 2016 (accessed May 5, 2023). https://www.cnn.com/2016/05/02/americas/puerto-rico-exodus/index.html.

Addiction Center. "How Much Do Drugs Cost: The Steep Price of Addiction." *AddictionCenter.com*. Accessed May 19, 2023. https://www.addictioncenter.com/drugs/how-much-do-drugs-cost/.

Alcoholics Anonymous (Fourth Edition). Alcoholics Anonymous World Services, Inc. 2002.

Alcoholics Anonymous. "The Twelve Steps." Accessed May 14, 2023. https://www.aa.org/the-twelve-steps.

American Anti-Vivisection Society. "Which Animals are Used." *AAVS.org*. Accessed May 11, 2023. https://aavs.org/animals-science/animals-used/dogs/.

American Music Therapy Association. "Music Therapy and Addiction Treatment." *MusicTherapy.org*. Accessed May 19, 2023. https://www.musictherapy.org/assets/1/7/FactSheet_Music_Therapy_and_Addiction_Treatment_2021.pdf.

American Society for the Prevention of Cruelty to Animals. "New ASPCA Survey Shows Overwhelming Majority of Dogs and Cats Adopted During the Pandemic Are Still in Their Homes." Organization press release. *ASPCA.org*. May 26, 2021 (accessed May 11, 2023). https://www.aspca.org/about-us/press-releases/new-aspca-survey-shows-overwhelming-majority-dogs-and-cats-acquired-during.

American Society for the Prevention of Cruelty to Animals. "Pet Statistics." *ASPCA.org*. Accessed June 14, 2023. https://www.aspca.org/helping-people-pets/shelter-intake-and-surrender/pet-statistics.

Animal Humane Society. "Pandemic Pets Are Being Returned to Shelters at Alarming Rates—Or Are They?" *AnimalHumaneSociety.org*. August 19, 2021 (accessed May 11, 2023). https://www.animalhumanesociety.org/news/pandemic-pets-are-being-returned-shelters-alarming-rates-or-are-they.

Anxiety & Depression Association of America. "Anxiety Disorders: Facts & Statistics." *ADAA.org*. Accessed May 28, 2023. https://adaa.org/understanding-anxiety/facts-statistics.

Balmaceda, Javier. "Tax Credit Expansions Expected to Significantly Reduce Poverty in Puerto Rico." *Center on Budget & Policy Priorities*. March 14, 2022 (accessed May 5, 2023). https://www.cbpp.org/blog/tax-credit-expansions-expected-to-significantly-reduce-poverty-in-puerto-rico.

Barton, Julie. *Dog Medicine: How My Dog Saved Me from Myself*. Think Piece Publishing. 2015.

Beagle Freedom Project. "Beagle Freedom Project Rescued 34 Dogs and 7 Cats from a

Testing Facility in Oklahoma." YouTube [Video]. 00:59. September 29, 2022 (accessed May 11, 2023). https://www.youtube.com/watch?app=desktop&v=xf6TBm3a4qE.

Bender, Kelli. "100,000 More Pets in Shelters Now Compared to January 2021 Due to Pandemic, Animal Group Finds." *People Magazine Online.* January 28, 2022 (accessed May 11, 2023). https://people.com/pets/100000-more-pets-waiting-shelters-due-to-pandemic/.

"Best Pets for Your First Year Sober." *IAmSober.com.* Updated December 10, 2021 (accessed May 19, 2023). https://iamsober.com/blog/pets-for-first-year-sober/.

Black, Thomas. "Americans Have More Guns Than Anywhere Else in the World and They Keep Buying More." *Bloomberg.com.* May 25, 2022 (accessed May 11, 2023). https://www.bloomberg.com/news/articles/2022-05-25/how-many-guns-in-the-us-buying-spree-bolsters-lead-as-most-armed-country#xj4y7vzkg.

Bogage, Jacob. "Americans Adopted Millions of Dogs During the Pandemic. Now What Do We Do with Them?" *The Washington Post Online.* January 7, 2022 (accessed May 11, 2023). https://www.washingtonpost.com/business/2022/01/07/covid-dogs-return-to-work/.

Campanile, Carl, Bruce Golding, and Bernadette Hogan. "Brandeis Warns Students Not to Say 'Picnic,' 'Rule of Thumb,' Calling Words 'Oppressive.'" *New York Post Online.* June 24, 2021 (accessed June 19, 2023). https://nypost.com/2021/06/24/brandeis-warns-students-not-to-say-picnic-rule-of-thumb/.

Centers for Disease Control and Prevention. "COVID Data Tracker." *CDC.gov.* Accessed May 19, 2023. https://covid.cdc.gov/COVID-data-tracker/#datatracker-home.

Centers for Disease Control and Prevention. "Synthetic Opioid Overdose Data." *CDC.gov.* Updated June 6, 2022 (accessed May 19, 2023). https://www.cdc.gov/drugoverdose/deaths/synthetic/index.html.

Chatterjee, Rhitu. "Overdose Deaths Continued to Rise in 2021, Reaching Historic Highs." *NPR.org.* May 11, 2022 (accessed May 19, 2023). https://www.npr.org/sections/health-shots/2022/05/11/1098314220/overdose-deaths-continued-to-rise-in-2021-reaching-historic-highs.

Cole, Linda. "Can Dogs Sense Bipolar Disorder?" *WagWalking.com.* April 10, 2018 (accessed May 28, 2023). https://wagwalking.com/sense/can-dogs-sense-bipolar-disorder.

Collins, Ronald K.L. "New Report: What Students Think About Expression at American Colleges." Middle Tennessee State University. *MTSU.edu.* October 11, 2017 (accessed June 25, 2023). https://www.mtsu.edu/first-amendment/post/63/new-report-what-students-think-about-expression-at-american-colleges.

Cutt, Hayley, BSc, Billie Giles-Corti, Ph.D., Matthew Knuiman, Ph.D., and Anna Timperio, Ph.D., and Fiona Bull, Ph.D. "Understanding Dog Owners' Increased Levels of Physical Activity: Results from RESIDE." National Institutes of Health. January 2008 (accessed May 19, 2023). https://pubmed.ncbi.nlm.nih.gov/18048786/.

Dale, Christopher. *Better Halves: Rebuilding a Post-Addiction Marriage.* Thornapple Press. 2022.

Deng, Mengjie, Zhening Liu, Xuan Ouyang, Brendan Ross, and Shuyi Zhai. "Factors Influencing Medication Adherence Among Patients with Severe Mental Disorders from the Perspective of Mental Health Professionals." BMC Psychiatry. *BMCPsychiatry.BiomedCentral.com.* January 7, 2022 (accessed May 28, 2023). https://bmcpsychiatry.biomedcentral.com/articles/10.1186/s12888-021-03681-6.

Des Marais, Saya, MSW. "Marriage After Sobriety: What to Expect." *PsychCentral.com.* Updated January 23, 2023 (accessed June 6, 2023). https://psychcentral.com/relationships/marriage-after-sobriety.

Ellerbeck, Stefan. "Half of US Teens Use the Internet 'Almost Constantly.' But Where Are They Spending Their Time Online?" World Economic Forum. *WEForum.org.* August 30, 2022 (accessed May 28, 2023). https://www.weforum.org/agenda/2022/08/social-media-internet-online-teenagers-screens-us/.

Evins, Anne Eden, Randy L. Gollub, Steven M. Niemi, Lori S. Palley, and Luke E. Stoeckel. "Patterns of Brain Activation when Mothers View Their Own Child and Dog: An fMRI Study." *Journals.PLOS.org.* October 3, 2014 (accessed May 23, 2023). https://journals.plos.org/plosone/article?id=10.1371/journal.pone.0107205.

"Fact Check: The Word 'Picnic' Does Not Originate from Racist Lynchings." *Reuters.* July

13, 2020 (accessed June 19, 2023). https://www.reuters.com/article/uk-factcheck-picnic-origin-lynchings/fact-check-the-word-picnic-does-not-originate-from-racist-lynchings-idUSKCN24E21V.

Finn, Robin. "Operation Paws." *The New York Times Online*. March 24, 2012 (accessed May 5, 2023). https://www.nytimes.com/2012/03/25/nyregion/christina-beckles-boxer-and-dog-rescuer.html.

Foundation for Individual Rights and Expression. "President Obama: College Students Shouldn't Be 'Coddled and Protected from Different Points of View.'" *TheFIRE.org*. September 15, 2015 (accessed June 25, 2023). https://www.thefire.org/news/president-obama-college-students-shouldnt-be-coddled-and-protected-different-points-view.

Foundation for Individual Rights and Expression/RealClearEducation. "2021 College Free Speech Rankings." *Reports.CollegePulse.com*. Accessed June 19, 2023. https://reports.collegepulse.com/college-free-speech-rankings-2021.

Gervais, Ricky, dir. *After Life*. 2019–2022 (3 seasons). Netflix. https://www.netflix.com/search?q=After%20Life&jbv=80998491.

Gervais, Ricky. [@rickygervais], "One of the main themes of AfterLife is that a dog can save your life. This is ramped up in season 3 & she becomes as important as any other character." Twitter post, August 13, 2021, 5:55am, https://twitter.com/rickygervais/status/1426120172096606210?lang=en.

Gibbs, Lynn. "After Life: 10 Moments Tony's Dog Stole the Show in Season 1." *ScreenRant.com*. January 23, 2020 (accessed June 30, 2023). https://screenrant.com/after-life-brandy-dog-season-1-best-scenes/.

Haidt, Jonathan, and Greg Lukianoff. *The Coddling of the American Mind: How Good Intentions and Bad Ideas Are Setting Up a Generation for Failure*. Penguin. 2018.

Haidt, Jonathan, and Greg Lukianoff. "The Coddling of the American Mind." *The Atlantic Magazine Online*. September 2015 (accessed June 25, 2023). https://www.theatlantic.com/magazine/archive/2015/09/the-coddling-of-the-american-mind/399356/.

Hampton, Ryan. *American Fix: Inside the Opioid Addiction Crisis—and How to End It*. All Points Books. 2018.

Hanson, Hilary. "Group Devoted to Puerto Rico's Stray Dogs Is Flying Dozens to Safety." *The Huffington Post*. September 30, 2017 (accessed May 5, 2023). https://www.huffpost.com/entry/dead-dog-beach-hurricane-maria-puerto-rico_n_59cfbadde4b05f005d3482c6.

Hecht, Julie. "Is the Gaze from Those Big Puppy Eyes the Look of Your Doggie's Love?" *ScientificAmerican.com*. April 16, 2015 (accessed May 23, 2023). https://www.scientificamerican.com/article/is-the-gaze-from-those-big-puppy-eyes-the-look-of-your-doggie-s-love/.

Hedgpeth, Dana. "So Many Pets Have Been Adopted During the Pandemic That Shelters Are Running Out." *The Washington Post Online*. January 6, 2021 (accessed May 11, 2023). https://www.washingtonpost.com/dc-md-va/2021/01/06/animal-shelters-coronavirus-pandemic/.

Heritage, Stuart. "Ricky Gervais Calls After Life the Best Thing He's Done. This Is Patently False." *TheGuardian.com*. March 11, 2019 (accessed June 30, 2023). https://www.theguardian.com/tv-and-radio/2019/mar/11/ricky-gervais-calls-after-life-the-best-thing-hes-done-this-is-patently-false.

Heterodox Academy. "Campus Expression Survey." *HeterodoxyAcademy.org*. March 2022 (accessed June 19, 2023). https://heterodoxacademy.org/wp-content/uploads/2022/02/CES-Report-2022-FINAL.pdf.

Humane Society. "Undercover Investigation Reveals Animal Suffering in Toxicology Laboratory." Organization Report. *HumaneSociety.org*. April 2022 (accessed May 11, 2023). https://www.humanesociety.org/sites/default/files/docs/HSUS_Inotiv-Investigation-Report.pdf.

"In Your Own Words: Mental Health on Campus." *The New York Times Online*. February 21, 2019 (accessed May 11, 2023). https://www.nytimes.com/2019/02/21/education/learning/student-responses-mental-health-on-campus.html.

Johnson, Anthony. "How Inflation Is Causing a Crisis at Some Local Animal Shelters."

Bibliography

ABC7ny.com. July 28, 2022 (accessed May 11, 2023). https://abc7ny.com/nj-animal-shelters-inflation-pets-pet-food-costs/12080158/.

Johnson, Chuck. "4,000 Beagles Will Be Rescued from a Virginia Breeding Facility." *CNN.com*. July 18, 2022 (accessed M ay 11, 2023). https://amp.cnn.com/cnn/2022/07/12/us/beagles-virginia-facility-rescue/index.html.

Keim, Brandon. "Antidepressants May Thwart Quest for True Love." *Wired.com*. February 25, 2009 (accessed May 23, 2023). https://www.wired.com/2009/02/antidepressants/.

Keliher, Irene. "These Mixed Breed Dogs Each Took a DNA Test. Can You Guess the Results?" *Rover.com*. Accessed May 8, 2023. https://www.rover.com/blog/mixed-breed-dogs-took-dna-test-can-guess-results/.

Knight Foundation. "College Student Views on Free Expression and Campus Speech 2022." *KnightFoundation.org*. January 25, 2022 (accessed June 25, 2023). https://knightfoundation.org/reports/college-student-views-on-free-expression-and-campus-speech-2022/.

Lancer, Darlene. *Codependency for Dummies*. For Dummies Publishing. 2015.

L.E.A.D. "Let's Empower, Advocate, and Do!" Accessed May 11, 2023. https://www.leadnow.org/.

Levenson, Michael, Catherine Pearson, and Matt Richtel. "Surgeon General Warns That Social Media May Harm Children and Adolescents." *The New York Times Online*. May 24, 2023 (accessed May 28, 2023). https://www.nytimes.com/2023/05/23/health/surgeon-general-social-media-mental-health.html?smid=nytcore-ios-share&referringSource=articleShare.

Levinson, Douglas F., M.D., and Walter E. Nicholas, M.D. "Major Depression and Genetics." Stanford Medicine. *Stanford.edu*. Accessed June 30, 2023. https://med.stanford.edu/depressiongenetics/mddandgenes.html.

Lidsky, Katya. "The Case for Codependency… with a Rescue Dog." *TheFix.com* (defunct). March 8, 2022. Link unavailable.

Lidsky, Katya. *KatyaLidsky.com* (blog/professional catalogue). Accessed July 2023.

Llera, Ryan, BSc, DVM, and Lynn Buzhardt, DVM. "How Dogs Use Smell to Perceive the World." VCA Animal Hospitals. *VCAHospitals.com*. Accessed May 28, 2023. https://vcahospitals.com/know-your-pet/how-dogs-use-smell-to-perceive-the-world.

Marschhauser, Brian. "Mahopac Resident Pleads Guilty to Animal Cruelty." *TapInto.net*. January 8, 2017 (accessed May 19, 2023). https://www.tapinto.net/towns/mahopac/sections/law-and-justice/articles/mahopac-resident-pleads-guilty-to-animal-cruelty.

Mayo Clinic. "Cyclothymia (cyclothymic disorder)." *MayoClinic.org*. Updated December 13, 2022 (accessed May 28, 2023). https://www.mayoclinic.org/diseases-conditions/cyclothymia/symptoms-causes/syc-20371275.

McKoy, Jillian. "Depression Rates in US Tripled When the Pandemic First Hit—Now, They're Even Worse." *bu.edu* (Boston University). October 7, 2021 (accessed May 11, 2023). https://www.bu.edu/articles/2021/depression-rates-tripled-when-pandemic-first-hit/.

McWhorter, John. "Even 'Trigger Warning' Is Now Off-limits." *The Atlantic Online*. July 4, 2021 (accessed June 19, 2023). https://www.theatlantic.com/ideas/archive/2021/07/brandeis-language-police-have-suggestions-you/619347/.

Megna, Michelle. "Pet Ownership Statistics 2023." *Forbes.com*. April 10, 2023 (accessed May 11, 2023). https://www.forbes.com/advisor/pet-insurance/pet-ownership-statistics/.

Meyer, Carin. "My Dog Alerts Me to My Bipolar 'Cycling.'" *BPHope.com*. November 8, 2018 (accessed May 28, 2023). https://www.bphope.com/pets/how-my-dog-senses-my-mental-health-struggles-before-i-do-and-provides-invaluable-comfort/.

Millan, Cesar. "Saving the Satos—Stray Dogs." *The Huffington Post*. May 2, 2012 (accessed May 14, 2023). https://www.huffpost.com/entry/saving-the-satos-stray-do_b_1470597?ref=travel.

Mithers, Carol. "Most Americans Have Pets. Almost One Third Can't Afford Their Vet Care." *TalkPoverty.org*. November 12, 2021 (accessed May 11, 2023). https://talkpoverty.org/2021/11/12/low-income-veterinary-care-affordability/.

Narcotics Anonymous. "Who, What, How, and Why." Pamphlet. 1976 (accessed May 14, 2023). https://na.org/admin/include/spaw2/uploads/pdf/litfiles/us_english/IP/EN3101.pdf.

National Health Service. "Exercise for Depression." *NHS.uk*. Last reviewed September 7, 2022 (accessed May 23, 2023). https://www.nhs.uk/mental-health/self-help/guides-tools-and-activities/exercise-for-depression/.

National Institute of Mental Health. "Major Depression." *NIMH.NIH.gov*. Updated January 2022 (accessed May 23, 2023). https://www.nimh.nih.gov/health/statistics/major-depression.

National Institute on Drug Abuse. "Drug Overdose Death Rates." *NIDA.NIH.gov*. Accessed May 19, 2023. https://nida.nih.gov/research-topics/trends-statistics/overdose-death-rates.

Office of U.S Congressman Gregory F. Murphy, M.D. "Murphy: 'Fentanyl Is Killing More Young Americans Than COVID-19.'" *Murphy.House.gov*. February 15, 2022 (accessed May 19, 2023). https://murphy.house.gov/media/press-releases/murphy-fentanyl-killing-more-young-americans-covid-19.

Owen, Quinn. "DEA Seized Enough Fentanyl to Kill Every American in 2022." *ABCnews.go.com*. December 20, 2022 (accessed May 19, 2023). https://abcnews.go.com/Politics/dea-seized-fentanyl-kill-american-2022/story?id=95625574.

Pembroke Animal Hospital. "Dr. Sims on Parvo: Everything You Need to Know About Canine Parvovirus." *pemah.com*. Accessed May 11, 2023. https://pemah.com/dr-sims-on-parvo-everything-you-need-to-know-about-canine-parvovirus/.

Ray, Michael. "Sandy Hook Elementary School Shooting." *Encyclopedia Britannica Online*. Updated April 24, 2023 (accessed May 11, 2023). https://www.britannica.com/event/Sandy-Hook-Elementary-School-shooting.

Reisen, Jan. "The Nose Knows: Is There Anything Like a Dog's Nose?" American Kennel Club. *AKC.org*. July 21, 2020 (accessed May 28, 2023). https://www.akc.org/expert-advice/news/the-nose-knows/.

"Rescue and Rehabilitation." *The Sato Project*. Accessed May 3, 2023. https://thesatoproject.org/rescue-rehabilitation.

Rescue Dogs 101. "Fostering a Dog—Foster Fail?" *RescueDogs101.com*. Accessed June 25, 2023. https://www.rescuedogs101.com/fostering-a-dog-foster-fail/.

Robinson, Ann. "'Dogs Have a Magic Effect': How Pets Can Improve Our Mental Health." *TheGuardian.com*. March 17, 2020 (accessed May 23, 2023). https://www.theguardian.com/society/2020/mar/17/dogs-have-a-magic-effect-the-power-of-pets-on-our-mental-health.

Robinson, Kara Mayer (medically reviewed by Brunilda Nazario, M.D.). "How Pets Help Manage Depression." *WebMD.com*. December 4, 2017 (accessed May 23, 2023). https://www.webmd.com/depression/features/pets-depression.

Rogers, Zachary. "Fentanyl Becomes Leading Cause of Death in Americans Aged 18–45." *KATV.com*. December 17, 2021 (accessed May 19, 2023). https://katv.com/news/nation-world/fentanyl-overdoses-surge-become-leading-cause-of-death-in-americans-aged-18-45-families-against-james-rauh-drug.

Rozenbaum, Mia. "The Science of Sniffs: Disease Smelling Dogs." *UnderstandingAnimalResearch.org.uk*. June 19, 2020 (accessed May 28, 2023). https://www.understandinganimalresearch.org.uk/news/the-science-of-sniffs-disease-smelling-dogs.

The Sato Project. "10 Years Since the *New York Times* Put a Spotlight on the Sato Project." March 2022 Newsletter. March 25, 2022.

Segarra, Marielle. "More Residents Are Expected to Flee Puerto Rico, Contributing to the Brain Drain." *Marketplace.org*. September 27, 2017 (accessed May 5, 2023). https://www.marketplace.org/2017/09/27/more-residents-are-expected-flee-puerto-rico-contributing-brain-drain/.

Shelter Animals Count. "Income and Outcome Data Comparison for Q1 of 2021 and 2022." *ShelterAnimalsCount.org*. May 3, 2022 (accessed May 11, 2023). https://www.shelteranimalscount.org/intake-and-outcome-data-comparison-for-q1-of-2021-and-2022/.

Shirk, Tim. "What Is Grit, Why Is It Important & How Can We Develop It?" *SchoolRubric.com*. April 5, 2020 (accessed June 19, 2023). https://schoolrubric.com/what-is-grit-why-is-it-important-how-can-we-develop-it/.

Social Media Victims Law Center. "Social Media's Effects on Self-Esteem." *Social*

MediaLawVictims.org. Updated May 17, 2023 (accessed May 28, 2023). https://socialmediavictims.org/mental-health/self-esteem/.

Sophie Gamand Photography. "Dead Dog Beach (2011–2013)." Accessed May 3, 2023. https://www.sophiegamand.com/deaddogbeach.

Streep, Peg. "6 Things You Need to Know About Empathy." *PsychologyToday.com.* January 23, 2017 (accessed June 25, 2023). https://www.psychologytoday.com/us/blog/tech-support/201701/6-things-you-need-know-about-empathy.

Terlizzi, Emily P., M.P.H., and Maria A. Villarroel, Ph.D. "Symptoms of Depression Among Adults, United States, 2019." Centers for Disease Control and Prevention. *CDC.gov.* September 2020 (accessed May 23, 2023). https://www.cdc.gov/nchs/products/databriefs/db379.htm.

U.S. Department of Justice. "Opioid Manufacturer Purdue Pharma Pleads Guilty to Fraud and Kickback Conspiracies." Organization press release. *Justice.gov.* November 24, 2020 (accessed May 19, 2023). https://www.justice.gov/opa/pr/opioid-manufacturer-purdue-pharma-pleads-guilty-fraud-and-kickback-conspiracies.

United States Drug Enforcement Administration. "Fentanyl." *DEA.gov.* Accessed May 19, 2023. https://www.dea.gov/factsheets/fentanyl.

Wallen, Joe. "India Has a Brutal Plan to Deal with Its Stray Dogs Problem." *The Telegraph Online.* March 9, 2023 (accessed May 5, 2023). https://www.telegraph.co.uk/global-health/climate-and-people/indias-stray-dog-days-finally/.

Walter-Warner, Holden. "University of Michigan Is Blasted as 'Parochial and Moronic' After 'Woke' IT Task Force Bans Words Like 'Picnic.'" *The Daily Mail Online.* December 24, 2020 (accessed June 19, 2023). https://www.dailymail.co.uk/news/article-9085007/University-Michigan-task-force-claims-words-picnic-brown-bag-blacklist-offensive.html.

Willingham, Emily. "Dogs Detect the Scent of Seizures." *ScientificAmerican.com.* March 28, 2019 (accessed May 28, 2023). https://www.scientificamerican.com/article/dogs-detect-the-scent-of-seizures/.

World Atlas. "Countries with the Most Dogs Worldwide." *WorldAtlas.com.* Accessed June 14, 2023. https://www.worldatlas.com/articles/countries-with-the-most-dogs-worldwide.html.

World Health Organization. "Depression—Overview." *WHO.int.* Accessed May 23, 2023. https://www.who.int/health-topics/depression#tab=tab_1.

Index

Numbers in ***bold italics*** indicate pages with illustrations

Abrams, Samuel 143
After Life (television show) 173-176
Aguadilla, Puerto Rico 123
Airplane! (film) 16
Al-Anon 115
Alcoholics Anonymous/AA (organization) 20, 58-59, 62-64, 68, 75, 79, 81, 93, 115
AllSides Media Bias 158
Altman, Bambi (dog) 47-49, 51-52, ***53***, 54
Altman, Daisy (dog) ***54***, 55
Altman, Kyrah 47-55, ***53***
Altman, Ollie (dog) 52-53, ***54***, 55
American Breeders: Puppies & Kittens 77
American Society for the Prevention of Cruelty to Animals 40, 130
Amigos de los Animales (Friends of the Animals) 11
Animal Humane Society 40
Animal Planet (television network) *see* Puppy Bowl
The Animal That Changed You (podcast) 185
anorexia 183; *see also* eating disorder
anxiety 17, 19, 27-30, 34-36, 51, 98, 100, 102-103, 105, 107-108, 137, 147
The Atlantic (magazine) 158
Austin, TX 183-184
Azabu University 90

The Beagle Freedom Project 48
beagle medical experimentation 48-49
Bear (dog) 128
Beckles, Bobby 11
Beckles, Boom Boom (dog) 11, ***12***
Beckles, Chrissy 11, ***12***, 13-16, 141
Belchertown, MA 155
Best Friends Animal Society 40, 162
Better Halves: Rebuilding a Post-addiction Marriage 20, 115
Better Together Dog Rescue 155, 160, 162, 164, 166
Biden, Commander (dog) 40
Biden, Jill 40
Biden, Joseph R. 40

bipolar disorder 98, 102-103, 105
Bipolar Hope 105
Boston, MA 100, 123, 143
Boston Globe 143
Bourdain, Anthony 94
Brandeis University 146
Brandy (dog, television show character) 173-176
Brooklyn, NY 12, 19, 59
bulimia 183-186; 189, 192

Caribbean 6, 8, 61, 83, 87, 97, 116, 140
The Case for Codependency... with a Rescue Dog 187
Cattet, Jennifer, Dr. 106-110
Centers for Disease Control 85
The Champions (film) 162
Chang, Deanna 41-45, ***46***, ***47***
Chang, Otto (dog) 44-45, ***46***, ***47***
Chang, Wing 42-45, ***46***
Claude, Boomer (dog) 15-16
Claude, Cheryl Jean 15-17
Claude, Cody (dog) 15-16
cocaine 19-20, 27, 59-60, 67, 72, 88, 112, 119-120, 124, 183
The Coddling of the American Mind (book) 158-159
"The Coddling of the American Mind" (magazine article) 158
codependency 187-189
Covid-19 pandemic 8, 42, 50, 54, 71-72, 85-87, 89, 97, 100, 123, 129 ; pet adoption uptick 39-40; psychological impacts 43
Cyclothymia 98, 102

Daisy (dog) 134, ***135***
Dale, Nicholas 22, 25-26, 58, 87, 137-138, ***139***, 140-143, ***144***, 145-147, ***148***, 149-151, 168-169, 176-178, 197
Dale, Stephen 86, 168-171, ***172***, 173-179
Darcy (dog) 108, ***109***, 110
Dead Dog Beach ***7***, 12, 66, 122; *see also* Puerto Rico

213

Index

Depression 3, 17, 27–30, 43, 51, 63, 85–96, 97–98, 101–102, 106, 112, 140, 169–172, 174, 176
Dick Clark's New Year's Rockin' Eve 13
dopamine 75, 90, 94, 167
Dopamine Reuptake Inhibitors 90
Doyle, Richard 77, 80
Drug Enforcement Administration 72

eating disorder 182–183; *see also* anorexia; bulimia
ehrlichia 5, 10, 30, 36, 61, 68, 177

Family Paws Parent Educator 180
fentanyl crisis 72–73, 82–83
The Fix (website, defunct) 187
Foundation for Individual Rights and Expression 144
Franz, Callie (dog) 155
Franz, Foster (dog) 153, *154*, 165
Franz, Jack 153–166
Franz, Jenny 152–166, *157*, *163*
Franz, Marty Byrde (dog) 155
Franz, Nate 153, 155, 159, 161, 164
Franz, William 155–166
Franz, Wren (dog) 155
Freedom Flights 13, *14*, 100; *see also* The Sato Project

Gamand, Sophie 7
George Washington University 50
Gervais, Ricky 173–174
Gina Galina (dog) *133*, 134
Glassell Park *see* Los Angeles
Glover (dog) *156*, 157, 159
The Guardian 89, 173
Guinness (dog) 49
Guzman, Stalin 97, 99
Guzman Caban, Missy Foo (dog) 100–103, *104*, 105, 124

Haidt, Jonathan 157–159
Harabin, Carmen (dog) 122–124, *125*, 126–127
Harabin, Cassidy (née Arocho) 122–124, *125*, 126–127
Harabin, Marek 122–124, *125*, 126–127
Harabin, Tito (dog) 127
heartworm 10, 15, 30, 61
heroin 72–74, 78, 82
Heterodox Academy 144
Humane Society of the United States 48
Hurricane Maria 8; *see also* Puerto Rico

I Am Sober (website) 76
India 6
Indianapolis, IN 105

Jacobs, Mark 13
John Jay College of Criminal Justice 73

Kanab, Utah 162
katyalidsky.com 190
Knight Foundation 159

Lanza, Adam 49
Laredo, TX 182–183
Last Chance Animal Rescue 39
LEAD (organization) 49–50; LEAD Academy (training program) 50
Leominster High School 49
Li, Patricia (Patty) 1, *2*, 16–22, 56, *57*, 58–63, 87, 111, *112*, 113, *114*, 115–121, 125, 127, 137–143, 147–151, 169, 197
Lidsky, Katya 180–184, *185*, 186–188, *189*, 190–193
Lidsky, Ophelia (dog) 180, *181*, 182, 184, *185*, 186–188, *189*, 190–193
Lopez, Nadja Caban 97–103
Los Angeles, CA 42, 128–130, 132, 183–184
Lucky Dog Animal Rescue 39
Luis Muñoz Marín International Airport 10
Lukianoff, Greg 158–159
Luving Paws Foundation 54

Manhattan (New York City borough) 15, 21, 58–59, 62
Manos por Patas (Hands for Paws) 11
Massachusetts 49–50, 54, 146, 155
McNicholas, June, Dr. 89–90
Medical Mutts (organization) 105–108
"Mental Health Promotion" (program) 50
Middle Tennessee State University 158
Murthy, Dr. Vivek 102

Naloxone 74
Narcan® *see* Naloxone
Narcotics Anonymous 59, 79
National Council for Behavioral Health 50
National Health Service (UK) 88
National Institute of Mental Health 86
National Institutes of Health 75
Navy (US military) 74, 80, 82
Neo, Perpetua, PhD 89
New Jersey 18, 21, 70, 124, 194
The New York Times 12, 50
New York University 18, 158, 183; Tisch School of the Arts 129
Newtown, CT 49
No-Kill Los Angeles Animal Shelter 130
Northwestern University 50

Obama, Barack 158–159
Odie (dog) 52
The Office (television show) 173
OKCupid 129, 131
Ophelia, I Feel Ya (blog series) 190–193
opioid epidemic *see* fentanyl crisis
OxyContin 72–73
Oxytocin 90

panic disorder 105
Paresky, Pamela 143
Parvovirus 45, 48, 184
Pepper (dog) 152–154, 165

Percocet 72
Pesky Moon Entertainment 185
Pew Research Center 101
Playa Lucia 7; *see also* Dead Dog Beach
PLOS ONE 89
postural orthostatic tachycardia syndrome (POTS) 105
psychiatric service dogs 105–110
Puerto Rico 6, 8–9, 11–15, 26, 30, 36, 60–61, 96, 97, 99–100, 122–124, 132; animal shelters 8; earthquake 8; poverty and economic crisis 8; population decline 8–9; *see also* Dead Dog Beach
Puppy Bowl 13
Purdue Pharma 72

Queenie (dog) 134, *135*

Ray (dog) 106–107
RealClearEducation 144
Rescue Dogs 101 156
Robinson, Ann 89
Roxy (dog) 127, 130–131, *132*, 133–135
Rutgers University 18

Sackler family *see* Purdue Pharma
Sanchez, Roselyn 13
Sandy Hook Elementary School 49
The Sato Project 12–17, 52–54, 61–62, 100, 122–124, 127, 141; Sanctuary 13; *see also* Freedom Flights
schizoaffective disorder 106
School Rubric 146
Scientific American 90
Screen Rant 174
Selective Serotonin Reuptake Inhibitors 90
Serotonin 90
Sharpley, Cindy 39
Shelter Animals Count 40
smell, canine sense of 104; diagnostic capabilities 105–108
social media 13, 89, 142–143, 158; adverse mental health consequences of 101–102; promotion of disingenuousness 120

Social Media Victims Law Center 102
Southern Utah University 161
Spade, Kate 94
Stephanie (last name withheld) 108–110
Supermutt 25

Thailand 6
Tiny Elvis (mouse) 164–165
Trump, Donald J. 39
12 Steps of Recovery 62–63

University of California, Los Angeles 128
University of Hawaii 128
University of Michigan 146

Vick, Michael 162
Vicodin 72
Virginia Tech University mass shooting 49
visual impairment 1, 19, 25–30; optic nerve 27; physical impacts 29; psychological impacts 29, 33–38; scotomas 27

W., Amber (dog) 70–71, 77–78, *79*, 80, *81*, 82–83
W., Joe 82
W., John 70–83
W., Joni 71, 83
The Washington Post 39–40
WebMD 89
Westchester, NY 73
Wiercyski, Desiree 89
Wilkins, Lauren 50
Wilma (dog) 25–26
Worcester, MA 53
World Health Organization 85

Xanax 73
Xena (dog) 31, 171, *172*, 175, 179

Yabucoa, Puerto Rico 7, 122
Yun (last name withheld) 127–136

Zoe (last name withheld) 127–136

www.ingramcontent.com/pod-product-compliance
Ingram Content Group UK Ltd.
Pitfield, Milton Keynes, MK11 3LW, UK
UKHW021845140426
5217IPUK00022B/1601